Outward Spirals

A Guide to Shaligram Stones

Holly Walters

TLS

ISBN13: 978-1-959350-50-7

 Set in: Georgia 10/11/12/17/24/30/36 pt

©The Three Little Sisters
USA/CANADA

CONTENTS

Kageni Village and the Kali-Gandaki River
(Mount Nilgiri in the background)

Kali Gandaki River
(Tiri Village below)

The Kali-Gandaki River near Kagbeni Village
(a popular site for finding Shaligrams)

Ananta Sesha Shaligram appearing in the river
(Below)

Sri Ram Shaligram (Showing his arrow)

Kalpvriksha Shaligram on the river bank

Vishnu-Chenrezig Mandir (Muktinath)

Shaligram Mandir (Yagyashala) at Muktinath

A Laksmi-Narayan temple Shaligram receiving blessings at Muktinath

The 108 Sacred Fountains at Muktinath

Sangdo (Sarwa) Gompa at Muktinath

Jwala Mai (Mother Flame) Gompa at Muktinath

A Home Shaligram Collection in Kathmandu

Temple Shaligram Puja: Mayapur, West Bengal, India

A Shaligram is placed on top of a Buddhist stupa at a crossroads in Mustang (white stupa in the center)

The Shaligram at the top of the stupa, placed with sacred juniper sprigs

A Krishna Shaligram sits in the offering window of a village stupa, along with clay images of the Buddha.

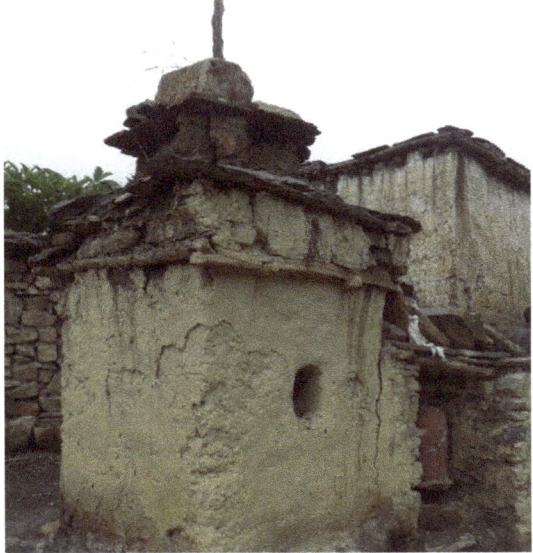

A large Krishna Shaligram sits in the offering window of the stupa, along with clay images of the Buddha

Ammonites from Chongur village

Ammonite Fossil Wash-out Near Chongur Village, Mustang, Nepal

A belemnite fossil cross-section emerging from the sediments, showing the distinctive "cow-hoof" structure read in Shaligrams as Krishna Govinda

A fossil belemnite bisected, read in Shaligram traditions as Shiva Linga

CHAPTER ONE

"The worse my drawings were, the more beautiful did the originals appear." ~
John James Audubon

In the Himalayas, I always carried two notebooks. The first; was a standard
pocket field book typical among anthropologists conducting ethnographic research,
the second was a sketchbook, filled with drawings and diagrams detailing each
Shaligram (as I encountered them) in graphite, charcoal, and ink. Shaligrams,
or Salagrama-shila (शालग्राम शिला), are the sacred fossil *ammonites*[1] of Himalayan
Nepal. Viewed primarily as manifestations (rupa) of Hindu gods and goddesses,
these aniconic deities are primarily obtained through pilgrimage to the Kali
Gandaki River Valley of Mustang. They are then brought home, to families and
communities all over South Asia and the Diaspora, where they are venerated as
divine beings.

Originally, I had chosen to start the second notebook because it was not always
permissible or even possible to photograph Shaligrams. This is because, in many
Hindu and Buddhist religious contexts, there are often restrictions on photography
in sacred spaces or prohibitions on creating additional representations of sacred
images. Later, I came to find that the drawings were exceptionally helpful in
comparing textual instructions on Shaligram identification with actual stones
whose meaningful characteristics and minute details could only be highlighted
through careful pictorial representations; which were then additionally important
since none of the early scriptural texts on Shaligrams contain pictures of the stones
they describe.

1 Ammonites are an extinct group of marine mollusks most closely related to modern-day squid
and cuttlefish. They are also known as index fossils because they link related rock layers from all
over the world to particular eras of time.

But as my research moved through Nepal and India, and I began to amass significant numbers of drawings, the notebook which contained my Shaligram drawings soon took on an entirely new meaning and focus: it became prodfoundly important to the practitioners I met. The first time I set the large paper-pulp notebook in my lap to draw a set of Shaligrams, I was sitting alone near a roadside shrine in India. I had set out that day to document some of the intricacies of village worship and sacred objects by carefully sketching them on the blank pages. As I outlined each stone in turn, an elderly man happened by to pray, when he stopped to glance down at what I was doing. Only a few minutes later, we both sat together on the uneven roots of a massive banyan tree as he inspected my drawings, commenting on the particulars of each Shaligram and correcting my mistakes as I struggled to make note of his explanations beside the corresponding image.

From that moment on, the Shaligram sketchbook became an integral part of my fieldwork. As a conversational ice-breaker, it facilitated long discussions about the specifics of Shaligram practice as families, ritual specialists, and life-long devotees paged through each drawing and related their own experiences with Shaligrams. As a source of documentation, Hindu and Buddhist pilgrims often asked to look through the drawings, wanting to see and learn as much about Shaligrams elsewhere in the world as they wanted to contribute their own knowledge (and often to have drawings of their own Shaligrams added).

As an object of Shaligram veneration, it was also the most popular piece of research I produced in all my time in Nepal and in India, since no extensive pictorial guide to Shaligrams exists, practitioners often asked if it could be published and if so, when could they get a copy for their own use. A return gift I am happy to now make. One of the challenges of writing ethnography however, is in taking the jottings and chaotic scribblings of field notebooks and turning them into some kind of cohesive account. Here, I was faced with an additional task. How to take the drawings of a sketchbook and turn them into a useful kind of narrative? For many Shaligram devotees, information about identifying Shaligrams is slim. Gurus and teachers are not always accessible, and published works difficult to come by.

My decision then, was to reproduce over five years of drawings and photographs, categorized by deity name, with all of the traditional interpretive descriptions I had encountered up until that point. This work also allows me to demonstrate the complex nature of Shaligram veneration by describing how Shaligrams are "read" by various religious traditions as they move outward from the **Kali Gandaki River Valley** in Mustang, Nepal to homes and temples throughout **South Asia** and in the diaspora. Learning how to read Shaligrams involved a great deal of questioning and the consideration of multiple religious perspectives. This has resulted in equal concerns about how to present this material in such a way as to accurately record Shaligram identification practices as they are described in text, as well as how they are actually carried out among practitioners and ritual specialists. In addition to the concerns of recording, the need to ensure respectful representation of Shaligrams and their meanings.

This work therefore walks a line between ethnography and religious exposition, where neither scientific taxonomy nor purely textual analysis can completely dictate the order and relationship of images to descriptions. As a result, ammonite evolution takes second place to Shaligram categorization and Scriptural definition.

The view here then is that of Shaligrams as **texts**—which can be read if the interpreter has a kind of fluency in the language of Shaligram characteristics as well as related myths, legends, stories, and histories. Similar to other types of studies in oral traditions, the following pages discuss Shaligram interpretation not just as variable takes on a master narrative embedded in a variety of South Asian religions but as attentive to the contexts of performance—where, when, and how Shaligrams are read in particular places and by particular peoples.

Incorporating Shaligram interpretive traditions into the ethnographic study of lived religion, not only opens up new venues of inquiry into the relationships between stories and objects generally but helps to extend the methodologies of fieldwork to include an engagement with "native texts" that do not neatly fit into preconceived notions of archives, writings, or performances. In other words, Shaligram interpretations are expressive traditions where no objective division between Shaligrams themselves, their body of histories and legends, and the people who read them exists. This reference guide combines Shaligram interpretive traditions as they are laid out in; Shastric, Tantric, and Puranic texts with the ways people describe them and narrate them; during rituals, on pilgrimage, and in their homes.

Shastric: a suffix used in Indian literature context, for technical or specialized knowledge in a defined area of practice

Tantric: A set of dialogic texts that discuss various techniques for expanding consciousness and liberating dormant energy, such as breathing, yoga, and meditation.

Puranic: is a vast genre of Hindu literature about a wide range of topics, particularly about legends and other traditional lore.

READING SHALIGRAMS

In typical Shaligram identification, practitioners take into account a variety of characteristics, the most important of which are:

» Set (how the Shaligram naturally sits on a flat surface)
» Shape
» The number and positioning of Chakras (ammonite shell spirals)
» The presence of Vanamala (a white quartz line representing the sacred thread)
» Vadana (meaning: mouths or large openings)
» Color (Shaligrams are usually black, but can also be red, brown, green, blue/light grey or yellow)
» Minor Markings, such as striated lines (rekha), small holes, "teeth," or other discernable shapes

These characteristics then form the foundations by which a Shaligram is determined to bare some iconic resemblance to a deity or divine person. In addition to physical characteristics, Shaligrams are also arranged into **hierarchies** of divine relationships, where the various gods and goddesses present may be discerned using references to specific religious texts or local histories that are compared to how the Shaligram was acquired or where it was found.

In the end, Shaligrams are primarily arranged, in practice, by their resemblances to deities and celestial beings, separated into name-type categories found in ancient religious texts. While I have decided to arrange Shaligram names and descriptions in this book by alphabetical order for better ease of use, it is important to note that many Shaligram ritual specialists tend to divide Shaligram name-types into three main categories.

The first category comprises Shaligram descriptions taken directly from Shastric, Tantric, and Puranic texts. These Shaligrams are not only mentioned by name within the texts but form the core hierarchy by which most other Shaligram identification practices are based. I have also included variations in identification when they appear as competing descriptions in different texts or where local practices of identification diverge from textual descriptions. This is because certain Shaligrams can actually be the same deity but only as that deity appears in specific stories. For example, there is both a Krishna Shaligram and a Gopala (Krishna as an Infant) Shaligram—where the former generally relates to Krishna as he appears in the Mahabharata epic and the Bhagavad-gita and the latter as he appears in Puranic compilations.

The second category is all Shaligrams which fall under the category of Devi or goddess Shaligrams. While goddess-identified Shaligrams are somewhat contentious in some Puranic writings, the practice of identifying specific Shaligrams with Hindu and Buddhist goddesses (or other representations of female divinity) is wide-spread and reflects areas of religious practices that more often venerate the feminine divine than in popular Brahmanical Hinduism. In other words, where female divinity is more common, goddess Shaligrams are more prominent, as is the case among the many shamanic and animistic religions of Nepal and in the Tantric and Shakti traditions of Hindu India regardless of their relatively brief inclusions in scriptural works.

Finally, the last (third) category contains Shaligram identifications and categories from local and regional traditions. These Shaligrams are almost never mentioned by name in standardized ritual texts, though their related lore and legends are equally drawn from religious stories. They do, however, comprise significant categories of use and practice at the local level. I must also emphasize that there is a significant portion of Shaligrams not included here. As divisions between text and practice often go, it is not unusual for practitioners and ritual specialists to read any number of deity combinations or mythic references in any given individual Shaligram. In other words, while Hindu texts tend to only list ideal types based on single deity manifestations, the reality of Shaligram practice is much more complex.

For instance, while a particular Shaligram may be read as an overall manifestation of Krishna (as in the previous example), it may also contain additional markings indicating Shiva, Ganesh, Krishna's consort Radha, his brother Balaram, the serpent Ananta, a set of favored weapons such as a bow or mace, or a wide variety of other characters and figures drawn from history, mythology, or literature. It is therefore impossible for any categorical discussion, even an extensive one, to cover all possible permutations or available forms of Shaligrams which may, depending on their characteristics and backgrounds, be one deity or many.

This also acknowledges, once again, Shaligrams as texts. Just as any book or poem may be read differently by different individuals, who may be encountering it for the first time or the hundredth time, Shaligrams are interpreted through multiple narratives, viewpoints, histories, and experiences. But as my long-time research participant and guide Sriram Bhavyesh explained, "One form or many forms, it is all the same. Infinite oneness appearing only as it must. This is how Shaligram speaks."

HOW TO USE THIS GUIDE

A guide is, at its heart, designed to help the reader identify objects in the natural world (plants, animals, minerals, etc.). It is generally anticipated that such a guide will be brought out into the 'field' or local area where such things exist to help distinguish one specific object from among similar objects. As such, a field guide is expected to include a description of the objects covered, together with paintings or photographs to help in discerning nuance so that each subject might be better organized by family, color, shape, location or other descriptors.

But field guides also serve to educate and create knowledge of a topic just as much they purport to simply reflect established knowledge. I caution then, that this work is in no way exhaustive and does not reflect all possible variations of Shaligram identification everywhere. Indeed, where I have noted, there is not even complete agreement on the meanings of certain Shaligram characteristics in Puranic texts, between various Hindu and Buddhist religious traditions, or among ritual specialists.

In some ways, these disagreements on Shaligram identification reflect the ways in which scientific taxonomies are also not fixed: indeed, it changes each time science makes new discoveries about evolutionary or genetic ancestry and forms what is sometimes called "the mythology of science." There are, however, systematic criteria and commonalities in Shaligram identification and it is these themes and patterns of practice which are most especially emphasized here. It is also difficult to generalize how any given field guide will be used, because this varies from one guide to another and partly depends on how expert the targeted reader is expected to be.

My intent then it to appeal primarily to the average Shaligram devotee, who is generally familiar with their own religious traditions and with Shaligram practice in general but who is interested in learning more about Shaligram identification or who wants to compare and contrast interpretive practices from multiple viewpoints. This guide is also useful for the general public as well. Because the main function of a field guide is to help the reader identify a bird, plant, rock, butterfly or other natural object down to at least the popular naming level, this guide may provide essential background to tourists and trekkers traveling to Nepal or India and who may encounter Shaligrams in the course of their journeys.

To this end some field guides employ simple keys and other techniques where the reader is encouraged to scan the drawings and illustrations in looking for a match to an object within their immediate purview. They may also be advised to compare similar-looking objects using information on their differences. While this guide may be useful in this regard, I still highly encourage anyone looking to identify a particular Shaligram to consult with religious specialists whose experience and knowledge on these topics simply cannot be reproduced in a few hundred pages of pictures and explanations.

Shaligram Interpretive Traditions

Scriptural references to Shaligrams typically take the form of a number of categorical lists of name-types followed by descriptions of markings. These categories are then compared across a series of texts which have been compiled at different times and by different spiritual philosophies and traditions to arrive at the general definition of a specific Shaligram. But the actual practice of identifying Shaligrams is far more complicated than these lists and brief summaries might otherwise imply. In practice, religious texts are more often used as a kind of systematic shorthand for identifying Shaligram varieties rather than as definitive authorities in determining which precise arrangements of features and characteristics ultimately indicate a specific Shaligram manifestation. Additionally, the variability of the texts is often taken to demonstrate the legitimacy of local interpretive variations that don't necessarily adhere to any specific list, combine lists, or add and subtract certain name-type descriptions.

In other cases, such as among many traditional Indian Brahmins, interpretation is a highly conservative endeavor where only certain texts are employed while the rest of the interpretive framework relies on extensive experience with Shaligram practice and a careful examination of each Shaligram's particular details. Despite this however, the near infinite variation of manifestations and their interpretations does not necessarily de-legitimize the practice of Shaligram reading. Rather, the vast majority of Shaligram practitioners note that because God Himself is capable of taking any number of forms He might deem necessary, it is no surprise that any given individual Shaligram might not strictly adhere to a specific textual reference.

Shaligrams are thus identified using a wide variety of characteristics, the most important being shape, size, color, the presence of absence of chakra-markings, the position of the chakra markings, the number of visible chakras and their respective sizes, the presence or absence of a vadana, and the presence or absence of other identifiable features such as a vanamala (garland) marking, an axe or an arrow marking, a conch shell marking, and so on.

In general, non-anthropomorphic Shaligrams, such as the avatars of Vishnu like Matsya (fish), Varaha (boar), and Kurma (tortoise), are identified using the overall shape of the Shaligram as well as distinctive markings other than the number of chakras the shila (Sanskrit: stone) contains. Therefore, a Shaligram with multiple visible chakras that also has the characteristic shape of a fish would still be identified as Matsya even though a Puranic description might denote the number of chakras as indicating a different possible category. A point I'll elaborate on further in Chapter 3.

In the same thread, a Narasimha (half-man, half-lion incarnation of Vishnu) Shaligram would be primarily identified by its gaping "mouth" and the presence of "fangs" rather than any number of chakras present on the outside of the shila (which would be 2 according to the Garuda Purana). Furthermore, it is also not uncommon to read additional chakras or markings on these specific Shaligrams as the presence of more than one deity. Therefore, it is possible to encounter Shaligrams whose names incorporate all of the identifiable deities present in a single stone (i.e., a Radha-Krishna-Balaram Shaligram, a Lakshmi-Narayan-Ananta-Samudra Manthan or a Mahavishnu-Lakshmi-Aditya Shaligram and so on). For anthropomorphic Shaligrams, the determination of markings as various weapons usually takes precedence in their identifications.

For example, an arrow and a quiver for Śri Ram, a sword for Kalki, an axe for Parasurama, and so on. A careful and detailed examination of each Shaligram is therefore necessary in determining its exact manifestation. For comparison, I have compiled a few of the most common textual descriptions identifying each Shaligram on their respective pages. Note particularly however, the ways in which various categories and name-types overlap, contradict, or complement other aspects of the interpretive frameworks. This is largely due to the fact that no single authority on Shaligram practice exists and many interpretive traditions have interacted, exchanged, and incorporated each other's various deities and practices over the centuries. For this reason, textual identification is only a starting point for understanding some of the general methods for reading Shaligrams and is by no means comprehensive since Shaligram interpretive traditions remain largely oral and generational.

There are several commentaries on Shaligram practices available though. An extensive interpretive framework detailing dozens of sub-types and Shaligram variations has recently been documented by Raghuvendra Srinath, a Madhwa Brahmin from Maharashtra who descends from a long line of Shaligram practitioners and who has been involved in the rituals and scholarship of Shaligrams since childhood. His work relies on interpretations largely drawn from the Dvaita School of Vedanta philosophy (Sripada Madhvacharya) for Shaligram identification, thereby eschewing the Praṇa-toshini Tantra in favor of using only the Padma, Skanda, Narasimha, Varaha, and Brahma Vaivarta Puranas[2].

This is because Madhwa traditions view religious hierarchies in very strict terms; hierarchies which include the Puranic texts themselves. Although Madhwas view all of the Puranas as written by Śri Vedavyasa, the Śrimad Bhagavata is considered the highest and most authoritative text followed by the rest of the five satvika Puranas[3]. This means that the remaining Puranas tend to be viewed as later additions by entirely human authors (though still important) and the Praṇa-toshiṇi Tantra and any other tantras as entirely non-authoritative. In this tradition, Shaligram identification begins with a set of guidelines (namely Puranic quotations) but then also requires a knowledgeable guru to help with the nuances of interpretation.

---

2 https://shaligrama.wordpress.com/different-forms-of-lord-and-identification/ (Accessed 12-11-2016)

3 Satvika refers to the list of Puranas considered authoritative by Vaishnava traditions. Which specific Puranas these are however, varies by the tradition in question.

Ideally, the practitioner will also have extensive previous experience with many representative Shaligrams (skills acquired through exposure over time) and a capacity to "see" the Shaligram beyond the basics of the texts, whose generalized descriptions often suit more than one sub-type in any give case (Srinath, personal communication). As such, his list contains some fifty-five primary categories, each with between two and upwards of fifteen sub-types, each with their own unique set of characteristics. Śrī Padmanābha Goswami's "Śālagrāma-śila" (1993) on the other hand, relies primarily on the Brahma Vaivarta, Bhaviśya, Agni, and Skanda Puranas along with the Gautamīya Tantra. Subsequently, his interpretive framework maintains a list of roughly forty Shaligram categories more in line with the Gaudiya Vaishnava/Hare Krishna theological lineage and which does not deviate into sub-categories[4].

Additionally, Vaishnavacharya Chandan Goswami's (a student of Padmanābha Goswami's) "The Sacred Shilas" (2017), contains an extensively detailed description of Puranic Shaligram references as well as a discussion on Shaligram puja requirements for daily worship and for festivals. Shaligram interpretation in this tradition is therefore somewhat more straightforward, and even today, many Gaudiya Vaishnavas reject extensive hierarchies of Shaligram types and sub-types in favor of shorter lists of single deity manifestations; viewing the former as unnecessarily esoteric and inaccessible to the lay-practitioner. Lastly, some traditions simply rely on the Śrī Vaishnava Vedanta Chatur-vyūha list of Shaligram descriptions.

Founded on the four Chatur-vyūhas ("four emanations") of Vishnu -- which comprise four of the six causes of creation: Narāyana ('thinking'), Vāsudeva ('feeling'), Samkarśana ('willing'), Pradyumna ('knowing'), Aniruddha ('acting'), and Vishnu himself as the final cause -- this theological tradition begins its Shaligram interpretations with the vyūhas as primary ideal name-types. Then basing the rest of the identification practices off of the story of the sage Shalankayana in the Varaha Purana (who becomes Shaligram himself after meditating beneath a śala tree on the banks of the Kali Gandaki River), this framework, which is more common in South India and in Indonesia, combines a wide variety of Shaligram references in various texts in terms of shape, color, and size.

---

4 1993. Śrī Padmanābha Goswami. "Śālagrāma-śila" Shanti Kutir. Radharamana Temple. Vrindavan, U. P. 281121. India.

It also bases the resulting sub-variations in name-type categories almost entirely on Dasvatara typology (the ten incarnations of Vishnu), which is said to branch out from the initial four vyūhas. Like many of the other interpretive frameworks, it also contains a series of repetitions (where specific Shaligrams are mentioned more than once but with different descriptions), conflicting criteria for identification, and textual ambiguities and therefore also benefits from the expertise of ritual specialists and gurus who have maintained and passed down the oral traditions of Shaligram identification and worship for generations. There are, without a doubt, many more local and regional methods of identifying Shaligrams not recorded here and many of these interpretive frameworks still remain largely confined to oral tradition, all with their own distinctive variations, sub-categories, and alternate manifestations.

Overall, however, I have begun by providing the name-type or category of the Shaligram in the following guide pages along with the Scriptural sources where the name-type is referenced. I have then included the Scriptural description which, where possible, can be compared and contrasted with the variant local or traditional descriptions drawn from Shaligram practitioners' and ritual specialists' own experiences. The result, hopefully, is a brief synopsis of the most common forms of Shaligrams that appear in worship along with a set of guidelines for identifying them by name.

PRIMARY TEXT SOURCES FOR SHALIGRAM INTERPRETATION

Chand, Devi. 1997 (2002). Atharvaveda, Sanskrit Text with English Translation. Munshiram.

Prana-toshini tantra. 1983. Ramatosana Bhaṭṭa and Ramadatta Shukla, trans. Prayaga: Shakta Sadhana Piṭha Publishers.

Puranas, Translated into English.2007. By A Board of Scholars. Motilal Banarsidas Publishers Pvt. Ltd. 74 Volumes.

Rao, S. K. Ramachandra. 1996. Shaligram Kosh [Śālagrāma – Kosha]. Sri Satguru Publications. Indian Books Center. Delhi, India.

Sharma, Ram Charan. 2000. Shaligram Purana. S.R.C. Museum of Indology & Universal Institute of Orientology Trust, 199. Digitized 2009. University of Michigan.

Singh, Chandra Shekar et. al.2017. The Puranas. Amazon Digital Services.

CHAPTER TWO

SHALIGRAM INTERPRETIVE TRADITIONS IN TEXT

The most definitive, and most widely distributed, work on Shaligram interpretation is, without a doubt, S. K. Ramachandra Rao's Śālagrāma-Kosha. This work, published in two volumes in 1996, is also the most often referenced work for devotees, pilgrims, and ritual specialists alike and forms the basis for the majority of current pilgrimage literatures and religious websites discussing Shaligram stones. While the books do a remarkable job of consolidating significant portions of traditional stories and scriptural references to Shaligrams (including a number of historical manuscripts never seen in print), they do not discuss actual Shaligram practices nor do they detail the methods for Shaligram identification outside of what is already laid out in the Puranas and what was compiled in Maharaj Krishnaraj Wodeyar III (1780-1865) of Mysore's Sri-tattva-nidhi. Unfortunately, as many practitioners point out, the book is also mired in esoteric theology and is, therefore, difficult for the lay reader to understand and make use of in their own practices.

Throughout my years of fieldwork on Shaligrams it also became clear to me that, prior to the publication of the Śālagrāma-Kosha, the details of most Shaligram interpretive traditions were almost entirely unavailable to anyone without access to temple libraries or ritual specialists and were therefore largely unknown by most lay practitioners beyond a few overarching themes. This is why the publication of Shaligram identification practices here must be viewed as not just consolidating the tradition and making it available, but also as possibly instantiating it as authoritative among non-specialists. The reasons for this are complex but just as the Puranic and Shastric texts don't always agree on the origins of Shaligrams, they also don't agree on the specifics of their identification. As a result, it is important to keep in mind that there are a wide variety of local, regional, and traditional variations of Shaligram interpretation that are not represented here. Rather, this guide represents the most common readings of Shaligrams drawn from the ethnographic study of Indian, Nepali, and Tibetan Shaligram practices since the 2010s.

SHALIGRAMS IN TEXT

According to the Skanda Purana (Nagarekhanda, 244: 3-9), in ancient times, Shaligrams were divided into twenty-four different types, each given the name of a specific manifestation of Vishnu: (1) Keshava, (2) Madhusudana, (3) Shankarshan, (4) Daamodara, (5) Vaasudeva, (6) Pradyumna, (7) Vishnu, (8) Maadhava, (9) Ananta, (10) Purushottama, (11) Adhokshaja, (12) Janaardan, (13) Govinda, (14) Trivikrama, (15) Shridhar, (16) Hrishikesha, (17) Nrisimha, (18) Vishvayoni, (19) Vaamana, (20) Naaraayana, (21) Pundarikaaksha, (22) Upendra, (23) Hari, and (24) Krishna. The Brahma Vaivartta Purana (Prakrtikhanda, chapter 21), however, categorizes Shaligrams into nineteen different varieties with the following Descriptions[5]

1. Lakshmi-Narayana: In color, he resembles a new cloud and has a single opening marked with four circular prints. A linear mark resembling a vanamala (a particular kind of garland held by Lord Vishnu, or series of forests) is also printed on his body.
2. Lakshmi-Janardan: The above type without the mark of vanamala.
3. Raghunatha: He has two openings with four circular marks. His body also is marked with the footprint of a cow, but not with any mark of vanamala.
4. Dadhivamana: Very small in size with two circular marks and having the color of a new cloud.
5. Shridhar: The above type with an additional mark of vanamala.
6. Daamodara: Big in size with a round shape and two circular marks, but not having the mark of vanamala.
7. Ranarama: round and middle in shape with prints of arrows all over His body. He must have two circular marks and prints of a quiver with arrows on His body.
8. Rajarajeshwara: Middle in size, having seven circular marks and also the marks of an umbrella and grass (or quiver) on His body.
9. Ananta: Big in size with the color of a new cloud and having 14 circular marks on His body.
10. Madhusudana: Round in shape, middle in size, and charming to look at. He has two circular marks and a footprint of a cow on His body.
11. Sudarshan: With single circular mark.
12. Gadadhara: With a hidden circular mark.
13. Hayagriva: With two circular marks and having the shape of the face of a horse.
14. Narasimha: Having a large opening with two circular marks and glittering to look at.
15. Lakshmi-Narasimha: Having a big opening with two circular marks, and also marked with a vanamala.
16. Vaasudeva: Evenly shaped and charming to look at, having two circular marks at the front of his opening.

---

5 Quoted in Rabindra Kumar Siddhantashastree. 1985. Vaishnavism Through the Ages. Munshiram Manoharlal Publishers Pvt. Ltd. pages 27-49

17. Pradyumna: With the color of a new cloud and having a small circular mark and several small holes on His body.
18. Shankarshan: He has two circular marks joined with each other on the top side of His body.
19. Aniriddha: Round in shape, glaced and charming to look at, and having the yellowish color.

The Shaligram categories provided in the Garuda Purana (Panchanan Tarkaratna, part I, chapter 45), while clearly similar, continue to deviate further:

1. Vaasudeva: White in color having two circular marks joined with each other at the opening
2. Shankarshan: Reddish in color, having two circular marks joined with each other, and also the mark of a lotus on the far side of His body.
3. Pradyumna: Yellow in color and long in shape with a small opening.
4. Aniruddha: Blue in color and round in shape with a hole at the top side of His body.
5. Narayana: Black in color with three linear marks at the opening.
6. Nrisimha: He holds the mark of a mace at the center of His body, and a circular mark at the lower middle portion, His upper middle portion being comparatively bigger.
7. Kapila: He holds three dot-like marks on His body or at His opening.
8. Varahashaktilinga: He holds two circular marks of unequal size.
9. Kumaramurthi: Big in size, blue in color and printed with three linear marks and one or more dots.
10. Krishna: Round in shape with a flat upper side.
11. Shridhar: Printed with five linear marks and a mace.
12. Vaamana: Round in shape with a comparatively smaller height and printed with one or more beautiful circular marks.
13. Ananta: Variegated in color with many circular marks.
14. Damodara: Big in size, blue in color with a deep circular mark at the center.
15. Brahman: Red in color with a small opening.
16. Prthu: Printed with a long linear mark, a circular mark and a lotus, and having one or more holes.
17. Hayagriva: With a big hole, a big circular mark, five linear marks and the marks of a Kaustubha gem, an Ankusha (spear head) several dots and a dark spot.
18. Vaikuntha: Blue in color, printed with a lotus and a circular mark, and glittering like a gem.
19. Matsya: Long in shape and printed with a lotus and two linear marks.
20. Trivikrama: Green in color, with a circular mark on His left side and a linear mark on His right side.
21. Lakshminarayana: Round in shape with a single opening. He has four circular marks at the opening and is decorated with a vanamala, one footprint of a cow and a golden linear mark.

In addition to the categories listed above, an additional thirteen more varieties of Shaligram are recorded in the Garuda Purana based on their number of circular marks (chakras). Amongst these additional varieties, each type, with the exception of the last two, bear the same name as given in the previous list. The difference between the last two categories is that, according to this particular text, a Shaligram with twelve circular marks is called Dwadashatman and one with thirteen or more marks is called Ananta (dvaadashaatma dvaadashabhirta oorddhvamanantakah - Garuda Purana, part I: 45:30).

The categories of Shaligrams that are detailed in the Garuda Purana list are then the same categories that are also listed in the Agni Purana[6] as well. The difference, however, is that the name-types of Kumaramurthi (9), Brahman (15), and Prthu (16) are not included in the Agni Purana. Conversely, the Agni Purana includes the name-types of Parameshtin, Kurma Sudarshan, Acyuta, Janardan and a few more name-types based on the number of chakras a Shaligram might have. A further point of divergence is also that the Vaasudeva type Shaligram in the Garuda Purana is white but, in the Agni Purana (and other sources), it is black in color. As a result, Shaligram interpretation using the Garuda Purana can be, unfortunately, somewhat confusing. For example, the list of Shaligram names by number of chakras is as follows:

1. Sudarshan
2. Lakshmi – Narayan
3. Acyuta
4. Janardan, Caturbhuja
5. Vaasudeva
6. Pradyumna
7. Sankarshan
8. Purushottam
9. Navavyuha
10. Dasavatara
11. Anirudda
12. Ananta
13. Paramatma (13+)

Because several name-types based on number also overlap with Shaligram name-types elsewhere (which are not identified using number of chakras), there is no hard standard in the texts which can be used to describe exactly how any given Shaligram should be ideally identified. For example, the Garuda Purana identifies a Pradyumna Shaligram as potentially any Shaligram with six chakras, but the Brahma Vaivarta Purana identifies Pradyumna Shaligrams as "the color of new clouds" (meaning light blue or grey) with a small circular mark and several additional small holes. The same is true of the distinctive Anirudda Shaligram, which according to the list of names by number of chakras would be a Shaligram with eleven circular markings. In practice, the Anirudda Shaligram is actually a tear-drop shaped bivalve (Retroceramus) marked with a wide variety and number of concentric ridges irrespective of number.

---

6 Agnipurana, Bengavasi ed., Panchanan Tarkaratna, Saka 1812, chapter 46.

Additionally, some stricter Vaishnava traditions use an alternative interpretation of the Garuda Purana, and other associated texts, to identify Shaligrams using a sequence of four, and only four characteristics, said to represent marks of a shankha (conch shell), chakra (disc), gada (mace) and padma (lotus flower) arranged in a particular order. With any perceived change in the order of the four symbols, the name of the Shaligram is then interpreted differently for a total of twenty-four possible permutations, each associated with a particular name of Vishnu. The identification of Shaligrams in this sense is then always relative to the order of the four symbols (Debroy, Bibek and Dipavali Debroy. The Garuda Purana. Shalagrama. p. 42.)

1. Shanka, chakra, gada and padma - Keshava
2. Padma, gada, chakra, shanka - Narayana
3. Chakra, shanka, padma and gada - Madhava
4. Gada, padma, shanka and chakra - Govinda
5. Padma, shanka, chakra and gada – Vishnu
6. Shanka, padma, gada, chakra – Madusudhana
7. Gada, chakra, shanka and padma – Trivikrama
8. Chakra, gada, padma, shanka - Vamana
9. Chakra, padma, shanka, gada - Shridhara
10. Padma, gada, shanka, charka - Hrishikesh
11. Padma, chakra,gada, shanka - Padmanabha
12. Shanka, chakra, gada, padma - Damodara
13. Chakra, shanka, gada, padma - Sankarshana
14. Shanka, chakra, padma, gada - Pradyumna
15. Gada, shanka, padma, charka - Aniruddha
16. Padma, shanka, gada, chakra - Purushottama
17. Gadha, shanka, chakra, padma - Adokshaja
18. Padma, gada, shanka, chakra - Narasimha
19. Padma, chakra, shanka, gada – Acyuta
20. Shanka, chakra, padma, gada - Janardana
21. Gada, padma, shanka, chakra - Upendra
22. Chakra, padma, gada and shanka – Hari
23. Gada, padma, chakra and shanka - Krishna
24. Shanka, chakra, padma, gada – Vasudeva

In another account, the Prapanchasara[7], Vishnu is described as having fifty different forms, any of which may appear in the form of Shaligram: (1) Keshava, (2) Narayana, (3) Maahava, (4) Govinda, (5) Madhusudana, (6) Trivikrama, (7) Vaamana, (8) Shridhar, (9) Hrishikesha, (10) Padmanabha, (11) Damodara, (12) Vaasudeva, (13) Sankarshana, (14) Pradyumna, (15) Aniruddha, (16) Chakrin, (17) Gadin, (18) Sharngin, (19) Khadgin, (20) Shankin, (21) Halin, (22) Musalin, (23) Soolin, (24) Paashin, (25) Ankushin, (26) Mukunda, (27) Nandaja, (28) Nandin, (29) Nara, (30) Narakajit, (31) Hari, (32) Krishna, (33) Satya, (34) Saatvata, (35) Shauri, (36) Shuri, (37) Janardana, (38) Bhudhaarin, (39) Vishvamurtti, (40) Vaikuntha, (41) Purushottama, (42) Balin, (43) Balaanuja, (44) Bala, (45) Vrishaghna, (46) Vrisha, (47) Hamsa, (48) Varaha, (49) Vimala, and (50) Nrisimha.

---

7 Which is also quoted in the Pranatoshini Tantra on page 373

Furthermore, the Saradatantra states that all the above fifty forms of Vishnu, when worshipped in an image, should be rendered using green colors (shyama) while holding a discus (chakra) and a conch in two of the hands. In the Fetkarini Tantra, on the other hand, the color of the deities should be that of "a new cloud" (again, light blue or grey) and they are to be clad in yellow clothes (meaning: having golden markings) with their shakti consorts depicted on their laps (interpreted through other minor markings). In general, however, what matters most in teaching Shaligram identification through scriptural texts is to ensure that devotees have a foundational understanding of shapes and surface characteristics: different shapes thus indicating different divine manifestations which then subsequently bring about different results in their worship.[8]

Which brings us, finally, to the Pranatoshini Tantra, a 565-page encyclopedic compilation of earlier scriptural texts composed in Bengal in the 19th century (regarding mantras, yantras, meditations, deity worship, and the six acts of magic). This work is another one of the most commonly referenced scriptural authorities on Shaligram identification today and is compiled from multiple Shaligram texts spanning several centuries. As such, the Pranatoshini Tantra (see pages 351-356) records an extensive listing of sixty-two types of Shaligrams along with a detailed description of the sub-types that may correspond with the primary category (i.e., the principal deity followed by whatever specific form or mood (bhava) that deity might be appearing in for that specific Shaligram). As a compilation of quotes and descriptions from a number of different ancient texts, this listing forms the basis for nearly all Shaligram identifications in practice.

This does not mean, however, that Shaligram specialists and devotees necessarily consult this list directly when "reading" a Shaligram (in fact, they almost never do), but that the concept of multiple sub-types and variations on the main categories forms the foundation for interpreting Shaligrams in most modern oral traditions. In this way, any given Shaligram may not necessarily conform exactly to the ideals set out in scriptural texts and may carry a name or demonstrate an incarnation not specifically mentioned; though it will always fall somewhere along the spectrum of categories contained in the authoritative texts of Hindu theology. In other words, though Krishna Govinda may not be specifically mentioned in the scriptures as a type of Shaligram, Krishna Shaligrams are widely referenced.

---

8 (chatraakaare bhavedraajyam varttule cha mahaashriyah duhkhancha shakatakaare shoolaagre maranam dhruram vikritaasya cha daadridryam oingale haanireva cha. lagnachakre bhaved vyaadhirvidiirne maranam dhruvam – Brahma Vaivarta Purana, Prakritikhanda, 21:78-79).

Shaped like and umbrella: A devotee will gain a kingdom
Round: Brings immense wealth
Shaped like a cart: Brings sorrow
Shaped like the top portion of a spear: Brings death
Deformed or having an ugly mouth: Brings poverty
Shaped with joint circular marks - chakras: Brings disease
Cracked: Brings death
Reddish-brown of any shape: Brings loss of wealth
(Brahma Vaivarta Purana, Prakritikhanda, 21:78-79)

Therefore, a Shaligram read as Krishna Balaram would fall under the auspices of, and be considered a version of, the Krishna-type Shaligram recorded in the sacred texts even if it would be addressed as Balaram during ritual worship:[9]

1. Keshava: (i) Marked with a small circular print, a garland and several golden dot prints. (ii) Marked with a conch and a circle on the lower middle portion.

2. Hayagriva: (i) Blue in color, shaped like a spearhead (Ankusha), and marked with a linear, a circular and several dot prints. (ii) With five linear marks, other characteristics being the same as above. (iii) Marked with a circle and a flag-print, other things being the same as above. (iv) Green in color, shaped like the head of a horse, and marked with a circle.

3. Paremeshthin: (i) With a hole at the top and having the marks of a lotus, a circle and several dots. (ii) White in color, having a decent hole and a picture at the top and marked with a discus and a lotus. (iii) Reddish in color with a circular and linear mark, and a hole at the top. (iv) Round in shape, yellow in color with a hole at the top. (v) Reddish or yellowish in color with the marks of a lotus and a circle on His body, its top portion being divided by a circular hole.

4. Hiranyagarbha: (i) With the color like that of honey and having a long shape. It has moon-like marks and several golden linear marks on His body. (ii) Black in color and round in shape with a circular glaced opening. A sweet sound is always formed inside His body. It is marked with a charming Shrivatsa (a circle formed of hair) at its top.

5. Chaturbhuja: He holds the color of a new cloud. It has a round shape with four circular marks on the body.

6. Gadadhara: Green in color with its lower middle portion raised upwards. It has a big hole at its top and is marked with long lines.

7. Narayana: (i) He holds at His front side a good-looking opening marked with a necklace, a golden bracelet (keyura) and other ornaments. (ii) It is marked with two circular prints on its either side with a clear circular mark at its opening.

8. Lakshmi-Narayana: (i) It has a single opening with four circular marks (or with a vanamala) (ii) Round in shape big in size, having a glaced opening marked with a flag, a cross and a spear-head. (iii) Round in shape with a circular opening marked with four circles, and also printed with a flag, a cross, a spear head, and a yellow spot. (iv) Green in color, round in shape, and marked with one or four circular prints. (v) Big in size with a comparatively high top, and marked with a flag, a cross, a spear-head, a garland and a few dot prints. (vi) With a small opening, having four circular prints and also marked with a garland. (vii) Marked with three circular prints. (viii) With the color of a new cloud and having a single opening marked with four circular prints, and also having the mark of a garland on His body.

---

9 This list was originally compiled by Rabindra Kumar Siddhantashastree. 1985. Vaishnavism Through the Ages. pages 27-49 and is available in summarized for online at http://www.salagram. net/shaligrams1.htm.

9. Naranarayana: Green in color with a charming shape, having reddish circular marks at the opening and golden spots on His body.

10. Rupinarayana: Marked with a pestle, a garland, a conch, a discuss and mace on his front side. It may also have the mark of a bow at His front.

11. Madhava: With a color like that of honey and marked with a mace and a conch.

12. Govinda: (i) Black in color and very charming to look at. He holds the marks of a mace and a discus on His right side and that of a mountain on the left. (ii) Black in color and middle in size, having His central portion raised upwards. He has a big opening beautifully marked with circles, and His body is also decorated with five different circles.

13. Vishnu: (i) Big in size and black in color with linear markings at the center of the opening. (ii) With the mark of the mace at the center of the opening things being the same as above.

14. Madhusudana: With a single circular mark at the opening and the marks of a conch and a lotus on His body.

15. Trivikrama: (i) Green in color, triangular in shape, and glittering to look at. He holds a single circular mark on His left side and a linear mark on His right side. (ii) With two circular marks, other things apparently being the same as above.

16. Shridhar: (i) Round in shape and decorated with five linear marks and a good-looking garland mark. (ii) With linear marks standing upwards on His both sides, other things are the same as above. (iii) Green in color, round in shape with a flat upper side and having a lotus mark at the opening. (iv) Very small in size and marked with two circles and a garland. (v) Glittering like a gem and having the marks of a flag and a circle. (vi) He has a glaced body with the mark of vanamala on it, and there are also linear marks on the upper side on his body.

17. Hrishikesh: (i) Shaped like a half moon. (ii) With a single circular mark and also with marks resembling the hair of a boar.

18. Padmanabha: (i) Reddish in color with a mark of a lotus on His body. (ii) With a full and half circular mark, and also with the mark of a petal (of a lotus) but there is no hair mark on the body.

19. Damodara: (i) Big in size with a small circular mark. (ii) Green in color and big in size with a very small opening. He has a big circular mark and one or more yellow spots on His body. (iii) He has a single opening not very deep, and two circular marks one above the other. There is also a long linear mark at His center.

20. Sudarshan: (i) Green in color and glittering to look at. He holds the marks of a mace and a discus on His left side and two linear marks on His right side. A lotus printed with linear marks is also found on his body. (ii) A circular mark at the top and a big opening is deeply dark.

21. Vaasudeva: White in color and glittering to look at. He has two circular marks closely printed but not joined, at His opening.

22. Pradyumna: (i) Yellow in color with a small opening and having several linear marks both at the top as well as on the sides. (ii) Blue in color with many holes at His small mouth and having a comparatively long shape.

23. Aniruddha: (i) Blue in color and round in shape and glaced and printed with a lotus and three linear marks. (ii) Black in color with a beautifully shaped opening and having the mark of a discus at the center, another on a side and a small circle at the top. (iii) Yellow in color, round in shape and very charming to look at.

24. Purushottama: (i) golden in color with a circular mark at the middle portion of His body and a bigger circular mark at the top. (ii) Yellow in color and marked with dot-prints on all sides. (iii) With openings on all sides numbering about ten.

25. Adhokshaja: Deep dark in color with red linear marks. He is round in shape with a single circular mark and a few reddish spots on His body. He may be either big or small in size.

26. Acyuta: With four circular marks on the right and left sides and two red circles at the opening. He is also marked with conch, discus, stick, bow, arrow, mace, pestle, flag, a white umbrella and a red spearhead.

27. Upendra: Green in color and glittering like a gem. He has a glaced body with one or more circular marks on His sides.

28. Janardana: (i) With two openings marked with four circles. (ii) With two circular marks on the sides and two others at the top. (iii) With one opening at the front side, and another at the back side, each marked with two circles.

29. Lakshmijanardana: With one opening printed with four circles.

30. Hari: Green in color, round in shape with one opening at the top. The lower portion of His body is marked with dot-prints.

31. Ananta: (i) Marked with the hood of a snake and many circles. (ii) With many holes on His body and marked with several circles. (iii) Variegated in color and marked with the hood of a snake and also with circular prints not less than 14 and not more than 20 in number. (iv) big in size, cloudy in color and marked with 14 chakra prints.

32. Yogeshwara: The type found at the top of the Shaligram mountain.

33. Pundarikaaksham: Printed with two eye-like marks either on a side or at the top.

34. Chaturmukha: With four linear marks rising from the sides, and also printed with two circular marks on the middle portion of His body.

35. Yajnamurthi: Reddish yellow in color, with a small opening and two circular marks, one at the bottom and one the other side on the right side.

36. Dattatreya: (i) With white, red and black spots all over His body and a mark of a rosary on the very topside (ii) Red and yellow in color, other things being the same as above.

37. Shishmaarga: Long in shape, with a deep triangular opening and having one or two circular marks on the front side and another on the back side.

38. Hamsa: Shaped like a bow with a mixed color of blue and white and having the marks of a discus and lotus on His body.

39. Parahamsa: Shaped like the throat of a peacock, with a glaced body and round opening. Inside the opening there are two circular marks with a sun-like print on the right side of them. There are also two linear marks forming the shape of a boar on His body.

40. Lakshmipati: Either the front or any one of his rear sides is shaped like the throat of a peacock. He is dark in color with a big opening and a small circular mark.

41. Garudadhvaja: Round in shape with the marks of golden horns and hoofs on the body. He is also printed with a circular mark with dark linear marks inside it.

42. Vatapatrashaayin: Round in shape with a mixed color of white, red and blue. He has also one circular mark with a conch on His left and a lotus on His right side. There are also four circular marks and three dot-prints inside His opening.

43. Vishvambhara: He has 23 circular marks on His body

44. Vishvarupa: With one opening and many circular marks.

45. Ananta: Bigger than Vishvarupa in size with five openings and many circular marks. He is also held as a variety of Vishvarupa.

46. Pitambara: Round in shape having some similarity with the buttock of a cow and printed with one circular mark.

47. Chakrapani: Round and glaced in shape, with a small circular mark and many other prints.

48. Saptavirashrava: Round in shape with a small circular mark and several golden dot-prints all over the body.

49. Jagadyoni: Red in color with a circular mark at the front of his opening.

50. Bahurupin: With many openings having the marks of a conch and discus in one of them.

51. Harihara: (i) With two circular marks and a print like a Shiva linga on His front side. (ii) With three circular marks on the sides, other things being the same as above. (iii) With four circular marks, other things being the same as above.

52. Shivanarayan: (i) a Harihara type with four different circular marks, and two openings. (ii) Without any opening, other things being the same as above. Both these varieties of Shivanarayan are forbidden to be worshipped; because they cause loss of wealth and land, and even they extinguish the family of their worshippers.

53. Swayambhu: Blue in color with a long and big opening, and having His body encircled by linear marks.

54. Shankaranarayana: Marked with the print resembling a Shiva linga either side on the right or the left side.

55. Pitaamaha: He has four different openings with a circular mark in each of them.

56. Naramurtti: Yellow in color with the marks of a Shiva linga on one side and a sacred thread on the other.

57. Shesha: Printed with linear marks forming the coiled body of a snake.

58. Pralambaghna: Red in color with the marks of a coiled body and a hood of a snake. this type is forbidden to be worshipped.

59. Suryamurtti: With twelve different circular marks either on the body or inside His opening.

60. Haihaya: (i) With one opening and different marks of hoods. Amongst these marks two take place on the right-side outside the opening. (ii) Shaped like a lotus leaf with a golden mark resembling an arc.

61. Vishnupanjara: Printed with several linear marks created by the insect called Vajrakita.
62. Garuda: (i) Shaped like a lotus with three linear marks one above the other, the central line being longer. (ii) Printed with long linear marks and having two, three or four golden spots on His body. In color he may be green, blue or white.

Dasavatara Shaligrams, the ten incarnations of Vishnu, receive similar treatment where each Shaligram incarnation includes a number of sub-types. This list of Dasavatara types is also included in the Pranatoshini Tantra (348-351)[10]. Again, this list is considered spiritually authoritative but is not necessarily directly referenced during actual Shaligram identifications:

1. Matsya or the Fish type
    ii. Long in shape, golden in color, and marked with three dot-prints.
    iii. Like bell metal in color, other characteristics being the same as above.
    iv. With the color of sphatika (crystal) other things being the same as above.
    v. Green in color and marked with a fish, and two circles.
    vi. Long in shape with three openings, having a circular mark inside the opening and another at the tail. He has the mark of a cart on His right side and a linear fish on His left side.
    vii. With a long shape having opening at the right side, and marked with three dot prints, one discus, one lotus and one conch.
    viii. Shaped like a fish with a long mark on His head.
2. Kurma or the Tortoise type:
    i. Shaped like a tortoise with the eastern side elevated.
    ii. Green in color, round in shape resembling a tortoise, His upper side being comparatively higher and printed with circular markings.
    iii. Shaped like a tortoise and printed with five different marks each resembling the sun.
    iv. Marked with foot-prints of a cow on His sides.
    v. Marked with a conch, a flag, and three golden dot-prints.
    vi. Long in shape with openings on the left and right sides and printed with five sun-marks.
    vii. Shaped like a snuhi (emphorbia antiquorum) flower with circular marks on both the sides.
    viii. Round and long in shape, having a circle and a tortoise printed on His sides. He has a mixed color of blue and red.
3. Varaha or the Boar type:
    i. Blue in color, big in size, and printed with circular marks in odd number, as well as three linear marks.
    ii. Printed with even number of circular marks, of which at least one takes place on His right side, and also with a vanamala. This last variety is also called Lakshmi-Varaha.

10 This list was originally compiled by Rabindra Kumar Siddhantashastree. 1985. Vaishnavism Through the Ages. pages 27-49 and is available in summarized for online at http://www.salagram.net/shaligrams1.htm.

4. Narasimha or the Man-lion type:
    i. With a big opening and two circular marks.
    ii. With a long opening and linear marks resembling the mane of a lion, and also with two circular marks.
    iii. Marked with three dot-prints other things being the same as above.
    iv. Uneven in shape with a mixed reddish color, having two big circular marks above it, and a crack at the front.
    v. Reddish in color and printed with several teeth like marks, three or five dot-marks and a big circular mark.
    vi. With a big opening, a vanamala and two circular marks. This type is popularly known as Lakshminrisimha.
    vii.   Black in color with dot marks all over his body and two circular marks on His left side. This also is a variety of the Lakshminrisimha sub-type.
    viii.   Printed with a lotus mark on His left side. This also is a sub-type of Lakshminrisimha.
    ix. When any of the above types of Narasimha is marked with five dot prints He is popularly called Kapilanrisimha.
    x. Printed with seven circular marks and golden dots and also having openings on all sides. This type is called Sarvotmukhanrisimha.
    xi. Variegated in color, having many openings including a large one and marked with many circular prints. This type is popularly called Paataalanrisimha.
    xii.   With two circular marks inside the main opening and eight others on His sides. This also is a variety of Paataalanrisimha.
    xiii.   Aakaashanrisimha: With a comparatively high top and a big opening and also printed with circular marks.
    xiv.   Jihvaanrisimha: Big in size, with two openings and two circular marks. He being the giver of poverty, His worship is forbidden.
    xv.   Raakshasanrisimha: With a fierce opening and holes, and also marked with golden spots. His worship also is forbidden.
    xvi.   Adhomukhanrisimha: With three circular marks one at the top and two on the sides, having His opening at the bottom.
    xvii.   Jvaalaanrisimha: Marked with two circular prints and a vanamala, and having a small opening.
    xviii. Mahaanrisimha: Printed with two big circular marks and a few other linear marks one above the other.

5. Vaman or the Dwarf type:

    i. Round in shape, small in size and marked with five linear prints.

    ii. Small in size and glittering to look at. He has a circular mark on each of His above and below sides with the print of a Garuda bird near the circular marks.

    iii. Not very small in size. Marked with a circular print at the centre and glaced to look at.

    iv. Yellow in color with a bit high top and having an indistinct circular mark.

    v. Cloudy in color, round in shape, marked with a vanamala and having a small opening.

    vi. Very small in size with the color of a cloud and marked with two circles. He is popularly called Dadhivaamana.

    vii.   Yellowish in color, marked with several dot-prints with one or more at the opening. He also is a variety of the Dadhivaamana sub-type.

N.B.: Regarding the shape of these Dadhivaamana varieties, the Matsyasukta(Matsyasukta quoted in Praanateshanitantra, page 350.) tells us that they may resemble either a vilva (woodapple) or vadara (berry) or even like the seed of any of these fruits.

6. The Parasuram type:

    i. Yellow in color and marked with a print resembling an axe.

    ii. With two prints resembling teeth, either at the top or on any two sides, other things being the same as above.

7. The Ramachandra type:

    i. Yellow in color and printed with the mark of the bow.

    ii. Green in color and glaced, having a stick like mark on the back side and two linear marks on the rear sides.

    iii. Ranaraama: Middle in size, round in shape and marked with two circles, and arrow, a quiver and several dot-prints.

    iv. Raajaraajeshvara: Round in shape, middle in size and printed with two circular marks at the opening. His body is marked with the prints of an umbrella, an arrow, a quiver, and several dots resembling the wounds caused by arrows.

    v. Sitaaraam: (a) Cloudy in color, with one opening, and printed with marks resembling teeth, bow, arrow, spear, umbrella, flag, chowry and garland.

8. With two openings each furnished with two circular marks and also with a circular print on His left side.

    i. Dashakanthakulaantaka Raama:

    ii. Like an egg of a hen in size, green in color, and having two openings with two linear marks at each of them, and also with the mark of a bow. His top side is comparatively higher.

9. Printed with a linear mark resembling a bow on each side, other things being the same as above.

   i. Viiraraama: Printed with an arrow, a quiver, a bow, an ear-ring, a garland, and a small circular mark decorated with petals.

   ii. Vijayaraama: Printed with an arrow, a bow, a quiver, and a big opening marked with red dots. A circular mark decorated with petals also is printed on His body or at the opening.

   iii. Raamamurtti: or Kavitavada Raama: Black in color and glaced, having one opening with a circular mark.

   iv. Dushtharaaraama: Cloudy in color with the mark resembling one's knee, and also with a bow and arrow on the top side and footprints of a cow on the rear sides.

10. The Sankarshan type:

   i. With two circular marks joined with each other on the top side.

   ii. Reddish in color with the glaced and spotless eastern side and marked with two circles joined with each other.

   iii. Balabhadra: Marked with seven circular prints.

   iv. Balarama: With five linear marks on the top side and a bow and an arrow on the rear sides.

11. The Buddha type:

   i. With a very small opening and without any circular markings.

   ii. This type is popularly called Niviita Buddha.

12. The Kalki type:

   i. With the color of a bee and printed with six circular marks, having a linear sword above the opening.

   ii. Shaped like a horse and marked with three circular prints.

A group of the Vaishnavas having been inclined to hold Krishna Vaasudev as the eighth prominent incarnation of Lord Vishnu, instead of Sankarshan, used to worship a new type of Saligram holding it a sacred symbol of the Lord, and giving the name Krishna type to it. With the passing of time this new type also was divided into different varieties in the following way:

13. The Krishna type:

   i. Marked with a vanamala and a discus on His right side.

   ii. Black in color with two equal circular marks at the opening.

   iii. Small in size with a yellow spot and several dot-prints on His sides.

   iv. With the upper side like that of a tortoise, and the entire lower middle portion resembling its mouth.

   v. Taarksya: (a) Black in color and long in shape resembling a pillar. (b) Shaped like a spear-head, and marked with two circles, one lotus, one ring, and one gem.

   vi. Baalakrsna: With a long opening having dot-prints on His lower side.

   vii. Gopala: Deep black in color, big in size with a good-looking opening. He has two circular marks, and the marks of vanamala and shrivatsa on His upper side, and also teeth like marks on a rear side.

viii. Madanagopal: A Gopala type holding a lotus mark on His upper or lower side.

ix. Santaanagopal: Long in shape, black in color with an opening of the half-moon shape.

x. Govardhanagopala: With a comparatively less height and round upper portion. Marked with a stick, a garland, a whistle and long lines and also having silver dots all over His body.

xi. Lakshmigopal: Shaped like the egg of a hen and marked with a vanamala, a plough, a whistle, and a ring on different sides.

xii. Kaliyamardana: Marked with a golden line and three dot-prints.

xiii. Syamantahaarin: Big in size, with the color of a sword, and having the marks of a vanamala and shrivatsa on His upper side.

xiv. Chanooramardan: Green in color with two red spots and a linear mark on each of the right and left sides.

xv. Kamsamardana: Blue in color, having a different color either at the front or on a rear side.

PILGRIMAGE LITERATURE

Today, because numerous and fractionated texts often fail to provide clear direction, multiple practitioners have, however, begun to write their own guides. The wide variety of variations, revisions, and combinations of these Shaligram name-type lists is thus now referenced and reproduced in any number of pilgrimage pamphlets and local guru literatures available throughout South Asia. One such example, for instance, is Ashoke Roy's "Bhagaban Vishnu and Saligram Shila," a Bengali Shaligram identification directory with limited distribution in West Bengal, Kathmandu, Nepal, and in Bangladesh. Roy's work is interesting however in that, though it provides photographs of many Shaligram variations, it does not appear to follow any particular Puranic list.

Rather, Roy groups the Shaligrams in his guide by the specific characteristics of their principal central spirals and includes ammonite fossils (which would not otherwise be considered Shaligram) from elsewhere in the world in his interpretive frameworks. As such, Roy's Shaligram guide leverages more modern regional interpretations of Shaligrams which bars any stone with an uneven shape or a spiked appearance from worship and includes such unique categories as Paramesthi, Padmanava, Baikuntha, Buddha, Ksheerabdishayan, Guru, and Shib Navi, along with many previously recognizable categories like Lakshmi-Narayan, Sudarshan, Damodar, and Sri Ram.

Beyond that, there are, in fact, a number of pilgrimage guides that also contain discussions of Shaligrams, along with the temple site of Muktinath where they are venerated, that have been written and published over the years. The most prevalent Hindu one available near Muktinath today is Madhu Sudhan Ramanujadas' Muktichhetra Mahatmyamam (2003), which includes large sections of Sanskrit, Hindi, and Nepali text drawn from the various Puranas that outline a multitude of Shaligram origin stories and identifying characteristics. Another is Pandit Bhavanishankar Shastri's Shalgram-Rahasyam ("The Mystery of Shaligram") published with the support of Subba Mohan Man Sherchan of Tukche village in 1947.

Furthermore, the obscure book Mustang Digdarshan[11] is another compilation occasionally referenced in terms of historical material on Shaligram pilgrimage, but given that it contains no citations, it is usually ignored in favor of more comprehensive texts, such as Rao's Śālagrāma – Kosha. And apart from religiously-oriented pilgrimage materials, some devotees also cite Ramesh Dhungel's "Damodarakunda: Ek Parichaya" (Damodar Kunda: An Introduction)[12] as especially helpful in researching the history of Shaligrams as well as his "Muktinath: Kehi Aitihasik Tathya" (Muktinath: Some Historical Facts)[13] and 'Dharmic Sahishnutako Prasanga Muktinath' (Muktinath: A Context of Religious Tolerance)[14]. Taken together, it is easy to see how complicated, and disorienting, learning about Shaligram interpretation can be.

ADDITIONAL RESOURCES

1. Mustang Digdarshan (Mustang: a Perspective) by Narayan Prasad Chhetri. Published by Kathmandu, 1987
2. A research paper in the possession of MFI (Muktinath Foundation International) and at Tribhuvan University.
3. 1988: "Muktinath (a Hindu Temple in North-western Nepal): Some Historical Facts" Ancient Nepal No. 102
4. 1988: "Context of Religious Tolerance in Mukti-Chhetra" (text in Nepali), Saiva Bhumi Vol. 3, No.3 (Journal of Pashupati Socio-religious Service Association, Kathmandu, Nepal)

CHAPTER THREE

SHALIGRAM INTERPRETIVE TRADITIONS IN PRACTICE

Beaming with joy in the high Himalayan sun, Naga Baba, a Nepali sadhu held up a large Shaligram. Though he typically spent the majority of the cold winter months at Pashupatinath Temple in Kathmandu, he was currently living just outside of Muktinath Temple in Mustang on what he explained was his thirtieth year of Shaligram pilgrimage. We had been on the Kali Gandaki River, walking along the banks of black, sandy, sediments, for several hours when he suddenly shouted to the small group of pilgrims (which included myself) that a Shaligram had appeared. As we rushed over to see the new deity, Naga Baba carefully sat down on a stony outcropping and began to gently turn the stone over and over in his hands.

"This is Shankaranarayana." He said, opening his hands for everyone in the group to get a better view. Several pilgrims immediately asked him to explain how he knew the Shaligram's name.

"The writings say that you will see two things." He replied. "There must be Vishnu and Shiva together and the stone must be large and very black. Here you see Vishnu." He indicated a moderately-sized ammonite spiral imprinted on the top of the Shaligram. "Here you see Shiva in the lingam." He then turned the stone over to trace his finger down the edge of a fossilized belemnite[15]. "But that is not all!" He continued. "This lingam has a golden color[16] and there is a vanamala going around the entire body. This means that he is meditating and is in the mood of renunciation. I do not see markings of trishula[17] though, just chakra. That also means that I cannot take him. A sadhu does not keep such Shaligrams."

"I've never heard of such a shila." One of the pilgrims said. "Are they very rare?"

Naga Baba smiled again. "You would call him Harihara. That is the name in your books. Harihara. That is not what I would call him but he is the same. I feel how heavy the shila is, I see how dark his body is, and I know his name. These Shaligrams only appear when someone is very conflicted, when they don't know what path is ahead of them. He has come to show someone the way."

---

15 Belemnites were marine cephalopods with characteristically long, thin, bodies and shells shaped like spear-points. Their closest living relatives are squid and cuttlefish.

16 Mineralized iron ore deposits are common in ammonite fossils in the Nepal Himalayas. As the ammonite then spends a long time tumbling down the Kali Gandaki River, the iron oxidizes into iron pyrites; which gives many Shaligrams their golden colors.

17 A trident weapon traditionally wielded by Shiva.

I spoke with Naga Baba several times while at Muktinath and he took great pride in his knowledge of Hindu scriptures as well as his extensive experience interpreting Shaligrams. I learned a great deal about Shaligram traditions from him and I once had the privilege of attending a Shaligram puja he conducted at Pashupatinath after leaving the Himalayas. Overall, his greatest concern though was that he saw fewer and fewer pilgrims to Mustang each year and he was now focusing his efforts on teaching Shaligram interpretation to several Nepali families in the Kathmandu area. I owe him a tremendous debt of gratitude for all that he was willing to teach me.

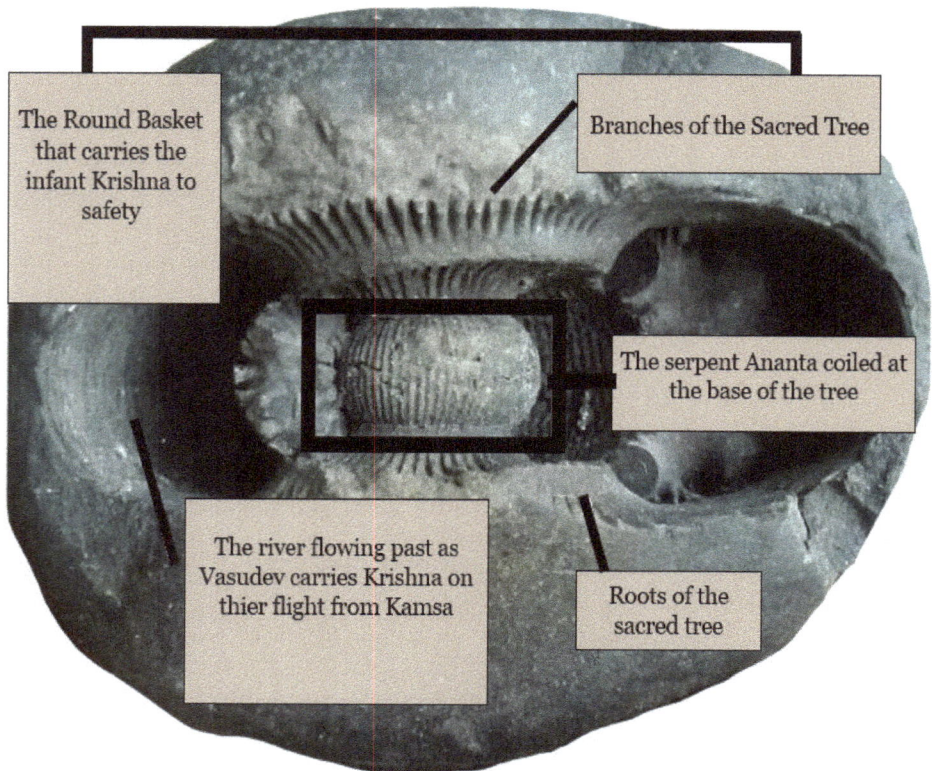

The Round Basket that carries the infant Krishna to safety

Branches of the Sacred Tree

The serpent Ananta coiled at the base of the tree

The river flowing past as Vasudev carries Krishna on thier flight from Kamsa

Roots of the sacred tree

Figure 1: Reading a Vasudev Shaligram

PRINCIPAL CHARACTERISTICS

Reading a Shaligram may begin with scriptural texts, but it ends with the final divination of the deity by way of each Shaligram's unique characteristics as they appear when the shila is acquired. The arrangement of these characteristics is then interpreted within the contexts of a given practitioner's life circumstances or experiences. For ritual specialists, interpreting a Shaligram typically follows three general steps: determining the name-type of the Shaligram (using a name-type list drawn from the practitioner's religious tradition), determining the specific deity manifested (rupa). Just like (bhava) is after mood or stance.

This is accomplished with the observation of six main types of characteristics: set (how the Shaligram rests on a flat surface), shape, color, chakra (number and type of spirals), vadana (number and type of mouths/holes), and vanamala (number of white lines). After that, any other minor markings a Shaligram contains will also be taken into account, such as rekha (striated lines), markings of weapons, markings of lotus flowers, tulsi leaves, or a conch shell and golden or white spots. One of my long-term teachers explained is thusly: "You first look at the shape." Sriram Bhavyesh placed a Shaligram in the palm of his right hand. "It's smooth, black, and almost perfectly round, but it has this one chakra on the bottom here which forms a ridge all along the edge. It makes the bottom flat, the top rounded, and there is this little protrusion here on the end, sort of pointed.

This is a Mahavishnu Shaligram. Others call it Dasavatara. It is Sri Kurma, the turtle incarnation of Vishnu as you see that it is shaped like a turtle. But you see this indentation here in the center of the shell?" He turned the Shaligram to show me the small, rounded, impression with a small amount of iron pyrites glittering in the center. "It is golden in color. This is the mark of Mount Mandara where it rested upon Kurma's back. From here the gods churned the ocean of milk and so this is Sri Kurma Mandar Parvat, the turtle who carries the mountain. This we find in Bhagavata Purana, in Vishnu Purana, and in Mahabharata."

"Would everyone agree?" I asked. "If I were to take this to another temple, would they say the same?"

Sriram laughed. "I am Sri Vaishnava, so I know it in this way. A Shaiva might say the same. So would a Smarta. They would know that it is Mahavishnu because this is what the scriptures tell us. They would also know that it is Kurma; that can be read no other way. But maybe they would see some other manifestation in the small things. Each tradition is different and different teachers can see different things. It depends on who you are when the Shaligram speaks to you."

In this way, both text and local tradition combine to read and understand each Shaligram in turn, where interpretation of text and the interpretation of stone become one and the same thing, and the gods themselves speak to devotees through the physical and symbolic processes of nature and narrative. As such, various ritual specialists often begin by broadly identifying the shila using their own categorical lists of Shaligram types and descriptions drawn from local traditions or from various ritual genealogies. They then work from general to specific; narrowing down the particular deity manifestation present in the individual Shaligram by reading the smaller characteristics that define the unique divine presence they are encountering.

In most cases, practitioner lists of Shaligram categories typically demonstrate strong overlap with the various Puranic lists (with the inclusion or exclusion of specific deities as per their preferences) but in a few other cases it should be noted that the type-lists were drawn almost entirely from regional stories and traditions. Among one group of Shaligram specialists in Kathmandu, Nepal, for example, their name-type list of thirty Shaligrams was based on a blending of Nepali Vaishnava theology (based on Dasavatara manifestations) and other regional and shamanic ritual practice systems (most notably including the Buddha, the Damodar Kunda -- a sacred mountain lake -- and the Jwala -- or sacred mother flame) resulting in the list: 1) Sudarshan, 2) Vishnu, 3) Shiva, 4) Lakshmi-Narayan, 5) Lakshmi-Narasimha, 6) Kurma, 7) Matsya, 8) Varaha, 9) Ram, 10) Vaman, 11) Parshuram, 12) Krishna, 13) Narasimha, 14) Buddha, 15) Kalki, 16) Balaram, 17) Santhan Gopala, 18) Laddu Gopala, 19) Hayagriva, 20) Damodar, 21) Hiranyagarbha, 22) Ratnagarbha, 23) Govinda, 24) Madhusudan, 25) Gopal, 26) Damodar Kunda, 27) Ugra or Jwala, 28) Balaji (Venkatesh), 29) Sita Ram, and 30) Panchayan – a combination of stones (or a single stone) that represents Ganesh, Durga, Surya, Shiva, and Vishnu.

This list was often then compared to another type-list of twenty-three categories being used by a group of Shaligram specialists from the Shakti Hindu tradition on the other side of the city: 1) Aditya, 2) Anirudda, 3) Damodar, 4) Govinda, 5) Hayagriva, 6) Hiranyagarbha, 7) Hrishikesh, 8) Janardan, 9) Kalki, 10) Keshav, 11) Krishna, 12) Kurma, 13) Lakshmi-Narayan, 14) Lakshmi-Narasimha, 15) Lakshmi, 16) Maha Shakti/Maha Devi, 17) Matsya, 18) Santan Gopala, 19) Shankha, 20) Shivling, 21) Shridhar, 22) Sudarshan, and 23) Surya. What is most notable then, within these lists, is the various inclusions and exclusions of deities and deity manifestations in accordance with the most commonly venerated gods and goddesses within each relative tradition. In other words, just as the Puranic texts relate to one other through a variety of compositions, authors, and time periods so too do Shaligram type-lists owe their composition to persons, traditions, and practices within certain historical, political, and geographical contexts that vary considerably.

CASTE CONCERNS

Various textual restrictions on Shaligram worship are also a topic of concern among a large number of Vaishnava Shaligram practitioners. The injunctions found in different sacred books tend to fall into two categories: the restriction of certain types of Shaligrams by caste and the general restriction of certain kinds of Shaligram from worship entirely (forbidden Shaligrams). According, once again, to the Pranatoshini Tantra, each of the four varnas (the principal caste divisions of early Hinduism) are entitled to worship a particular type of Shaligram for securing the material and karmic merits suited to their specific caste dharmas.

In this tradition, the Vaasudeva-type Shaligrams are preferred by brahmanas; the Sakarshan-types by kshatriyas; Pradyumna-types by vaishyas and Aniruddha-types by shudras (see Hemadri quoted in Pranatoshini Tantra, 357). Brahmanas, however, are always authorized to offer worship on behalf of others, which not only explains why all Shaligram types are typically "permitted" among brahmanas but may also play a part in explaining why Shaligram worship is particularly visible among high-caste devotees.

In fact, Eleanor Zelliot mentions one such episode involving a disagreement about Shaligram worship between a Brahmin and shoemaker (an untouchable leather-worker) in her discussion of the hagiography of the 15th century bhakti poet-saint Ravidas (himself low caste and in his own words a "Chamar" whose trade is low and whose labor is degrading). In this account, a Marathi version of Ravidas' life appearing in an 18th century hagiography of Mahipati, a Brahmin comes to visit the house of Ravidas [Rohidas] and complains of his use of leather while worshipping Shaligram. Though lengthy, it bears repeating in full.

"22. Now it happened on a certain day that this bhakta of Vishnu was sitting performing his worship of God. He had withdrawn to be alone with materials of worship, and he held his fickle mind in restraint. 23. He brought a bottle of leather and placed it there filled with water. His mat and his sacred bag and casket were also made of leather. 24. Rohidas was sitting down with all his vessels made of leather and just then a Brahman came to his house to explain to him the [astrological] Calendar. 25. The Brahman sat down by the holy and beautiful tulsi altar. Rohidas at once arose and with reverence made him a namaskar. 26. The Brahman said to Rohidas, 'You are worshipping God while sitting upon a leather seat. What do you expect from that?' 27. We Brahmans worship Shaligram, the idol of Vishnu. How is it that you have placed Him in a leather bag? 28. How is it you have placed in a leather bag Him who dwells in Vaikunth [heaven], the Life of the world whom Yogis contemplate? How is it you have placed Him in a leather bag? 29. He who dwells upon the sea of milk, the Recliner upon Shesha, and who cannot be described adequately by the Shastras though you might search there for Him, you have made a leather bag and placed Him in it [...]

31. Hearing what the Brahman said, Rohidas replied, 'What object have you ever seen which has not leather connected with it? 32. Musical instruments and drums are used in the praise-service of Hari [...] 33. The black cow has a leather skin and yet her milk is holy [...] 34. Animate things that are born, those hatched from eggs, and those produced from seed, all three are covered with skin and Atmaran (God) is in them alike. 35. Shudras, Vaishyas, Kshatriyas, and Brahmans are covered with skin [...] 37. [...] And from a leather shrine (the human body) Atmaran (God) speaks with His gentle voice. 38. [...] If the Pervader of the universe, the Life of the world, is in a leather bag, how can you regard Him as defiled by the leather?" [...] 43. The Brahman now replied, 'The emblem of Vishnu (Shaligram) is a holy pebble and so if a shoemaker worships Him, He is defiled thereby [...] 45. We alone should worship the Lord of Vaikunth (heaven). Among the four races we Brahmans are the highest. 46. Shri Hari is chief among the gods. The Brahmans are the highest among the four races. They alone have the authority to invest themselves with the sacred thread and they alone can worship Vishnu.'

47. Hearing this remark, Rohidas replied, 'Oh Swami, I will show you my sacred thread.' 48. Then with his sharp tool he ripped open his stomach, and showed the sacred thread within it. 49. The Brahman then exclaimed, 'You are indeed a bhakta of Vishnu, I was thoughtless and persecuted you [...] 50. [...] In persecuting you I have but advanced your glory [...] 55. You are a supreme bhakta of Vishnu. Worship the Shaligram at your pleasure.' Thus speaking, the good Brahman went back to his home." (2010: 89-91).

This does not mean that only high-caste devotees venerate Shaligrams (far from it) but that the brahmana traditions of Shaligram worship tend to be the most often referenced, the most published about, and the most discussed in terms of "ideal" Shaligram worship. The texts also go on to mention that kshatriyas are entitled to offer worship to three different Shaligram types other than their primary one.

Similarly, a vaishya may lawfully offer worship to the Pradyumna and Aniruddha-types while a shudra, unsurprisingly, to the Aniruddha-type only. In practice, however, very few if any of these kinds of caste restrictions are followed nor, as I noted several times in my field notes, even taken into serious consideration. The relatively anti-caste and anti-elite approaches of the majority of modern Vaishnava bhakti have long since rejected many ritual-caste divisions and none more so than Hindus and Buddhists of the global Diaspora who undertake pilgrimage for Shaligrams.

This isn't to say that caste is never considered or discussed, but that the majority of Shaligram ritual specialists today have stated that, in the time of Kali Yuga (the current and final age), it is more important that Shaligram traditions be continued and passed down regardless of caste, gender, or political divisions. Different scriptural authorities however, denote a few types of Shaligrams which should not be worshipped by householders and a number of other types which should be avoided by sadhus and ascetics.

In the texts, the reason for this, as you may recall from earlier, is that certain types of Shaligrams are said to bring undesirable results to householders and their families, such as loss of wealth, the deaths of wives and children, and a danger of creating worldly attachments to material goods. Some of the noted forbidden varieties of Shaligrams are those that offer no result at all from veneration:

   i. triangular in shape
   ii. uneven in shape
   iii. without any opening or with deformed or incorrect kinds of openings
   iv. broken ones
   v. shaped like a half of the moon

And those that bring sorrow, disease, and death:

   i. with an ugly mouth
   ii. broken
   iii. uneven in shape
   iv. with different circular marks joined together
   v. A Nrisimha type with uneven lower portion
   vi. a Kapila type with uneven circular or linear marks

Again, in Sri Vaishnava Chatur-vyuha theology, the suitability of Shaligrams for worship is a combination of color, shape, and wear patterns divided up caste-varna.

The details to be examined are the shape and the colour of the stone, the number and location of chakra-marks, the type of filaments that are present in the crevices and fissures and the deity-identity. Of the large number of deity-specific salagrama-stones, three are held especially sacred: Vishnu-salagrama (identified by the chakra in the shape of a garland, and by the marks of conch, mace and lotus), Lakshmi-narasimha-salagrama (having two chakras on the left side of the opening or vadana, and dots and specks all over the body), Matsya-murti-salagrama (fish shaped flat stone with a single opening and two chakras, one of them inside the opening and the other outside; having dots and specks on the body resembling a foot-print). A salagrama with no openings but having two chakras on the surface is usually considered ferocious (ugra) and is either avoided or worshipped especially elaborately. The Matsya-murti-salagrama is particularly recommended when it has a chakra on the tail portion (viz. Rear).

Authorities like Vrddha-gautama indicate that brahmanas may worship five Salagramas, kshatriyas eight, vaishyas seven and shudras seven; for ascetics four Salagramas are suggested.

For brahmanas: i) Lakshmi-narayana; ii) Ananta, iii) Hiranya garbha; iv) Purushottama; and v) Chaturbhuja.

For kshatriyas: i) Lakshmi-narayana; ii) Ananta; iii) Krishna; iv) Aniruddha; v) Garuda-dhvaja; vi) Gopala; vii) Rama; and viii) Sridhara.

For vaishyas: i) Lakshmi-narayana; ii) Vasudeva; iii) Pradhyumna; iv) Damodara; v) Pitambara; vi) Hari; and vii) Gadadhara.

For shudras: i) Lakshmi-narayana; ii) Madhava; iii) Krishna; iv) Achyuta; v) Aniruddha; vi) Kesava; vii) Pitambara.

For ascetics: i) Narsimha; ii) Hayagriva; iii) Mukunda; and iv) Maha-nila.

However, Puja-prakasa suggests that the Vasudeva-murti-salagrama is suitable for the brahmanas, Samkarshana-salagrama for the kshatriyas, the Pradyumna-salagrama for the vaishyas and the Aniruddha-salagrama for the Sudras. Vishnu-dharmottara has the same prescription and adds that the brahmanas may worship four salagrama-stones, the kshatriyas three, the vaishyas two, and the shudras one.

WHICH STONES TO BE AVOIDED?

According to the Brahmanda Purana, there are several types of forbidden Shaligrams. Those which have chakra markings that cross each other (tiryak-chakra), which have "bound" chakras (baddha-chakras, meaning thereby the chakra markings showing constraint).

Which are deformed (kurupa), have rough openings (nishthurasya), have a terrific aspect (karala), look ferocious (vikarala), are tawny-coloured (kapila), have uneven spirals (vishamavarta), have openings too wide (vyalasya), are hollow inside (kotara), do not stand steadily (asana chalana).

Which are broken (bhanga), are very large (maha-sthula), have a crevice in the bottom joined with a single chakra (asane sushiram yasyas chakrenaikena samyuta), are cracked (dardara), which have a large number of chakras (bahu-chakra); has chakras that are broken (bhagna-chakra), has an opening below (adhomukhi).

Has a hole or fissure (sa-chhidra), is very red in colour (su-rakta), has a wide, spreading chakra (brhacchakra), is criss-crossed by numerous lines (bahu-rekha-samyukta), is an elongated chakra (dirgha-chakra), has chakras in a row (pankti-chakra), has been put in a fire (pradagdhika), which has no mark whatsoever (achihna), has fang-like projections (krura-damshtra-samayukta) or has swellings like water-bubbles (sphota-budbuda-samyuta) to be avoided.

The triangular, uneven shaped and crescent-shaped stones must not be worshipped. The salagrama-stones which have irregular angles, which are burst, burnt, stained, or warm to touch must be avoided, as also those without chakras, or those which have been embrocated (rubbed and frayed), or which have crooked apertures. Likewise, the stones with numerous chakras, crooked chakras and chakras at the bottom, must be avoided.

The stones with many arrow-like lines, or with chakras which cannot be deciphered at all; the stones which are shaped like unripe bread-fruit (Artocarpus integrifolia) or like the deep-brown vegetable (Caculus melanoleucus). The stones which are fettered (clasped or joined) or obstructed, the stones which have a cruel, terrible and awesome aspect, and the stones which have crooked snouts must be avoided.

The stones which are broken or burst open, the stones which are burnt, and the stones which are triangular in shape must be avoided, as also those which have internally split, and damaged; and the stones which have many scratches and fissures must also be avoided."

Modern day Shaligram practice, however, is still largely passed down generationally and through oral traditions. This means that so many of these scriptural restrictions are almost never referenced and even more infrequently practiced when it comes to Shaligrams already established within community networks. For example, most Shaligram interpretive traditions do not restrict any shila by shape.

Rather, they only expressly forbid the worship of Shaligrams that are broken, completely worn off, or have been intentionally modified (cut, sanded, or tooled); a point I will return to below. In any case, though texts comprise an important aspect of Shaligram veneration and are still referred to as authoritative in terms of spiritual ideals, actual ritual practice, the incorporation of Shaligrams into daily life, the respectful care for and interaction with the manifest deity, and the intentions of the devotee weigh far more heavily on the minds of practitioners than strict adherence to multiple, and often conflicting, scriptural authorities.

As one Nepali pilgrim explained, "I have read the texts and I understand them, but they can only tell you so much. They are good guides, but they cannot tell you everything you need to know. You must "see" (darshan) Shaligram, you must hear it and touch it and experience it. Shaligram must speak to you, and when it does, you must listen. Without this, there is nothing." This focus on action, and on individual ties with specific Shaligrams, rather than on authoritative doctrine is one of the hallmarks of Shaligram veneration worldwide.

COLOR CODING AND SIZE

Various Puranic texts describe Shaligrams as being black, red, yellow, white/whitish, sky-colored/blue, or brown. In regards to color, the Pranatoshini Tantra quotes an additional writing called the Yogaparijata that describes any Shaligram with a white color (or displaying "white teeth marks") as particularly inclined to bring good fortune to the devotee. Any given Shaligram might also contain a combination of colors, such as white quartz bands, reddish or golden iron pyrites, or green calcite.

The Skanda Purana (also in Pranatoshini tantra, page 347) references twenty categorical divisions of Shaligrams based on color and texture: (1) Glaced (meaning polished), (2) Black, (3) Brown, (4) Yellow, (5) Blue, (6) Red, (7) Rough, (8) Curved, (9) Big, (10) Unmarked, (11) Reddish brown, (12) Variegated, (13) Broken, (14) With many circular marks (chakras), (15) with a single circular mark, (16) with a long opening, (17) with a big circular mark, (18) having two or more circular marks joined with each other, (19) having a broken circular mark, and (20) having opening at the base.

The Skanda Purana then goes on to explain the likely results of worshipping each of the color-type varieties:

1. Glaced: By worshipping it daily in the proper way, a devotee secures his salvation very easily.
2. Black: Brings fame to its worshippers.
3. Brown: Removes sin.
4. Yellow: Brings children into the family.
5. Blue: Grants good fortune to the devotee.
6. Red: Daily worship will surely invite diseases. This Shaligram should not be worshipped in homes.
7. Rough: Daily worship invites great anxieties. This Shaligram should not be worshipped in homes.
8. Curved: Daily worship brings poverty. This Shaligram should not be worshipped in homes.
9. Big: Brings untimely death to a devotee. Individual worship should be carefully avoided.
10. Unmarked: This Shaligram is unable to offer any result, good or bad. Its worship is useless.
11-12. Reddish-Brown and the remaining nine types can only offer mental pain to their worshippers, and each as such, no devotee should offer worship to any of these types.[18]

---

18 Interestingly, this text also describes the characteristics of reading Dwarka shilas, which are also divided into a number of different varieties according to their colors and outward appearances (Padma Purana, quoted in Pranatoshini tantra, page 360.)

(1) The blue type: It is the giver of untimely death
(2) The reddish brown: It brings in serious dangers.
(3) Variegated: It gives insanity
(4) Yellow: It causes destruction of wealth.
(5) Smoky Color: It causes untimely death of children.
(6) The broken type: It causes death of wife.
(7) The white type with dot prints: It fulfils all desires.
(8) The type with unbroken circular marks: It removes poverty and sorrow.
(9) The type having glaced circular shape: It gives the same results as above.
(10) The type with quadrangular shape: It gives the same result as above.
(11) The type with even number of circular marks: It gives bliss and worldly pleasure.
(12) The type with odd number of circular marks: It causes sorrow and worldly pain.

The same authority adds that one should not offer worship to any of the following types because of their habit of giving undesirable results

(1) The type with one or more holes on its body.
(2) The broken one.
(3) That which is neither round, nor has angles on its sides.
(4) That which has odd number of circles marked on its body.
(5) That which is shaped like the half part of the moon.

A color-type and size list compiled by a Sri Vaishnava ritual specialist, however, includes another wide variety of possible combinations:

"The sacred stones may be white, yellow, red, black, green, tawny or ash-coloured; they may contain stains, and they may be multi-coloured. The colours might be excessive or faded; the colours may otherwise be difficult to determine. The stones occur thus in many colours and forms. The salagrama-stone is described as the "field" for the presence of Godhead. The differentiation in this regard are dependent on the colours.

The Vasudeva-salagrama is white in hue; the Sridhara-salagrama is yellow; Vishnu-salagrama is black stone; Narayana-salagrama is greenish (blue-black) in colourNarasimha-salagrama is red; Damodara is represented by the blue-coloured stone and Vamana-salagrama is like the atasi flower in colour. Multi-coloured stones indicate Ananta and stones which are bright-white in colour Adhoksaja. The stones which are reddish brown like honey represent Brahma and tawny coloured stone represents Narasimha.

The colours have their own effects and influences. The ash-coloured salagrama stone is especially suitable for worship by ascetics. The stones which are stained bring decay and destruction, the multi-coloured stones are also unfit for worship, unless it be Ananta-salagrama. Highly coloured stones cause misery; the faded colours destroy the lineage; the colours which are indistinct and uncertain make for death.

The tawny-coloured stone is consort-killer; the bluish-stone brings wealth; the black-stones cause nourishment and prosperity; and the red-stone brings in sovereignty. Excessively red-stone, however, deals death; the fair-coloured stone (viz. White) bestows wealth; multi-coloured stone makes for prosperity, while the faded colours are not useful when worshipped.

White coloured stones facilitate the obtainment of emancipation, and the stone with indistinct and uncertain colours destroy everything. The salagrama stones also differ with regard to their circumference (parimana), which is measured in terms of the size of the aperture.

The wise one will tie round the middle of the salagrama-stone a thread; and if the aperture is located at the spot which marks one-eighth of the thread's length, then the stone is of superior variety; it may also be of the middling variety.

However, the stone having an opening in the one-third part is to be rejected. (However, Brahmanda Purana has a different prescription: There are different effects in terms of locations of operators. If the aperture is downward, it is terrible; the aperture on top will be useful only in magical rites of driving away the enemy; The apertures being even are especially meritorious, while the aperture on the sides will take away fortune.

If the aperture is crooked, it causes disease; if long-mouthed it devours everything (viz. Makes one impoverished). One should carefully examine the stone before ascertaining the deity-specification. A large salagrama is by definition eight finger-breadths (of the worshipper) in width; larger than that is recognized as "very large" and is regarded as unsuitable for a householder to worship."[19]

According to the Yogaparijata, the veneration of broken, unusually large, or rough Shaligrams also causes loss of wealth, of intellect, and of lifetime longevity respectively. Additionally, the Pranatoshini tantra[20], describes various results of worship based on the number of circular marks (chakras) along the surface of a Shaligram.

The Prayogaparaijata section, however, describes the results of worshipping different colors of Shaligrams that contain only a single circular mark, all of which relate to the expected behavior of the Shaligram once it returns home with a devotee (Prayogaparaijata quoted in Pranatoshini tantra. page 361):

» One chakra: Sudarshan - Brings enjoyment and salvation (bhukti-mukti)
» Two chakras: Lakshminarayana – Brings the kingdom of heaven to earth
» Three chakras: Acyuta; Trivikrama - Brings wealth
» Four chakras: Janardan; Caturbhuja – Brings the destruction of one's enemies
» Five chakras: Vaasudeva - Brings freedom from the cycle of birth and death
» Six chakras: Pradyumna - Brings fame and prosperity
» Seven chakras: Sankarshan; Balabhadra – Brings sons and grandsons into the family
» Eight chakras: Purushottama – Brings the fulfilment of desires
» Nine chakras: Navavyuha - Brings high social or political positions
» Ten chakras: Dasavatara – Brings/strengthens kingship
» Eleven chakras: Aniruddha - Brings immense wealth
» Twelve chakras: Ananta – Brings the fulfilment of desires
» Thirteen or more chakras: Paramatma - Brings bliss and liberation
» White: Pundarika - Brings liberation from the karmic cycle
» Red: Pralambaghna – Bring disease and death
» Reddish Brown: Rama - Brings quarrels and strife in relationships
» Mixed of Two Colors: Vaikuntha - Brings poverty
» Mixed of Many Colors: Vishveshvara – Brings dependence on others

---

19 Balasubramanian, Venkatesh. 2003. Sri Ranga Sri "The Story of Shaligram." Ibiblio Archives. http://www.ibiblio.org/sripedia/srirangasri/archives/dec03/msg00007.html. Accessed 2 Dec 2016.

20 The Pranatoshini tantra is one of the two largest and most comprehensive scriptural compendia of tantric practices from northeast India, along with the 16th century Bṛhat Tantrasāra. See: Hugh B. Urban. 2009. The Power of Tantra: Religion, Sexuality and the Politics of South Asian Studies. I. B. Tauris Publishers.

Pranatoshini tantra. प्राणतोषणी. 1983. Ramatoṣaṇa Bhaṭṭa and Ramadatta Shukla, trans. Prayaga: Shakta Sadhana Pīṭha Publishers.

The scriptures therefore advise that only the first five color-types of Shaligram recorded in the Skanda Purana should ever be worshipped by devotees. The rest should either be turned over for temple care or simply avoided entirely. In general, the Puranic texts remain primarily concerned with the quality of Shaligrams as far as they might be considered ritually viable. For example, most of the scriptures also contain injunctions against worshipping Shaligrams that have been cracked (by long-term worship or by intention), Shaligrams that are broken into pieces, have holes that continue all the way through the shila, Shaligrams that have been burnt by fire, Shaligrams that have been stolen by a violent person or an enemy, or those that have lost their circular marks because of long-term handling.

The reasons given for this is that the deity is likely to abandon a worn or defective body in the same way that a person discards old clothes or, in some cases, the way the elderly give up their worn and used up bodies in death (dehe jirune yathaa dehi tyktvaanyamupagacchati lingaadini tu jirnaani tathaa munchati devataa - quoted in Pranatoshiṇi Tantra, page 361.) In practice, red Shaligrams were typically of the greatest concern and were described, more than once, as the most inauspicious form a Shaligram could take and that these were not worshipped due to the trouble they tended to bring.

On the rare occasion that a red Shaligram was found, most devotees either immediately returned it to the river or packed it securely in cloth for transport to a temple where, as several explained, it would be looked after by a temple priest (pujari or brahmacharya) so that its unusual potency would not inadvertently cause problems for devotees elsewhere. In other cases, devotees pointed out that such Shaligrams were mostly associated with disease and death and therefore, should only be worshipped by especially knowledgeable and skilled practitioners.

When I asked if this was why the red-orange "mountain" Shaligrams were also similarly shunned, many devotees responded affirmatively. Their formations were spiritually pure but their colors were a warning. (This concern, however, was not extended to a particular formation of Shaligrams called Ratnagarbha, a small, translucent, pebble-like shila that, when held up to a bright light source, turned bright red, yellow, or occasionally blue.)

In other cases, different colors of Shaligrams were associated with different effects. The standard black Shaligrams were sometimes said to bestow fame or general good fortune while brown Shaligrams were thought to remove sins committed in previous lives. Yellow Shaligrams were also occasionally described as particularly beneficial to children and blue (or "sky-colored") Shaligrams as bringers of wealth and prosperity. These color categories, however, though mentioned in the Puranic texts almost never translated to actual practice. In the end, as far as practitioners were concerned, black was the only color of a true Shaligram but any other color besides red was also acceptable.

Living Fossils

A Shaligram is thus a living fossil in a very different sense of the term. As ammonites, they hold clues to the existence of an ancient world filled with living creatures who once swam the waters of a primordial ocean back in an era when the earth was young. As deities, they live on, born out of the geological processes that once transformed animal into mineral, they transform once more from stone to person through a journey across a vast mythic landscape. Shaligrams challenge the notion of life's progress; a series of linear assumptions from birth to death that embody a belief in the continued march of history. Rather, they lived once in another form, in another kind of history, and then passed on, only to be reborn as stone and then as deity through four thousand years of human movement, heritage, practice, and spiritual imagination.

They live as gods and family members in temples and homes. They are born from the river, are given names, travel the world, share in home-cooked meals and daily bathing. They become persons, participate in relationships, and eventually even die; returning to the river with the cremated remains of their loved ones or retired to temples, too old and worn to carry on. And then they are reborn again, reappearing in the river to a new devotee or passing down into the hands of a new generation, continuing along in the karmic life cycle of the Hindu world.

This is also a world where landscapes themselves are bodies, constructed from the bits and pieces of the gods and men who traverse them. In this land as body, the endless cycle of erosion and reconstruction recapitulates the karmic life cycle of all living things; where geological space has become mythological time. Given enough time, both the works of Nature and the works of Man are then reduced to the same dust. Rocks are eroded to sediment, sediment is hardened into rocks, rocks are elevated above sea level through the movement of tectonic plates and transformed into mountains. Mountains weather away and become sediment once again. So too do homes and temples and bodies live and die and live again. This is the great wheel of Earth and the Shaligram has endured them all.

CHAPTER FOUR

SHALIGRAM PUJA

G enerally speaking, Brahmin and other high-caste Shaligram practices are more well known, but as a permanent, material, form of God that anyone may carry, Shaligrams are considered by most to be accessible to all. For many devotees, this means that assembling a Shaligram collection and selecting specific Shaligrams for their homes can be very complicated. The Śālagrāma-Kosha provides a translation of the Tattva-Nidhi text which concerns the selection of appropriate Shaligrams for worship. "The wise one will tie round the middle of the Salagrama-stone a thread; and if the aperture is located at the spot which marks one-eighth of the thread's length, then the stone is of superior variety; it may also be of the middling variety. However, the stone having an opening in the one-third part is to be rejected."

The Brahmanda Purana, however, contains a different prescription on deciding Shaligram suitability: "There are different effects in terms of locations of operators. If the aperture is downward, it is terrible; the aperture on top will be useful only in magical rites of driving away the enemy; the apertures being even are especially meritorious, while the aperture on the sides will take away fortune. If the aperture is crooked, it causes disease; if long-mouthed it devours everything (meaning: makes one impoverished). One should carefully examine the stone before ascertaining the deity-specification."

Shaligrams are typically worshipped without any prathisthana (installation ritual; as is done while installing man-made deity icons), since the deities are already present in the Shaligram of their own free will as a revelation to devotees. The Śālagrāma-Kosha enumerates in this by explaining that: "In the worship of Salagrama, no initiation is required; there is no special hymnology or specific procedure of worship, nor any need for a qualified priest or master of ceremonies. Worshipped anyhow, it will bestow the benefits; and there is no error of any kind." As a result of this, it was not uncommon for Shaligram practitioners to comment on what they deemed to be the most important aspect of Shaligram worship: that because Shaligrams were natural manifestations of the divine, they could not be corrupted by human hands. No mistake, no failure, no ritual gone wrong could ever "harm" a Shaligram.

SHALIGRAM RITUAL WORSHIP

In most cases, ritual worship of a Shaligram begins with a prayer. This could be any one of a wide variety of chants, mantras, or invocations specific to a religious tradition but the most popular opening recitation is the use of portions of the Shaligram Stotram.

SRI SHALIGRAM SHILA STOTRAM (PRAYER)
(Given by Krishna to Yudhishthira, Bhagavad-Gita)[21]

"Asya Shree Saligram strotra mantrasya/ Shree Bhagavan Hrishi Narayano Devata Anustup Chhandah/ Shree Saligram strotra mantrajape viniyogah"

I chant this Shaligram Strotra Mantra in front of Lord Narayan Hrishi

Yudhistiro Uvacha
   King Yudhishthira asked
"Shree Dev Dev devesa Devarchanamutamam
   Tat sarbam srotaumichhami Bruhime Purushotamam / 1/
   My dear Supreme Lordship Purushotam, I request you know the
   significance of the Shaligram shila.

Shree Bhagavan Uvacha - The Lord Replied
"Gandakyam Chotare Tire Girirajshchya Dakshine
Das Yojan Vistirnam Mahachhetra Vasundhara //2//
"Saligramo Vabet Devo Devi Dwara Bati Vabet
Uvayo Sangamo Yatra Mutistratrana Sansaya //3//
"Saligramo Sila Yatra Yatra dwara Bati Sila
Uvayo Sangamo Yatra Mutistratrana Sansaya //4//
   The mountains known as the Himalaya are situated on the bank of river
   Gandaki. In the south of this Himalaya is the land where Shaligram shila
   appear. This is the place where Devi Dwarabati begins. This place is called by
   those who know, Sri Muktishetra.
"Ajanma Krita Papanam Prayaschitam Ya Ichati
Saligram Silawari Paphari Namastute //5//
" Akal Mritu Haranam Sarvabyadhi Binasanam
Vishu Padodakam Pitwa Shirasha Dharyamyaham //6//
"Sankha Madhya Sthitam Toyyam Vramitam Keshavopari
Angalagnam Manukshanam Bramha Hatya Dikam Dayat //7//

---

21 See also: https://stotranidhi.com/en/sri-shalagrama-stotram-in-english/

Shaligram shilas found here are very precious and significant. These shilas are considered to be directly Lord Vishnu Himself and the person who worships or even keeps in the house or bathes the Shaligram and drinks water or pour those waters on their head, that man becomes free from all sin and it prevents from untimely death. That person becomes free from all sin and all material disease. The most feared sin of Bramahatya (killing of a Brahmin) is also washed away simply by worshiping the Shaligram.

"Snano Dakam Piben Nityam Chakrankita Sirot Vabam
Partkshallya Sudham Tatoyam Bramha Hatya Byapohati //8//
"Agnistomasahasnani Vajapaya Satanicha
Samyak Phalama Bapnoti Visnornai Vedya Vakshina //9//
That person who does snan (bathing) of Shaligram with chakra everyday get gets rid of all sin like Bramahatya, and if he drinks such water daily gets the equal boon of a thousand havan (fire sacrifices) of Lord Vishnu.

"Naivadyayuktam Tulsim cha Misritam Vishesta Pada Jalen Vishnu
Yoshnati Nityam Purato Murari Prapnoti Yazya Uta Koti Pundyam //10//
The person, who worships Shaligram with Tulsi leaf daily, gets the boon of a million Yajna also.
Khandita Sphutita Viina Vandi Dakdhya Tathi Va Cha
Saligram Sialyatra Tatra Dosho Na Vidyate//11//
Even if a Shaligram is damaged or broken, all shila are good to worship

Namantra Pujanam Naiva Natirtham Na cha Bhabanaa
Na stutir Na uppachars cha Saligram Silar cha ne //12//
Bramha Hatya Dikam Papam Manobak Karya Sambhamam
Shirgram Nachyati Tatsarvam Saligram Silrchana//13//
Without worship, without offering any sweets or without any pilgrims - only chanting this Shaligram mantra is enough to wash away all sins and is the fulfillment of all desire.

"Nanabarna Mayam Chiva Nana Bhogena Vestitam
Tathavarprasadena Laxmi Kantam Balamhayam //14//
"Narayanorbhabo Dev Chakramadya Cha Karmana
Tathavarprasadena Laxmi Kantam Balamhayam//15//
There are various kinds of size and shape of Shaligram in which Lord Vishnu is situated representing all the different incarnations.

"Krishane Sila Taneyatra Susmam Cakram Cha Drisyate
Saovagyam Santatim Dhatye Sarva Sakshaym Dadhaticha//16//

   Good Luck increases and one gets satisfaction from children, and in every
way in every aspect, all good enters one's life by worshipping Shaligram black
in color with little chakras.

Vashu Devschya Chinhani Distwa Papai Pramuchyate
Sridhar Sukare Bame Harivbarnatu Disyate//17//
"Varaha Rupenam Devam Kurmangai Rapi Chinhitam
Gopadam Tatra Dissheta Varaham Vamanam Tatha //18//

   A person who gets the chance to see the Vasudev shila, that person he
became free from sins. Shreedhar, Sukar, Vamanadev, Harivarna,Varaha,
Kurma and lots of other type of Shaligram are available also. Some Shaligram
has marking of cow's foot marks and some that of Narshimha Avatara (half
lion half man).

"Pitavarnam Tu Devanam Rakta Varnam Vayabhaham
Narashinho Vawet Devo Mokshadam Cha Prakrititam//19//
Sankha Chakra Gada Kurma Sankho Yatra Pradisyate
Sankha Varnaschya Devanaman Vame Devaschya Lakshanam//20//
"Damodarm Tatha Sthulam Madhya Chakram Pratisthitam
Purna Dwarena Sankrina Pita Rekha Cha Drischyate //21//
"Chhatrakare Vabet Rajam Vartule Cha Mahasreeya
Chipite Cha MahaDukham Sulagretu Ranam Dhrubam//22//

   A yellowish Shaligram is as auspicious as the Lord Himself (Pitambara) but
a reddish Shaligram is considered to bring fearful situations and is dangerous
to worship. The sacred symbols of Shankha (conch), Chakra (disc), Gada
(club), and Kurma (tortoise) are printed on the Shaligram stones.

   Shaligram with a Shankha (conch) sign is considered to be Vamanrup
(Vamandev) of Lord Vishnu, whereas chakra in the middle is considered as
Damodar Shaligram.

   Shaligrams of different shapes; round, umbrella shape which has white
lines are also available; worshipping this kind of Shaligram gives wealth and
reputation in society. Flat shaped Shaligram creates sorrow in a family and
Shaligram with sharp front side creates war, fighting, and tension in family.

"Lalate Shesha Vogastu Siropari Sukanchanam
Chakrakanchanavarnanam VamaDevaschya Lakshnam//23//
Vamaparbe Cha Bai Cakre Krishna Varnas tu Pingalam
Laxinarshimhadevanam Prithak Varnastu Drisyate//24//

Shaligrams which have a chakra around the head or in the forehead but the rest of its parts are clean and smooth is considered very auspicious and this type is to be considered as Vamandev shila. Yellowish or black in left side with a chakra is considered as Lakshmi-Narshimha shila.

Lamboste Cha Dalidram Syat Pingale Hani Revacha
Lagna Cakre Vabet Baydhir Bidare Maranamdrubam//25//

Worshipping a long shaped shila creates poverty, and Shaligram having lagna (rising) chakra create long term chronic diseases, even death.

Padom Dakamcha Nirmalyam Mastake Dharayet Shada
Visnor Dristam Vakshitabyam Tulsi Jal Misritam//26//
Kalpa Koti Sahasrani Vaikunthe Basate Sada
Saligram Sila Vinur Hatya Koti Vinasanam//27//

Any person who offers a Tulasi leaf while worshipping the Shaligram gets salvation and can stay at Vaikuntha (Heaven) for a million years.

Tasmat Sampujayet Dhyatwa Pujitam Chapi Sarvada
Saligram Silas Trotram Yah Pathecha Dijotam//28//
Sa Gakshet Parmam Sthanam Yatra Lokeshworo Hari
Sarva Pap Binir Muktwa Vishnu Lokam Sa Gashati//29//

Therefore always worship Shaligram, and chant Shaligram Stotra which is very beneficial for mankind. We can get one a higher position on Vishnu Lok (Vaikuntha) simply by doing so. All sins will also be destroyed and it is guaranteed that one gets to Vishnulok simply from this process of worshiping the Shaligram.

Dusovataro Devanam Prithak Varnastu Disyate
Ipsitam Labate Rajyam Vishnu Pooja Manukramat//30//
Kotyohi Vramhahatyanamgamyagamya Kotaya
Ta Sarva Nasamayamti Vishu Nai Vidya Vakshanat//31//
Vishno Pador Dakam Pitwa Koti Janmaghanasanam
Tasma Dasta Gunam Papam Ghumou Vindupatnat//32//

There are various types of descriptions available for Lord Vishnu's ten primary incarnations (Dasavatara) and also the Lord's incarnation in Sri Shaligram's worship, the Prayer to the Shaligram and drinking the Lord's bathing water wash away sins of million lives and one gets great prosperity, wealth and reputation through this, so everyone everywhere the Shaligram should be worshiped.

Iti Shree Vishotara Purane Shree Saligram Sila-stotram Sumpurnam!!..

SIMPLE PUJA

Note: In South India, it is more common for Shaligrams to be put away in a box or puja mandir while not actively engaged in ritual, while in North India and Nepal, Shaligrams tend to remain in the open. The most common and most basic form of Shaligram puja is the daily simple puja, which only requires that the devotee offer water, tulsi leaves (or flowers/fruit if none available), and a short prayer to the Shaligrams each day.

In many cases, the simple puja is also favored among practitioners who travel or who are actively on pilgrimage since it is possible to bring one or two important Shaligrams along and to perform the puja as a kind of morning or evening prayer even under the most difficult circumstances. In many households today, simple puja is the standard, with more elaborate pujas performed on special occasions or at certain times of year.

As a corrective to modern concerns about the potential spiritual dangers of keeping Shaligrams, many gurus also now recommend the simple puja, elaborating that it is more important to give what an individual is capable of giving in order to keep Shaligrams in the home (and the tradition alive) than the alternative of never interacting with Shaligrams at all. In other words, as one teacher explained, "Shaligrams are not monsters. They are here for us, to help us. If simple puja is what you can offer. Offer that. The rest will come in time, when it is time."

SRI VAISHNAVA TRADITION

If a Shaligram is to be formally worshipped in a temple context, all the details of worship must be carefully observed. Additionally, many small Shaligrams are also often strung together in the form of a garland using metallic casings made of silver and placed on the moolavar - the Dhruva bera (main temple deity) deity in Vaishnava temples. (108 in number representing the nine planets comprising the 27 stars and its four navamsa divisions – 27x4 = 108). Large Shaligrams (typically the larger than a man's hand) are also routinely made into iconographic murti (Lord Krishna, Rama, Vishnu, etc.) and worshipped in temples and Vaishnava mutts. Such icons are further believed to have extraordinary powers owing to their materials and origins.

Depending on the religious tradition in question, the ritual protocols for Shaligram worship vary considerably. However, the most commonly referenced method of Shaligram puja comes from the Sri Vaishnava tradition, where there is a more standardized procedure for the everyday worship of Shaligrams for temples, mutts, and home shrines. Generally, Shaligrams are almost always worshipped using water and tulsi leaves (holy basil). The Yagna (Yaga) Samskaram also prescribes procedures for the Bhagavad Aradhana (Aradhana is a method of worship; a Sanskrit word meaning an act of glorifying God or a person) of Sriman Narayana -Vishnu or His manifest form of Shaligrams.

There are two forms of Aradhana: Bahya (External) and Manasika (Internal). Shaligram puja in a temple context thus usually begins when the attendant pujari or brahmacharya initiates the Samskaram through Sanskrit verses before offerings are made. The following protocol is translated into English by Anand K. Karalapakkam:

"After Achamanam (sipping and swallowing water two or three times during which the twenty-four names of Vishnu are repeated), wearing Oordhvapundram, prostrating to the Lord (Sriman Narayana), sit in a seat. After pranayamam (yogic control of the vital breath), perform japam (repetition of Lord's name) with Dhyana slokas (divine hymns-Ashtakshara, etc). Later, worship the Lord Sriman Narayana residing in one's heart (Manasika Aradhana). Then with water from the vessel placed left of Sriman Narayana (Shaligram), sprinkle water on flowers and other materials for worship and vessels for arghyam (offering of rice, etc.), padyam (offering of water for washing the feet), etc. From water in an arghya vessel, sprinkle water on flowers etc. (for worship) and also on yourself."

"After welcoming the Lord, offer arghyam, padyam; Achamaniam and give Abisheka (ritualistic bath). Then offer cloth, Yajno Pavitha (sacred thread), sandal paste, flower, incense, and light, in that order. Offer Achamana, honey and again Achamana. Later offer food comprising of pudding, rice, vegetables, water, pan-betel etc. After prostration, restoring status quo is the procedure of worship of Vishnu."

Thus, the sishya (disciple) learn to perform Bhagavad Aradhana (prayer of the divine) to Sriman Narayana's archa-avatara as a Shaligram. Additionally, since the food a Sri Vaishnava eats should only consist of the remnants of food offered to Sriman Narayan, Saligrama Aradhana is considered to be especially important. Additionally, among Sri Vaishnavas, the Saligrama Aradhana is typically performed only by the male members of the upper three varnas (Brahaman, Kshatriya and Vaishya).

In this tradition, women are prohibited from touching or performing Aradhana of a Shaligram, though this prohibition is not universally shared. However, even in these cases, women have an important role of assisting the performance of the ritual by making the necessary preparations for the worship including cooking the food for offerings to the deity.

Women may also be responsible for arrangements in terms of preparing food, gathering and making flower garlands, or gathering and directing the participants as the ritual progresses. In general, however, most practitioners consider the participation of the entire family in Shaligram puja to be vital to the health and prosperity of the household.

SHAIVA TRADITIONS

Protocols for puja as set out by ritual specialists at Pashupatinath Mandir (from principally Shaiva and Smarta traditions) in Kathmandu, Nepal incorporate a slightly different sequence. In Puja Vidhi, Shaligram is worshipped in the same way as one worships Lord Vishnu. Normally tulsi is used and also a conch shell (Shankh) is kept near the Shaligram. Daily worship with purity of heart and body is required to get full benefits from Shaligram. (Ref.: Shrimaddevi Bhagwat and Pashupatinath Mandir).[22]

To perform puja of the Shaligram which you have selected to install in your altar of worship, you will need the following 'samagri' or ingredients: Ganga Jal (water from the Ganges River), Panchgavya (a mixture of 5 auspicious articles that include: cow dung, cow's urine, milk, ghee and curd), fresh tulsi leaves, kusha grass, pipal leaves, incense sticks, camphor, sandal paste, a lamp burner, and a conch shell. You may substitute any item that is not available with uncooked rice. Offerings made to the Shaligram can also be of milk, fruits, flowers, sweet dishes or a coconut.

PUJA:

1. Sit in a position in which you can face the East or North-East direction.
2. Wash the Shaligram with Ganga Jal poured from the conch shell. Then wash it again with Panchgavya, and then wash it once more with Ganga Jal.
3. Place some kusha grass in a stainless-steel glass filled with water to sprinkle over the Shaligram.
4. Now, put the Shaligram on some pipal leaves placed on a plate. Light the camphor, incense sticks, and the lamp filled with ghee.
5. Apply some sandal paste on the Shaligram and place some fresh tulsi leaves in front of the Shaligram.
6. Light the lamp and move it in a circular, clockwise movement of the hand in front of the Shaligram.
7. Chant the Shaligram mantra nine times. Other mantras may be substituted according to tradition.
8. Offer milk, fruits or sweets to the Shaligram. Offer some money and then give that money to a poor person.

If you are worshiping more than one Shaligram, make sure they are in even number. This means you should have either two, four or six Shaligrams (etc.). Place a tulsi mala (garland) around them or offer fresh tulsi leaves everywhere. It is important to remember that even the water that has touched the Shaligram becomes 'amrit' (holy water), while you are bathing it, it takes on the properties of the Shaligram. If you drink this water, it can help bring relief from various physical ailments and poor health.

---

22 http://pashupatinathmandir.com/?page_id=880 Accessed 12-11-2016

Because each specific Shaligram is read and interpreted in different ways, most Shaligram practitioners consider it essential that a Shaligram be properly examined and identified before they are taken for worship. In many Shaiva traditions, characteristics of particular focus are the shape and color of the Shaligram, the number and location of chakra marks, the type of lines or grooves that are present in the crevices and fissures, or any other distinctive feature which may indicate the deity's general identity.

Testing Shaligrams for suitability of worship may also involve any number of other rituals before the Shaligram is determined to be acceptable. In one such ritual, for example, the Shaligram is placed on the ground to see if it is steadily poised or unsteady; the former being preferred because worship will then result in prosperity, while the worship of the latter -- more unsteady -- Shaligram may lead to familial instability or in the loss of a devotee's home.

If the Shaligram rests too far on its sides, the worship of this shila is said to generate anxiety, and if the shila is uneven and wobbles, its worship will cause sorrow. The genuineness of Shaligram for worship is also tested by immersing it in a bowl of milk or rice of equal weight overnight and observing the milk or rice the following morning to determine if they show signs of increase or decrease. If the milk or rice has maintained or increased, the authenticity of the Shaligram is confirmed.

Smarta Traditions and Panchayatana Puja

In Smarta Traditions, the practice of Panchayatana Puja consists of the worship of five deities set in a *five-point cross pattern "Diagram of the five pointed cross pattern in various practices" on page 65*. As a rule, these five deities are Shiva, Vishnu, Devi or Durga, Surya, and an Ishta Devata (a term meaning one's favorite or tutelary deity) such as Ganesha, Skanda, or another god specific to the devotee's practice. On rare occasions, an Ishta Devata may also be included as a sixth deity in the puja.

In Shaligram Panchayatana Puja, Shiva is often represented as a lingam stone from the Narmada River in India, the Devi/Shakti using a Srichakra (a Mandala-shaped quartz crystal or coin), and Ganesh, Vishnu, and Surya as Shaligrams. As per the tradition, any one of the represented deities can be placed in the center as the main or presiding deity.

This deity is then the one who generally occupies a central role in the worship of the household and for whom the rest of the deities will be arranged around them (as is also mirrored in temple architecture from Odisha to Karnataka to Kashmir; and the temples containing fusion deities such as Harihara (half Shiva, half Vishnu).

Theologically, the Smarta tradition emphasizes that all murti are icons of saguna Brahman, a means to realizing the abstract Ultimate Reality called nirguna Brahman. The five or six icons are then viewed by Smartas as multiple representations of the one saguna Brahman (meaning a personal God with material form), rather than as distinct beings in and of themselves. The ultimate goal in this practice is to transition past the use of icons, then follow a philosophical and meditative path to understanding the oneness of Atman (soul, self) and Brahman as infinite and immaterial.

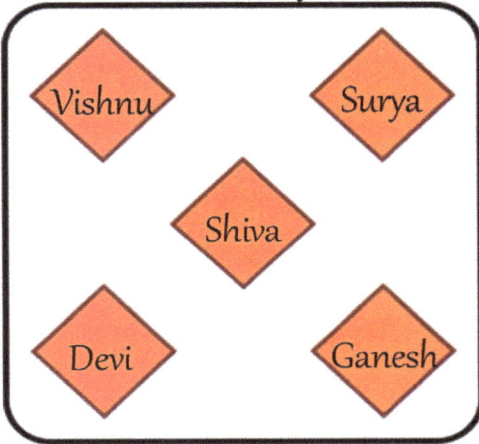

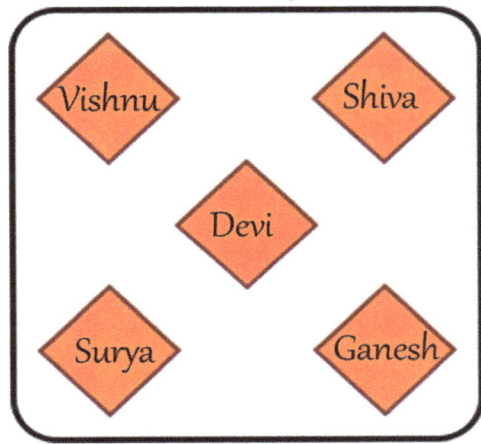

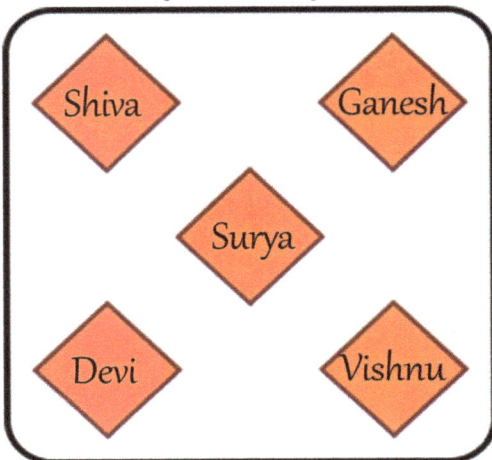

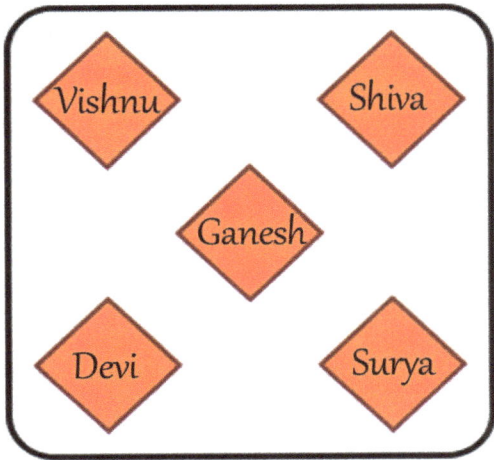

Diagram of the five pointed cross pattern in various practices

GAUDIYA VAISHNAVA AND HARE KRISHNA TRADITIONS

Sri Padmanabha Goswami's "Śālagrāma-śila" (1993) also details another puja sequence more common in the Gaudiya Vaishnava and Hare Krishna traditions. He begins by explaining that the worship of Shaligram is not different than the worship of any other installed deity and in any case where reverence or respect to a deity would be performed, so must it be performed for Shaligram, with individual attention paid to each shila present. He then goes on to say that the worship of Shaligrams should be "conducted in accordance with Puruṣa-sukta." (1993: 32).

If a devotee wishes to adorn a Shaligram with ornaments, this is acceptable but that an offering of rice should never be made (in contrast with the Sri Vaishnava tradition mentioned previously). Women are allowed to worship Shaligrams, but should refrain from doing so during their menstruation and finally, that the specific mantras one should recite vary depending on the Scriptural texts used and should therefore be whatever mantras are most well-known to the initiated Vaishnava. The sequence for puja and the offering of five items; gandha, puṣpa, dhūpa, dipa, and naivedya (tulsi is always required) or sixteen items then commences as so (additional descriptions for each piece of the sequence given in the text, pgs. 33-39):

1. Wake the Lord
2. After the Lord has risen, chant idam puspanjali samarpayami and offer flowers.
3. Asana (a seated posture) – while offering asana, chant idam asanam samarpayami
4. Svagata (welcome) – while offering svagata, chant susvagatam, susvagatam
5. Padya (poem, verse) – while offering padya, chant idam padyam samarpayami
6. Arghya (libation) – while offering arghya, chant idam arghyam samarpayami
7. Acamana (sipping water) – while offering acamana, chant idam acamaniyam samarpayami
8. Madhuparka (honey and milk) – while offering madhuparka, chant idam madhuparka samarpayami
9. Punaracamana (sipping water again) – while offering punaracamana, chant idam punaracamaniyam samarpayami
10. Snana (bathing) – while offering snana, chant idam snaniyam samarpayami
11. Vastra (clothing, or a cloth) – while offering vastra, chant idam vastram samarpayami
12. Upavita (sacred thread) – while offering upavita, chant idam upavitam samarpayami
13. Abhushana (ornaments, embellishments) – while offering abhushana, chant idam abhushanam samarpayami
14. Gandha (fragrance) – while offering gandha, chant idam gandham samarpayami
15. Tulasi (tulsi leaves) – while offering tulasi, chant idam tulasim samarpayami

16. Puspa (flowers) – while offering puspa, chant idam puspam samarpayami
17. Dhupa (incense) – while offering dhupa, chant idam dhupam samarpayami
18. Dipa (lamp) – while offering dipa, chant idam dipam samarpayami
19. Naivedya (an offering to God; i.e., a promise, a willingness, etc.) – while offering naivedya, chant idam naivedyam samarpayami

Incidentally, he also mentions that the mantra: om yajneshvaraya yajnasabhavaya yajnapataye govindaya namo namah from Hari-bhakti-vilasa (15/530) also suffices for all steps from padya to dipa.

Daily Care

Outside of ritual worship, Shaligrams also generally require basic daily care. For some practitioners, this means that their shilas are kept either in a dedicated cabinet or puja mandir in a room of the house dedicated to religious practices. For others, Shaligrams are commonly kept in areas of the house where they can observe the daily life of the family. In any case, a household's Shaligrams are kept in such a way that they can "live" with their families as active members. They participate in meal times, receive baths, are dressed in clothing that suits the climate, and oversee important gatherings and conversations. For this reason, puja is only the beginning of dedicated Shaligram practice and knowing a Shaligram's name is just the first step to welcoming a new deity, and a new person, into your life.

ACYUTA

Acyuta Shaligram
Top

Common formation of an
Acyuta Shaligram

Acyuta Shaligram Bottom

In some Hindu traditions, the Acyuta Shaligram is related to the Mahavishnu Multichakra-type Shaligrams and are described as any Shaligram bearing three distinct chakra marks. In most interpretive descriptions, Acyuta is referenced as another name of Vishnu and appears as the 100th and 318th names in the Vishnu Sahasranama. It is also often used in the Bhagavad Gita as a personal name of Krishna. According to Adi Shankara's commentary on the 1000 Names of Vishnu, Acyuta means "one who will never lose his inherent nature and powers." The name also means "immovable," "unchangeable," and as such is used to mean "the One who is without the six transformations, beginning with birth."

In other interpretive traditions, the Acyuta Shaligram contains four vadana (mouths or apexes) and eight chakras representing kundalas (coiled serpents), shankas, chakras, a mace, a bow, an arrow, a sword, a pestle, a flag, an umbrella and a lotus or an elephant goad. Interpretations of the Garuda Purana, however, identify Acyuta Shaligrams as containing four distinct markings in order: Padma (lotus), chakra (disc), shanka (conch shell), gada (mace). In practice, Acyuta Shaligrams tend to be complicated formations involving multiple circular marks (shells), holes, ridges and lines, and other features and markers that represent a series of possible objects such as a conch shell, a chakra, a gada (mace), a bow, or an elephant goad, and so on.

Reading Shaligrams of this type might therefore be exceptionally difficult and often requires specialist consultation. Lastly, in some cases, the shape of the Acyuta Shaligram may be similar to that of the Hamsa Shaligram, but each is identified using different markings. Veneration of the Acyuta Shaligram is therefore equally complex but tends to follow similar practices as the Mahavishnu Shaligram where the shila itself is considered quite versatile, accepting of almost all forms of ritual worship, and capable of destroying sin and karmic debt for the entire household.

TEXTUAL REFERENCES

Pranatoshani Tantra pg. 361, Agni Purana; Bengavasi ed., Panchanan Tarkaratna, Saka 1812, Ch. 46

Descriptions Pranatoshani Tantra (Divisions of Shaligrams by Number of Chakras)

1. Sudarshan
2. Lakshmi – Narayan
3. Acyuta
4. Janardan, Caturbhuja
5. Vaasudeva
6. Pradyumna
7. Sankarshan
8. Purushottam
9. Navavyuha
10. Dasavatara
11. Anirudda
12. Ananta
13. Paramatma

With four circular marks on the right and left sides and two red circles at the opening.

He is also marked with conch, discus, stick, bow, arrow, mace, pestle, flag, a white umbrella and a red spearhead. (P)

ADDITIONAL REFERENCES

1. Maharishi Mahesh Yogi on the Bhagavad Gita, a New Translation and Commentary, Chapter 1–6. Penguin Books, 1969, p 42 (verse 1:21), p 47 (verse 1:25)

ADHOKSHAJA

The Adhokshaja Shaligram does not appear often in Shaligram practice and is mentioned only by name in the Skanda Purana, where it is described as dark in color with red linear marks, a round shape, with a single chakra, and a few reddish spots. Adhokshaja is also one of the 1000 names of Vishnu and is typically translated as "One who has eternal knowledge" or "One who is beyond knowledge acquired through the senses." As such, these Shaligrams, when they do appear in practice, are strongly associated with responsibility, a stable or calm nature, and humanitarianism.

Occasionally, they are further associated with a desire for a calm and harmonious home life, but more commonly, Adhokshaja Shaligrams are exchanged in circumstances where the practitioner is experiencing problems with a chaotic environment (both physically and socially) or is suffering from anxiety and excessive worry. In Gaudiya Vaishnava traditions, Adhokshaja Shaligrams are representative of Krishna as "being beyond the range of limited sense perceptions" (Srimad Bhagavatam 1.8.19) and are sought after as temple Shaligrams to be placed at the feet of Krishna icons where they assist in devotees' abilities to properly "see" (receive darśan) of the deity.

As a result, these Shaligrams are considered to be highly auspicious when they are found and indicative of better times to come. Adhokshaja Shaligrams are rare in comparison to other types of Shaligrams but are typically identified using the reddish to reddish-brown spots or lines that appear over the body of the shila. In some descriptions, these spots might conversely be brown or tawny (light brown) in appearance rather than uniformly red but the rest of the Shaligram should otherwise be rounded and black in color.

These Shaligrams also almost always have either a single, deeply-embedded chakra mark or a single, small, vadana (which may have chakra marks inside of it). It is also possible for Adhokshaja to have any number of additional indentations, holes, or striations and in some interpretive traditions, it is considered especially good if the markings on the body of the shila are arranged in the shape of a face or of eyes since it helps newer initiates to focus on learning how to engage in darśan practices.

Textual References

Praanatoshani Tantra pg. 361, Skanda Purana, Nagarekhanda, 244: 3-9. Also, Srimad Bhagavatam: Canto 4 - Chapter 17

Description: Deep and dark in color with red linear marks. He is round in shape with a single circular mark and a few reddish spots on His body. He may be either big or small in size. (Sk and P)

Additional References

1. Desai, Kalpana. 2011. Iconography Of Visnu (In Northern India, Up to The Mediaeval Period). Abhinav Publications; 1st edition

ADITYA

In Hinduism, Adityas (meaning "of Aditi"), refers to the offspring of Aditi, the mother of the gods (devamata) in the Vedas. The name Aditya in the singular, however, usually refers to Surya, the Sun God. As such, the characteristics of this Shaligram are similar to Surya/Suraj Shaligrams in a few respects, including the wide ray-like striations encircling the outer portion of the shila and the relative characteristics of the Sun as a spiritual entity. The Bhagavata Purana, for example, lists of a total of twelve Adityas as sun gods.

In each month of the year, a different Aditya is said to shine and each, therefore, is representative of a different expression of Vishnu in the form of the sun. As such, Aditya Shaligrams tend to demonstrate a relatively wide degree of variation and in some interpretive traditions, are read not only as Aditya but also as one of twelve possible variations depending on the time of year. In other words, this means that the minor characteristics of each Aditya Shaligram may indicate a specific Adityas or a specific mood (bhava) that the Sun may be in.

In the Rig Veda, however, the Adityas are devas, a distinct class of gods who are set apart from other classes such as the Maruts, the Rbhus, or the Viśve-devāh. In this way, Aditya Shaligrams are also sometimes interpreted as celestial "associates" of larger or more "potent" Shaligrams and are therefore worshipped in combination with other Shaligrams depending on the tradition in question.

In practice, Aditya Shaligrams are strongly associated with the pursuit of religious enlightenment and are specifically related to healing illnesses of the eyes, mouth, and joints. This is largely due to this Shaligram's capacity to "illuminate" the causes of illness or misfortune and they are therefore commonly possessed by or given as gifts to both physicians and religious healers.

Overall, Aditya Shaligrams bear similar characteristics to Surya/Suraj Shaligrams but usually contain prominent grooves and ridges, whereas Surya Shaligrams are almost always presented in relief. This means that an Aditya Shaligram will have a series of "ray-like" lines around its outer edge with a round or oval center that is smooth and unmarked. Note however that Aditya Shaligrams also bear some resemblance to typical Lakshmi-Narayan Shaligrams but unlike those Shaligrams, the striated ridge does not typically extend all the way around the outer edge of the shila.

Textual References

Aditya Shaligrams are not specifically mentioned in the Puranic texts by name but are typically interpreted as variations or as subtypes of the Surya/Suraj Shaligram.

Additional References

1. Desai, Kalpana. 2011. Iconography Of Visnu (In Northern India, Up to The Mediaeval Period). Abhinav Publications; 1st edition

AGNI

Agni is a Sanskrit word meaning "fire" but it also refers to the fire deity of Hinduism. As a deity, Agni is commonly represented as a guardian and is typically, though not always, found in southeast corners of Hindu temples. In classical Hindu cosmology, Agni as fire is also one of the five inert impermanent elements or creation (pañcabhūtá) along with space (ākāśa), water (ap), air (vāyu) and earth (pṛthvī); the five then combining to form what is understood as empirically perceived material existence (Prakriti).

In Vedic literature, Agni is a major deity who is often addressed in conjunction with Indra and Soma and who is considered the "mouth of the gods" (meaning, a medium that conveys offerings to them in homa rituals or who acts as a mediator between Earth and Heaven). Agni also appears extensively in Buddhist texts (Pali: Aggi) as well as in Jain theology as a complex concept related to fire-bodied beings, the cycle of reborn souls, and classes of reincarnated beings.

The Agni Shaligram is equally complex in practice and has several variations depending on the religious tradition in question. S.K. Ramachandra Rao's Shaligram Kosh [Śālagrāma – Kosha] contains translations of the Lakshana Sloka however that states that an Agni Shaligram "should be of the sun's color with 7 rekhas (lines/streaks) and either the shape of an arm (bahu) or a horse's mane." For this reason, Agni Shaligrams tend to bear some resemblance to Surya Shaligrams (much like Aditya Shaligrams do) but are completely brown or reddish-brown in color (with some rare appearances of yellow) with at least two chakra "layers." This means that they should have at least two distinct sections of striated lines with notable separation between them set into a smooth, unmarked, and slightly elongated body. Agni Shaligrams can also have the overall shape of a horse's head or mane but they should not be confused with Hayagriva or Varaha Shaligrams, which have similar shapes but are uniformly black in color.

Finally, as Agni is also considered to be the master of all wealth, practitioners often recommend the veneration of Agni Shaligrams to those facing financial issues. More commonly though, the worship of Agni Shaligrams is associated with karmic penance and the purification of past misdeeds and faults. Agni Shaligrams are then described as bestowing their devotees with purity of thought and the success of virtuous endeavors. It is important to note though that the traditional ban on home worship of red/red-brown Shaligrams also means that Agni Shaligrams tend to appear more often in temples than in households since the Puranas warn against red Shaligrams as being volatile, demanding, and potentially dangerous if not treated properly.

For those who perform fire rituals or similar forms of puja, Agni Shaligrams are further said to ensure the success of sacrifices because whatever sacrifice is made in the presence of these shilas goes directly to the deity invoked; who is then invited to reside in the household of the devotee along with the Shaligram.

ADDITIONAL REFERENCES

1. Chapple, Christopher Key (2006). Jainism and Ecology: Nonviolence in the Web of Life. Motilal Banarsidass.

2. Lochtefeld, James G. (2002). The Illustrated Encyclopedia of Hinduism. Vol. A–M. The Rosen Publishing Group.

3. Kramrisch, Stella; Burnier, Raymond (1976). The Hindu Temple. Motilal Banarsidass.

4. Rao, S.K. Ramachandra. (2009). Salagrama-Kosha, Sri Satguru Publications.

5. Vatsyayan, Kapila (1995). Prakṛti: Vedic, Buddhist, and Jain traditions. Indira Gandhi National Centre for the Arts

6. Wynne, Alexander (2007). The Origin of Buddhist Meditation. Routledge.

ANANTA/ANANTA-SESHA

"Cobra Hood" variations of the Ananta Shaligram

A typical appearance of the Ananta-Sesha Shaligram showing the chamber lines

This variation of the Ananta Shaligram is sometimes interpreted as Shimshumara rather than Ananta.

As one of the many names of Vishnu, Ananta is a Sanskrit term meaning 'endless,' 'limitless,' or 'infinite.' As an artistic representation of the Vedas themselves, Ananta also carries connotations of infinite wisdom or the expansion of knowledge and perception without limitation. In more classical interpretations, Ananta is the Śeṣanāga, the celestial snake-god, on which Vishnu reclines.

In the Vedanta School, Ananta is typically used in the phrase "anadi (beginning-less) ananta (endless) akhanda (unbroken) sat-chit-ananda (being-consciousness-bliss)" which is a reference to infinity as a single non-dual reality. In the Yoga School, Ananta is the serpent of infinity who eavesdropped on the secret yogic teachings that were imparted to the goddess Parvati by Shiva.

After being caught by Shiva, Ananta was subsequently charged with imparting those teachings to humanity. As a result, Ananta then assumed a human form called Patanjali, author of the Yoga Sutras. The Ananta Shaligram is mentioned multiple times in the Puranic and Tantric texts and has a variety of possible forms based on those descriptions.

In practice though, it most commonly appears as a fan-shaped shila whose shape is reminiscent of a cobra's hood. Like its rarer variation, the Ananta-Basuki Shaligram, these shilas are associated with wisdom, memory, and learning. For this reason, they are often given to students, ascetics, or people pursuing skilled or religious professions.

More complex Ananta Shaligrams also occasionally appear as whole shilas with a "base" formed from a complete ammonite cast with at least part of the curved top ridge arching over the central spiral; a similar shape to a coiled serpent whose head hovers above its body.

Typical Ananta Shaligrams however, are comprised of a complete ammonite that has two specific characteristics: a grooved or striated ridge that mostly or completely encircles a smooth, rounded, central nodule and the presence of a few "serpentine" or twisted lines.

These lines are the remnants of the ammonite's internal chambers (after the outer shell has completely worn away) and will be mainly visible on the outer edge of the shila. Finally, it is important not to confuse the characteristics of the Ananta-Sesha Shaligram with an "Ananta marking." Some Shaligrams, such as the Vasudev Shaligram, contain minor markings indicative of the additional presence of Ananta but these characteristics are not the same thing as the manifestation (rupa) of Ananta within a whole shila.

In any case, despite its Scriptural descriptions, Ananta Shaligrams in practice tend to be comprised of the partial sections of larger Shaligrams that have been broken and worn smooth by the heavy silts of the Kali Gandaki River. Their crescent or fan-like shape is distinctive and are highly sought after by Hindus and Jains alike.

Somewhat less commonly, however, some traditions interpret any whole Shaligrams with a large central nodule and a thin worn chakra ridge as Ananta. Ultimately, the extensive variation of descriptions over time is why some Shaligram traditions are unclear about the specific identification of this Shaligram. One practitioner, for example, described Ananta as always cold to touch but shines like a blaze of fire while another ritual specialist stated that Ananta has an even number of minute chakras (up to 14) along with the marks of the classical five weapons of Vishnu (conch, discus, mace, bow and sword) and a Sri-vatsa (triangular) mark "on the chest."

TEXTUAL REFERENCES

Praanatoshani Tantra pg. 348 and 351 - 356, Praanatoshani Tantra pg. 361, Skanda Purana, Nagarekhanda, 244: 3-9, Brahmavaivartta (Prakritikhanda, Ch. 21), Garuda Purana (Panchanan Tarkaratna, Part 1, Ch. 45), Agni Purana; Bengavasi ed., Panchanan Tarkaratna, Saka 1812, Ch. 46

DESCRIPTIONS

1. Big in size with the color of a new cloud and having 14 circular marks on His body. (BV)
2. Variegated in color, many circular marks (G). Having 12 chakras (G).
    i.   Marked with the hood of a snake and many circles.
    ii. With many holes on His body and marked with several circles.
    iii. Variegated in color and marked with the hood of a snake and also with circular prints not less than 14 and not more than 20 in number.
    iv. big in size, cloudy in color and marked with 14 chakra prints. (P)
    v.   Bigger than Vishvarupa in size with five openings and many circular marks. He is also held as a variety of Vishvarupa. (P)
    vi. Shesha: Printed with linear marks forming the coiled body of a snake.

ADDITIONAL REFERENCES:
1. Chapple, Christopher Key (2006). Jainism and Ecology: Nonviolence in the Web of Life. Motilal Banarsidass.
2. Lochtefeld, James G. (2002). The Illustrated Encyclopedia of Hinduism. Vol. A–M. The Rosen Publishing Group.
3. Kramrisch, Stella; Burnier, Raymond (1976). The Hindu Temple. Motilal Banarsidass.

vii.

ANANTA VASUKI/SESHA

Ananta-Vasuki Shaligram

An elongated Ananta-
Vasuki Shaligram

This Shaligram is a generally
accepted variation of the Ananta-
Vasuki Shaligram but in some
traditions, because it is a partial
shila, this would be read as a Tulsi
Shaligram instead.

Ananta-Śeṣa ("endless serpent"), also known as Śeṣanāga as noted previously, is the multi-headed king of all nāgas and one of the primal beings of creation. In the Puranas, Ananta-Śeṣa is said to hold all the planets of the universe on his hoods and to constantly sing the glories of Vishnu from all his mouths. According to legend, when Ananta uncoils, time moves forward and creation takes place; when he coils back, the universe ceases to exist.

Vasuki is also the name of one of the serpent-gods in both Hinduism and Buddhism who has a gem called Nagamani on his head. Additionally, Vasuki is often depicted as Shiva's attendant snake and in Chinese and Japanese stories, he is also one of the "Eight Great Dragon Kings" (Hachi Ryuu-ou).

The Ananta-Vasuki Shaligram is a variation of the Ananta Shaligram which typically contains a distinctively large black central nodule with a chakra composed of interlocking sections on one side and either a full or partial chakra on the opposite side.

Also associated with the tale of the churning of the milky ocean (Vasuki acted as the churning rope), Ananta-Vasuki Shaligrams are described as providing immense protection from occult forces, curses, or malicious magic. These Shaligrams are popular in Vedic astrology, where worship of this shila provides release from Kaal Sarp Dosha.

Kaal Sarp Dosha or Kaal Sarp Yog is formed in a horoscope when all seven planets become trapped between Rahu and Ketu (Rahu referring to the serpent's head and Ketu, the dragon's tail).

The presence of Kaal Sarp Yoga in a horoscope is considered particularly harmful because all the planets are surrounded by the serpent and thus lose their positive impacts, making a person unlucky or creating problems in their life. In ritual worship, these Shaligrams are said to prevent a household's loss of wealth and act to prevent thefts.

In some Hindu traditions, only the heavily grooved or interlocking (chambered) chakra side is interpreted as Ananta-Vasuki. The opposite side is then read as the presence of another deity, often Lakshmi or Pradyumna. In other traditions, the entire shila is Ananta-Vasuki without the presence of any other deity unless the minor markings present elsewhere on the stone indicate otherwise.

Finally, there are several types of elongated partial Shaligrams which are also called Vasuki. These Shaligrams are similar to Ananta Sesha but are usually larger, with a longer "body," and a less distinct "hood."

This can be complicated to interpret in practice however, because some traditions designate these types of shilas as Tulsi Shaligrams (the interlocking chambers being viewed as leaf markings) rather than as manifestations of Ananta. As a result, the difference between the two tends to be read in the overall shape of the Shaligram: Ananta-Vasuki if the shila is elongated and Tulsi if the Shaligram is round or flat.

In most cases though, Ananta-Vasuki Shaligrams are identified by the stark differences between their opposing sides (which is what sets them apart from the similar looking Kalpvrisha Shaligram). The interlocking sections of the chakra are the result of significant wear to the exposed ammonite, appearing as the complete loss of the ammonite's outer shell structure and revealing the internal chambers. The opposite side, however, which has remained protected, contains a chakra-shell spiral which either remains largely intact and visible or is still wholly or partially obscured by shale accretions.

TEXTUAL REFERENCES

Praanatoshani Tantra pg. 347

DESCRIPTION:

Shesha: Printed with linear marks forming the coiled body of a snake. (P)

Pralambaghna: Red in color with the marks of a coiled body and a hood of a snake. this type is forbidden to be worshipped. (P)

Haihaya: (i) With one opening and different marks of hoods. Amongst these marks two take place on the right-side outside the opening. (ii) Shaped like a lotus leaf with a golden mark resembling an arc. (P)

Vishnupanjara: Printed with several linear marks created by the insect called Vajrakita. (P)

Rudra Ananta: Ananta-Sesha with 11 chakras along with a Shiva Nabhi (navel) is a Rudra Ananta. If there is no Nabhi, then it is Shuddaananta. (P)

Shuddaananta has a flag sign in the center; snake shape; very big size; 7 chakras.

ADDITIONAL REFERENCES

1. Chapple, Christopher Key (2006). Jainism and Ecology: Nonviolence in the Web of Life. Motilal Banarsidass.

2. Lochtefeld, James G. (2002). The Illustrated Encyclopedia of Hinduism. Vol. A–M. The Rosen Publishing Group.

3. Kramrisch, Stella; Burnier, Raymond (1976). The Hindu Temple. Motilal Banarsidass.

ANIRUDDA

A standard Anirudda Shaligram
-Left-

This Kurma Shaligram also
demonstrates the presence of Anirudda
(emerging from the left side)-Above

A "mountain" Shaligram of
Anirudda-Left

Anirudda ("The one who cannot be obstructed or resisted" or just "unconquered"), is a form of Bhagavan Vishnu (the Supreme God), a son of Pradyumna, and the grandson of Krishna. Along with Pradyumna, Sankarshan, and Vasudev, Anirudda is considered one of Vishnu's four vyuha avatars who received specific attributes or functions of Vishnu but not his entire incarnation (See also Pradyumna Shaligram).

In one of his most well-known stories, Anirudda's eternal consort, Usha, captured and sequestered him in the palace of her father, Bana. He was then rescued by Krishna, Balaram, and the Yadav army as a prelude to the story of Krishna and Shiva's battle at Banasura in the Bhagavata Purana. He is also, however, associated with the iconography of the boar (in terms of Vishnu's aspect as the avatar Varaha).

For this reason, Aniruddha often appears as a boar in some of the Caturvyūha statues, where he is an assistant to Vaasudeva, and in the Vaikuntha Chaturmurti when his boar's head protrudes from the side of Vishnu's head. This is why, in many Vaishnava Shaligram traditions, Anirudda and Varaha Shaligrams are paired together during worship.

The Anirudda Shaligram is particularly distinctive though in that it appears as a teardrop shaped (or what some practitioners refer to as "hibiscus shaped") shila with a series of curved parallel grooves marking the majority of the surface.

In many cases, the presence of Anirudda is also noted in other Shaligrams where the unique shape of the Anirudda Shaligram can be discerned emerging from somewhere along the other Shaligram's body. In the second image, for example, this Kurma Shaligram (note the turtle-like shape) has also been interpreted as bearing the influences of Anirudda in the characteristic concentric markings across the top portion of the stone.

In the final image, a small Anirudda Shaligram is taken out of the mountain rather than the river (sometimes called Kshetra or Mountain Shaligrams). Ultimately, the formation of this Shaligram involves the partial to near-complete weathering of one of two bivalve species also found in the same strata as contemporary ammonoids. It is, therefore, one of the few Shaligrams not comprised of an ammonite.

Rather, Anirudda Shaligrams are a type of bivalve called Retroceramus. Anirudda Shaligrams are typically associated with the comforting of householders, with blessings of wisdom, wit, and conviction, and with providing a "Vaikuntha" (heavenly or otherworldly) like atmosphere conducive to students, architects, administrators, and politicians. In other traditions, Anirudda Shaligrams are broadly associated with happiness and are worshipped as friends to the family. Finally, some Shaligram traditions recognize a few variations of this Shaligram.

The most common are:

1. Pitavarna Aniruddha: which is round; yellow; has 3 lines; and the mark of a lotus at bottom.

2. Susthira Anirudda: which sits stably and has many holes; is elongated or round; and blue in color

3. Trirekha Aniruddha: which has 3 lines; one or more lotus marks; is black in color; and has two very small chakras at the opening of a single vadana

TEXTUAL REFERENCES

Praanatoshani Tantra pg. 347, Praanatoshani Tantra pg. 361, Brahmavaivartta (Prakritikhanda, Ch. 21), Garuda Purana (Panchanan Tarkaratna, Part 1, Ch. 45)

DESCRIPTIONS

Round in shape, glaced (meaning "polished"), and charming to look at, yellowish color (BV).
Blue color, round shape, and hole at top side (G). Having 11 chakras (G).
i.   Blue in color and round in shape and glaced, and printed with a lotus and three linear marks.
ii. Black in color with a beautifully shaped opening and having the mark of a discus at the center, another on a side and a small circle at the top.
iii. Yellow in color, round in shape and very charming to look at. (P)

ADDITIONAL REFERENCES

1. Srimad Bhagavatam: Canto 10 - Chapter 61. bhagavata.org. Retrieved 11 July 2022.
2. Sharma, Yedathore Subbaraya. 1971. The Inner Meaning of Bharatha and Bhagavatha (the Torch Leading to the Path of Liberation). University of Michigan.
3. Gopal, Madan. 1990. K.S. Gautam (ed.). India through the ages. Publication Division, Ministry of Information and Broadcasting, Government of India.
4. Rangarajan, Haripriya. 1997. Varāha Images in Madhya Pradesh: An Iconographic Study. Somaiya Publications.
5. Srinivasan, Doris. 1979. "Early Vaiṣṇava Imagery: Caturvyūha and Variant Forms". Archives of Asian Art. 32: 39–54

BASUDEV/VAASUDEV

Vasudev carries a wide variety of meanings depending on the particular Hindu tradition in question. In Indian epic poetry, Vasudeva is the father of Krishna. He was the brother of Nanda Baba, the chieftain of the cowherder tribe, who was a Surasena (an ancient Indian region corresponding to the present-day Braj region in Uttar Pradesh) who also became the foster father of Krishna.

His sister Kunti was famously married to Pandu, both significant figures in the Mahabharata. In other interpretations, Vasudeva was a partial incarnation of Rishi Kashyapa (a famous Hindu sage) as well as one of Vishnu's four vyuha avatars who received specific attributes or functions of Vishnu but not his entire incarnation (See also the Anirudda and Pradyumna Shaligrams).

Additionally, following the advent of Bhagavatism in the 1st-millennium BCE, the patronymic Vāsudeva (with long ā) has also remained a popular name of Krishna. According to many Shaligram traditions, the Vasudev Shaligram is marked by both Śesha (Ananta), the eternal serpent who appeared to protect the infant Krishna as Vasudeva carried him across the river during his flight from the demon-king Kansa, and Kalpvriksha, the sacred tree along the river banks.

Typically, these Shaligrams are then identified using their long oval shapes (described as "basket-like") and the appearance of a central spiral within the opening (vadana) representative of the serpent Śesha. Ideally, they will also contain a tree-like marking of grooves or lines somewhere else along the internal surface of the vadana, though this is not always required. As a result, Vasudeva Shaligrams are identified primarily through a combination of features that link them to the narrative of Vasudev and Krishna.

In practice, Vasudev Shaligrams are more commonly associated with the stories of Krishna than with Vishnu specifically. As such, they are said to grant enormous physical strength to devotees in times of trial and to encourage all practitioners in their vicinity to adopt stout hearts and minds whenever troubled. This "never give up" atmosphere of ritual veneration also makes them especially popular as gifts to those who are ill or who have recently suffered tragic circumstances in their lives. Conversely, Vasudev Shaligrams are often paired with Krishna Shaligrams during worship, especially Gopala Shaligrams; where they can then carry out the circumstances of Krishna's rescue again and again for festivals and special occasions.

REFERENCES

Praanatoshani Tantra pg. 348, Praanatoshani Tantra pg. 361, Skanda Purana, Nagarkhanda, 244: 3-9, Garuda Purana (Panchanan Tarkaratna, Part 1, Ch. 45), Agni Purana; Bengavasi ed., Panchanan Tarkaratna, Saka 1812, Ch. 46

DESCRIPTION:

» Evenly shaped and charming to look at. Has two circular marks at front of opening (BV).
» White in color, having two circular marks joined together at the opening. (G) Having 5 chakras (G).
» Black in color, having two circular marks joined together at the opening (A).
» White in color and glittering to look at. He has two circular marks closely printed but not joined, at His opening. (P)

ADDITIONAL REFERENCES

1. Srinivasan. Doris. 1997. Many Heads, Arms, and Eyes: Origin, Meaning, and Form of Multiplicity in Indian Art. BRILL Academic. pp. 211–220.

2. Flood, Gavin D. 1996. An Introduction to Hinduism. Cambridge University Press. pp. 119–120.

3.Bopearachchi, Osmund. 2016. Emergence of Viṣṇu and Śiva Images in India: Numismatic and Sculptural Evidence. Paper presented at Education Studios, Asian Art Museum, San Francisco.

4. Singh, Upinder 2008. A History of Ancient and Early Medieval India: From the Stone Age to the 12th Century. Pearson Education India. p. 436–438

BRAHMAN (PARAMATMA)

The Brahman Shaligram is virtually absent from routine Shaligram practice largely due to its red color—an inauspicious type of Shaligram often prohibited in home worship. The relationship between Scriptural references to the Brahman and interpretation of this particular Shaligram are, however, the closest between text and practice. In Hinduism, Brahman connotes the highest Universal Principle, the Ultimate Reality in the universe.

In major schools of Hindu philosophy, it is the material, formal, and final cause of all that exists. It is therefore a pervasive, genderless, infinite, eternal truth and enlightenment which does not change, yet is the cause of all changes. Ultimately, Brahman is then often enacted as a metaphysical concept to refer to the single theological unity behind the diversity of forms in the universe. In terms of Shaligram veneration, the Brahman Shaligram is exceptionally rare and when it does appear, is described as reddish-brown to orange-red in color with several small markings or chakras covering its outer surface.

In most traditions, these Shaligrams are never kept in household shrines and are almost always turned over to temples when found. This is because red Shaligrams generally, and Brahman Shaligrams specifically, are often described as "chaotic" or "intensely demanding."

Their ritual care therefore requires strict adherence to rules of purity and practice that many consider to be outside the abilities of a single home practitioner. Attempting to keep such a Shaligram would then be to invite potential disaster if daily worship cannot be maintained.

Brahman is also synonymous with the concept of Atman; the soul or the self that is personal, impersonal, or Para Brahman (the Supreme deity, usually Vishnu or Shiva) or a combination of these qualities depending on the philosophical school.

As such, the Brahman Shaligram is also said to contain far too many divine connections to be safely worshipped by individuals and should never be incorporated into home use. This does not mean, however, that all red Shaligrams are Brahman. Rather, several Shaligram types do occasionally appear in a red color.

Brahman Shaligrams are typically set apart from other red Shaligrams by their multiple chakras and golden markings which indicate their various connections.

Overall, this means that the Brahman Shaligram is a shila whose composition is not that of the typical black shales of other Shaligrams, but instead is made up of Himalayan schists, gneiss, or sandstones which can appear as red, red-brown, or orange.

The red color of these shilas can also sometimes be challenging to differentiate from brown Shaligrams (which are permitted for worship) but most practitioners describe Brahman Shaligrams as distinctly crimson or flame-orange.

Most commonly, these Shaligrams also do not contain whole chakras, but rather a few small casts and impressions of shell-spirals throughout the main portion of the stone.

REFERENCES

» Garuda Purana (Panchanan Tarkaratna, Part 1, Ch. 45) -- Not found in Agni Purana; Bengavasi ed., Panchanan Tarkaratna, Saka 1812, Ch. 46.
» In the Pranatoshani Tantra pg. 361, this Shaligram is called Paramatma.

Some Shaligram traditions recognize two possible variations of the Brahman Shaligram:

1. Brahma-Parameshthi, which is whitish or yellowish in hue and perfectly round. It also has a single chakra and a mark of a lotus near the rear portion of the shila or near a small vadana.
2. Vishtara-sravo-murti, which is a large red Shaligram, elongated in shape, that has apertures (vadanas) on both of its sides. It also has at least one chakra marking and the mark of a vanamala going around its body.

DESCRIPTIONS

Red in color, small opening (G).
Having 13 or more chakras (G)

ADDITIONAL REFERENCES

1. Fowler, Jeaneane D. 2002. Perspectives of Reality: An Introduction to the Philosophy of Hinduism. Sussex Academic Press.
2. Michaels, Axel. 2004. Hinduism. Past and present. Princeton, New Jersey: Princeton University Press.
3. Puligandla, Ramakrishna. 1997. Fundamentals of Indian Philosophy. New Delhi: D. K. Printworld (P) Ltd.
4. Raju, P. T. 1992. The Philosophical Traditions of India. Delhi: Motilal Banarsidass Publishers Private Limited

BUDDHA

In addition to the prominence of Siddhartha Gautama in modern Buddhist traditions, the Buddha is also considered to be the ninth incarnation of Vishnu in the Dasavatara sequence by some Hindu traditions (though this is not universal, especially among traditions that consider Krishna's brother Balaram to be the ninth avatar).

Furthermore, because Buddhist teachings do not rely on the Vedas, are non-theistic, and deny the reality of the self or Ātman; many Hindu philosophers classify Buddhism as nāstika or heterodoxy within the larger scheme of Hinduism; making the Buddha Shaligram something of an enigma.

Regardless, the Buddha is described in a number of important Hindu scriptures, including almost all major Puranas. However, not all references to the Buddha are necessarily to the same person. Some references are to other persons and some mentions of 'buddha' simply mean 'a person possessing buddhi.'

The majority of references however, refer specifically to the founder of Buddhism. Unsurprisingly, this tends to mean that the Buddha Shaligram appears more commonly in regions where Buddhism is more prevalent and where Buddhism has blended with other local religious practices.

The Buddha Shaligram is typically included as one of the primary Dasavatara Shaligrams and is said to be especially auspicious for ascetics and sannyasis (or anyone interested in pursuing a materially-detached spiritual life). Buddha Shaligrams are also associated with charity, philanthropy, and patience.

Worshippers of this Shaligram are then bestowed with great concentration, satisfaction, and fulfillment in the face of scarcity. Buddha means "Awakened one" or "The Enlightened One" and is also the title for the first awakened being in an era. In most Buddhist traditions, Siddhartha Gautama is regarded as the Supreme Buddha of the current age.

As such, the Buddha Shaligram is often sought by Indian and Nepali Buddhists as meditation stones for their home altars or for use in the management of spirits or other energies. The Buddha Shaligram is also heavily associated with travel in the Himalayas and is sought after by both Hindu and Buddhist pilgrims in the region.

As a manifestation of Siddhartha Gautama (Shakyamuni), these Shaligrams also represent the teachings on which Buddhism was founded (in the Shakya region of the Himalayan foothills) and are therefore also associated with austerity, spiritual searching, and service to humanity.

In most interpretations, the Buddha Shaligram takes the overall shape of a man in a seated, meditative position. For this reason, Buddha Shaligrams are commonly triangular in shape, with a rounded top nodule, wider base, and occasionally a partial chakra ringing their bottom sections or angled up the back in the manner of an upright "spine."

It is important to note that only some Shaligram interpretive traditions recognize Buddha Shaligrams. In traditions where the Buddha is not recognized as a significant religious figure, these Shaligrams are interpreted differently; as a manifestation of the Devi in Shaktism (see Mahashakti Shaligram) or as a variation of the Kurma Shaligram. In practice, devotees also sometimes describe Buddha Shaligrams as having two openings and two chakras within the interior.

Shilas that have such characteristics are then differentiated from similar looking Shaligrams because the chakras will be "upward-inclined at the head" or they will appear along the sides of the Shaligram.

In these cases, Buddha Shaligrams are additionally likely to be multi-colored. This description was echoed by other practitioners throughout Nepal who further identified the Buddha Shaligram as being "muddy colored" (i.e., brown or dark grey) with spots on it or unclear (meaning smoothed out) chakra markings that are dark grey.

REFERENCES

Praanatoshani Tantra pg. 348

DESCRIPTION:

With a very small opening and without any circular markings. This type is popularly called Niviita Buddha (P)

ADDITIONAL REFERENCES:

1. Carrithers, M. 2001. The Buddha: A Very Short Introduction. Oxford University Press.

2. Cousins, L.S. 1996. "The Dating of the Historical Buddha: A Review Article". Journal of the Royal Asiatic Society. 3. 6 (1): 57–63

3. Ñāṇamoli Bhikkhu. 1992. The Life of the Buddha: According to the Pali Canon. Buddhist Publication Society

4. Gethin, Rupert, M.L. 1998. Foundations of Buddhism, Oxford University Press.

5. Gopal, Madan. 1990. K.S. Gautam (ed.), India through the ages, Publication Division, Ministry of Information and Broadcasting, Government of India, p. 73.

DADHIVAMANA (VAMANA)

While it is listed as Dadhivamana in the Brahma Vaivarta Purana, this Shaligram is often described as a variation of the more common Vamana Shaligram of the Dasavatara sequence of Vishnu's incarnations (See Vamana Shaligram).

Its description differs from the Vamana Shaligram however, in that the Dadhivamana Shaligram is often identified by ritual specialists as having a "raised head, being yellowish in color, sometimes with white spots, and containing unclear chakras."

The Dadhivamana Shaligram takes its name from the Dadhi Vamana Stotra (Prayer to Vamana) where Vishnu takes the incarnation of Vamana, his fifth avatar, to destroy the pride of the great Asura king Mahabali. Though a demon, Mahabali was a benevolent emperor. But he usurped the Deva kingdom and as such, Vishnu took the form of a young, dwarf, Brahmin boy called Vamana and requested that he be granted three steps of land as measured by his feet.

In spite of his guru's opposition, Mahabali agreed. Vamana then took the gigantic form of Trivikrama and measured all of the three worlds in two steps. When Mahabali offered his head as a third step, Vamana then requested that instead, Mahabali should live forever in Patala (the underworld).

In Kerala, devotees celebrate Mahabali's home-coming during the festival of Thiruvonam and in Karnataka, devotees believe that he visits them every year on the Bali Padyami. In this way, the Dadhivamana Shaligram is often brought out during these festival seasons as a presiding deity over the occasion.

In practice, the Dadhivamana Shaligram is usually recognizable as an uneven shila with a round or oval shape and one or more openings that appear yellowish in color. The body of the Shaligram itself is also typically mottled with yellow or orange infiltrates throughout a general grey to dark blue color.

The spots on this Shaligram are markings directly associated with splatters of curd and it is this characteristic that primarily differentiates this shila from the more traditional Vamana Shaligram. Lastly, if the Shaligram does contain chakra markings (and not all of them do), they should be "unclear;" meaning heavily worn, smooth, or barely visible.

The worship of this Shaligram is associated with Vamana's preference for anointing sacred beings in curd (dadhi) or offering rice mixed with curd where he confers strength to the tongue (so as to speak nothing but the truth) and gives a pleasing odor to the mouth.

Veneration of this shila is therefore described as bestowing good speech and a need for spoken truth. In some traditions, this Shaligram is associated with the purification of food and is offered prasadam (sacred food) before it is offered to other deities.

REFERENCES

Brahmavaivartta (Prakritikhanda, Ch. 21)

DESCRIPTIONS

Small in size with two circular marks (BV).
Very small in size with two circular marks, and having the color of a new cloud. (BV)

ADDITIONAL REFERENCES

See also: Pratima Kōśā, sixth volume, pg.108-109, which further mentions forms of Dadhivamana in the Meru-tantra, the Sāradā-tilaka and the Mantra-devatā-prakāśikā.

DAMODAR

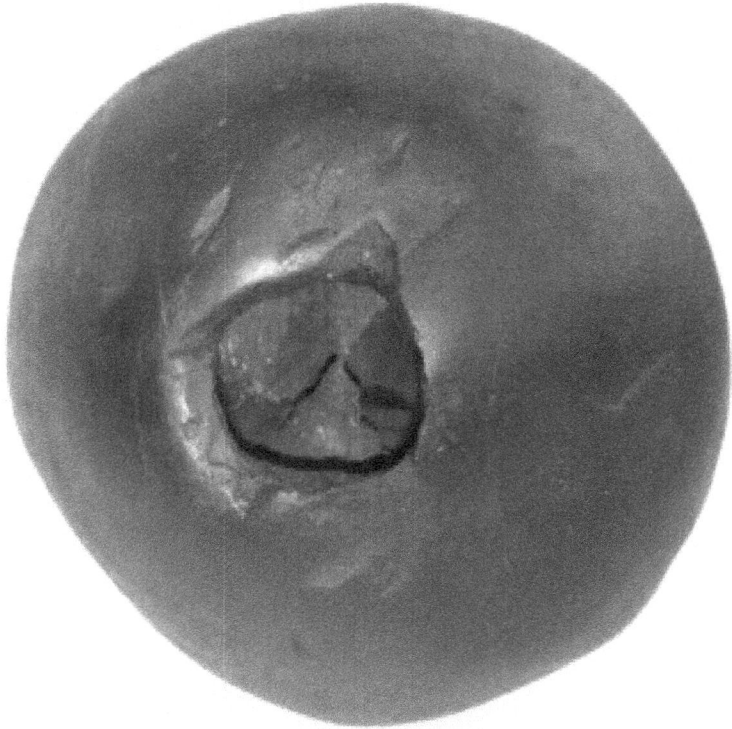

Damodar (also spelled Damodara) is the 367th Name of Vishnu from the Vishnu Sahasranama. The most popular interpretation of the name is "The Lord when He was tied with a cord (daama) around His waist (udara)," a phrase denoting the story of Krishna's mother Yashoda who bound the child Krishna around the waist as punishment for stealing butter.

In other usage, Damodar also means "One who is known through a mind which is purified (Udara) by means of self-control (dama)" or "One in whose bosom rests the entire universe." Most commonly associated with the story of Krishna as the Butter-Thief, the Damodar Shaligram is often given to students or young devotees because it is said to increase memory and concentration.

Damodar Shaligrams are also associated with the performance of meditation, austerities and personal sacrifices, and philanthropic activities. More importantly, these Shaligrams are linked to children and family. Practitioners describe the benefits of these Shaligrams as that of sons becoming obedient and all the children in a household experiencing a sense of calm as they develop a strong sense of proper actions.

As a result, Damodar Shaligrams are often venerated as deities of family life and are often kept permanently in multigenerational households. As such, worship of this Shaligram tends to focus on removing bad habits and resolving conflicts for the entire family.

Damodar Shaligrams are generally identified by the large central opening with two internal chakra impressions on either side of the central spiral column. This central opening however, is balanced against the overall shape of the Shaligram, which may be similar to that of the Gopala Shaligram (round, ball-like) or elongated in a shape similar to that of Krishna Shaligrams.

But in the latter case, a Damodar Shaligram will also have a ridge, groove, or striated line (rekha) representing the binding cord. Identification of Damodar Shaligrams is also sometimes tricky because they can appear very similarly to two other Shaligrams. In some cases, they resemble the Lakshmi-Narayan Shaligram.

A Damodar Shaligram, however, is distinguished from this form by the uneven and heavily marked outer ridge surrounding the central opening (i.e., the cord markings). In other cases, these Shaligrams are mistakenly identified as Narasimha Shaligrams due to the wide vadana (mouth) but these shilas do not contain the notable "teeth" of Narasimha Shaligrams.

Damodar Shaligrams also have numerous variations depending on the interpretive tradition in question. Some practitioners describe them as having a "big belly," for example, while others categorize them as any Shaligram with a small opening, two medium chakras and a vanamala.

OTHER VARIATIONS INCLUDE:

1. The Srighana Shaligram (Srighana is a pilgrimage place name). Which is white in color and exceedingly smooth to touch. It has a great many spots on the surface and a chakra.
2. Durvabha Damodara: A grass green shila that is large in size, with a chakra at the center and yellow lines at the opening.
3. Gadakara Damodara: A large shila with a center chakra, a round and smooth body that protrudes at the right side.
4. Kapila Damodara: Also large in size but with a small opening and two chakras.
5. Lakshmi Damodara: Which has a round body, is black in color, with a center chakra and white dots.
6. Nilamegha Damodara: Which is blue-black in color and has a vanamala covering the body with lines in the central portion.

REFERENCES

Praanatoshani Tantra pg. 347, Skanda Purana, Nagarkhanda, 244: 3-9, Brahmavaivartta (Prakritikhanda, Ch. 21), Garuda Purana (Panchanan Tarkaratna, Part 1, Ch. 45), Agni Purana; Bengavasi ed., Panchanan Tarkaratna, Saka 1812, Ch. 46

DESCRIPTIONS

Big in size, round shape, two circular marks but no mark of a vanamala (BV).

Big in size with a round shape and two circular marks, but not having the mark of vanamala. (BV)

Big size, blue color, deep circular mark at the center (G).

i. Big in size with a small circular mark.

ii. Green in color and big in size with a very small opening. He has a big circular mark and one or more yellow spots on His body.

iii. He has a single opening not very deep, and two circular marks one above the other. There is also a long linear mark at His center. (P)

ADDITIONAL REFERENCES

See also: Damodarashtakam (found in the Padma Purana of Krishna Dwaipayana Vyasa)

GADA DHAR

Shaligrams representing the
four sacred objects in Vishnu's
hands. From top left, clockwise:
Sudarshan chakra, Padma lotus,
Gada mace, and Shankha conch.

In Gaudiya Vaishnavism, Krishna is said to have been reincarnated on Earth in the 15th century as five distinct individuals: Chaitanya Mahaprabhu, Nityananda Prabhu, Advaita Acharya, Gadadhara Pandita, and Srivasa Thakura. Together, they form the Panchatattva (the Five Truths) who spread Krishna bhakti (devotion) throughout India.

In other interpretations, Gadadhar is a name that is taken to mean "One who has the gada (mace) as his weapon," a reference that can mean either Vishnu or Krishna. Interpretations of the Gadadhar Shaligram vary considerably depending on the Hindu tradition in question. For the most part, however, practitioners agree that this particular Shaligram can be identified using its flattened, embedded, or faint "mace" marking on an otherwise smooth and unmarked shila.

In other variations, however, the Gadadhar Shaligram has the overall shape of the gada (mace) -head and should be worshipped in combination with Shanka (conch), Sudarshan (chakra), and Padma (lotus) Shaligrams; thus representing the four sacred objects held in Vishnu's hands.

Note especially the last photo (opposite), where the Gadadhar Shaligram is located on the bottom right. Clockwise to the left is a Shankha Shaligram, Sudarshan Shaligram, and Lotus Shaligram (See also Padmanabha Shaligram and Kamal-Narayan Shaligram).

It is important to note that in some interpretive traditions, the Lotus Shaligram here could also be described as the first type of Gada Shaligram; but the two are typically differentiated by the overall shape of the marking (i.e., Lotus Shaligrams have a wider "blossom" and a long, thin, "stem").

Associated with worldliness, hard work/labor, patience, and pliability, it is not uncommon for Gadadhar Shaligrams to be sought after by craftsmen, laborers, and construction workers. This is because Gadadhar Shaligrams are said to impart harmonies between work and family life, ensuring a balance between providing for a family and participating in it.

In more regional interpretations, this Shaligram is viewed as a representation of the gada (mace) common in South Asian history and literature. As a representation of the gada, this Shaligram is therefore occasionally associated with great warriors of the Hindu epics, such as Bhima, Duryodhana, or Jarasandha (and may be addressed by those names instead).

For this reason, it may also be given to soldiers, politicians, or law-makers. In some traditional variations, this Shaligram is referred to as either Kaumodaki (which is the name of Krishna's mace in the Mahabharata) or Gadadevi (where it is personified as a goddess with Vishnu resting his hand on her head).

REFERENCES

Pranatoshani Tantra pg. 347, Brahmavaivartta (Prakritikhanda, Ch. 21)

DESCRIPTIONS

Hidden circular mark (BV)

Green in color with its lower middle portion raised upwards. It has a big hole at its top, and is marked with long lines. (P)

Having one chakra only, which will not be bright (Sk)

ADDITIONAL REFERENCES

1. Desai, Kalpana. 2013. Iconography of Visnu. Abhinav Publications.
2. Sivaramamurti, C. 1955. "The Weapons of Vishṇu". Artibus Asiae. Artibus Asiae publishers. 18 (2): 128–136

GANESH

Ganesha, also known as Ganapati and Vinayaka, is one of the best-known and most worshipped deities of the Hindu pantheon. The characteristic image of the elephant-headed god is found throughout India, Sri Lanka, and Nepal and it is not uncommon for a variety of South Asian and Southeast Asian traditions to worship him regardless of other deity affiliations. Devotion to Ganesha is also widely diffused among Jains and Buddhists.

Ganesha emerged as a distinct deity in the 4th and 5th centuries AD, during the Gupta period, although he inherited traits from a number of Vedic and pre-Vedic precursors. He was formally included among the five primary deities of Smartism in the 9th century and was later elevated to the status of supreme deity by the Ganapatya sect.

The worship of Ganesha is generally considered complementary with the worship of other deities; however, Hindus of all traditions often begin prayers, important undertakings, and religious ceremonies with an invocation of Ganesha. The "worship of the five forms" (pañcāyatana pūjā) system, which was popularized by Adi Śaṅkarācārya, also invokes the five deities Ganesha, Vishnu, Shiva, Devī, and Sūrya and is still common throughout South Asia today, particularly in Nepal.

Ganesha is widely revered as the remover of obstacles, as a patron of arts and sciences, and as the god of intellect and wisdom. As the god of beginnings, he is often honored at the start of rituals and ceremonies and is invoked as patron of letters and learning during classes or in academic conferences. As such, the Ganesha Shaligram is used similarly; as a gift during weddings or other festivals and as a focus of worship prior to the undertaking of new endeavors in school, business, or life in general.

More broadly, Ganesh Shaligrams are associated with an ability to face challenges, resolve conflicts, or surmount difficulties in life and are most often included in household altars that make a point to collect Shaligrams of the "five forms" worshipped in the household. The Ganesh Shaligram is often easy to identify. It always bears the distinctive shape and markings of an elephant's head; either turned sideways (with "trunk" curling downwards as in photo 1) or forward (with the "trunk" splitting the shila down the center as in photo 2).

In rarer variations, the Ganesh Shaligram combines a series of features, including "ears" of the bivalve (Retroceramus) – similar to the Aniruddha Shaligram -- and additional markings indicative of a seated man with a rotund belly. Ganesh Shaligrams also commonly have several smaller markings, such as a white vanamala, that indicate the presence of Shiva, Parvati, or other deities.

REFERENCES

While not typically included in Puranic lists of Shaligram categories, the Ganesh Shaligram is widely used in practice and is often included as a local variation of other Shaligram name-types, particularly Shiva and Shiva-Parvati Shaligrams. Some regional Shaligram name-lists further include the Ganesh Shaligram under other names, such as Vighnesha, Ekadanta, Heramba, or Gajanana.

ADDITIONAL REFERENCES

1. Brown, Robert. 1991. Ganesh: Studies of an Asian God, Albany: State University of New York.

2. Heras, H. 1972. The Problem of Ganapati, Delhi: Indological Book House

3. Martin-Dubost, Paul. 1997, Gaṇeśa, the Enchanter of the Three Worlds. Franco-Indian Research. pp. 412–416.

4. Ramachandra Rao, S.K. 1992. The Compendium on Gaṇeśa, Delhi: Sri Satguru Publications

GARUDA

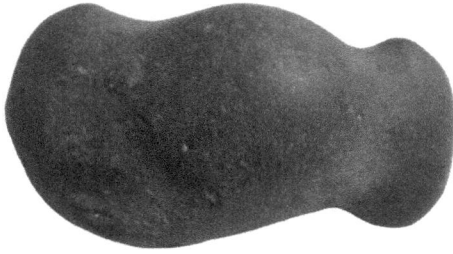

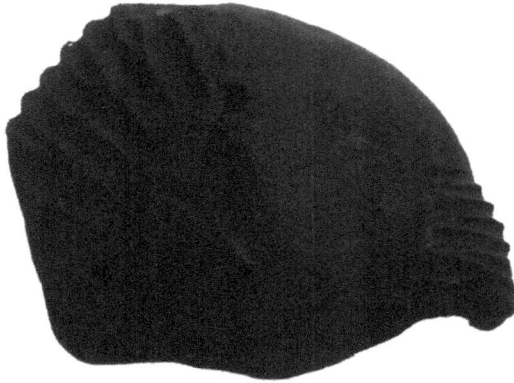

Garuda is a large mythical bird, bird-like being, or humanoid bird that appears in both Hinduism and Buddhism. In Hindu depictions, Garuda most often appears as the mount (vahana) of Vishnu. Additionally, Garuda is also the Hindu name for the constellation Aquila. In other artistic styles, the brahminy kite and the phoenix are considered by many to be the contemporary representations of Garuda. Especially popular in Indonesia, Garuda's depiction as a Javanese eagle also acts as the national symbol.

In Hinduism, Garuda is typically shown as having a golden body (either bird or man) with a white face, red wings, and an eagle's beak wearing a crown on his head. In some descriptions, he is further said to be so massive as to block out the sun. Garuda is also known as the eternal sworn enemy of the Nāga serpent race and is said to feed exclusively on snakes. The image of Garuda, and in many cases his Shaligram, is then often used as an amulet to protect the bearer from snake bites or death by snake poison, since the king of birds is so known as the "devourer of serpents."

The Garuda Shaligram is usually identified through a combination of overall shape and markings of wings and a crown (a partial chakra-spiral). The main portion of the Shaligram may be "bird-like" or a mix of bird and human characteristics. The majority of Garuda Shaligrams in practice, however, have no chakra markings and are comprised of a central, rounded, shale nodule with two protruding (slightly ridged) side sections representative of Garuda's extended wings.

Note that Garuda Shaligrams with golden markings are especially prized but such characteristics are not necessary for the Shaligram to be identified as such. The Garuda Shaligram is most often placed near a Vishnu Shaligram or Vishnu deity for worship (where he carries Vishnu on his back). Strongly associated with protection from snakes, this Shaligram is said to bestow protection from poisons and illnesses. It also associated with success in legal matters and in deliverance from war, disaster, or political conflicts.

REFERENCES

Pranatoshani Tantra pg. 361, 351-356.

DESCRIPTIONS

» Garudadhvaja: Round in shape with the marks of golden horns and hoofs on the body. He is also printed with a circular mark with dark linear marks inside it. (P)

» Shaped like a lotus with three linear marks one above the other, the central line being longer.

» Printed with long linear marks and having two, three or four golden spots on His body. In color he may be green, blue or white. (P)

ADDITIONAL REFERENCES

1. Daniélou, Alain, December 1991. Gods of India: The Classic Work on Hindu Polytheism from the Princeton Bollingen Series. Inner Traditions / Bear & Co. p. 161.

2. George M. Williams. 2008. Handbook of Hindu Mythology. Oxford University Press. pp. 21, 24, 63, 138

3. Helmuth von Glasenapp. 1999). Jainism: An Indian Religion of Salvation. Motilal Banarsidass. p. 532.

4. Robert E. Buswell Jr.; Donald S. Lopez Jr. 2013. The Princeton Dictionary of Buddhism. Princeton University Press. pp. 314–315.

5. Roshen Dalal. 2010. Hinduism: An Alphabetical Guide. Penguin Books. p. 145.

GOVARDHANA

Govardhana Shaligrams

Govardhana silas

Govardhana, Mount Govardhana, Giri Raj or the Royal Hill, is a sacred pilgrimage site in the Mathura district of Uttar Pradesh, India. It is located on an 8 km long massif which is situated in the area of Govardhan and Radha Kund, about 20 km (12 mi) from the holy town of Vrindavan. This hill crest is also the sacred center of Braj, the region where Krishna is said to have been born and grew up. In fact, the visible stone formation of the hill is often identified as a naturally-manifested form of Krishna himself (called a Govardhana shila).

Govardhan is also most famous not just because it is considered the place wherein Krishna, his brother Balaram, and Krishna's consort Radha carried out their past-times, but for the story of the lifting of Govardhan hill by Krishna when he defeated Indra, the god of thunder and lightning, by lifting the mountain to protect the villagers and their cattle from rain and flooding as a result of Indra's wrath.

There is often some confusion between the Govardhana Shaligram and the Govardhana shila: one being the manifestation Krishna-Govardhana from the Kali Gandaki River and the other being a stone taken directly from Govardhana Hill. Govardhana Shaligrams however, are most often described as being "mountain shaped" (triangular, with a wide base) which may contain golden markings at the top (or the marks of Surya as the rising sun at the tip) or a faint, partially obscured, chakra along the bottom edge.

Conversely, Govardhana shilas are usually brown or reddish-brown and come in a variety of geometric shapes as they are broken off from the hill itself. Their worship is often combined with puja altars that contain Shaligrams as well as Dwarka shilas (coral) and Banalinga (forms of the Shiva Lingam).

Worship of the Govardhana Shaligram is said to bestow an uncommonly peaceful environment and to prevent distractions or time-wasting actions that do not benefit the harmonious working of the household. These Shaligrams are also prized for bestowing strength, stability, and protection (usually from natural disasters) to their devotees.

Furthermore, Govardhana Shaligrams are described as being very adept at "making impossible things happen." Generally speaking though, Govardhana Shaligrams are more commonly found in Vaishnava practices (given their specific links to Krishna) but, on occasion, Govardhana and Samudra Manthan/Sona Parbat Shaligrams will be worshipped simultaneously (even identified as being one another) during special events and festivals from a variety of traditions (such as Govardhan Puja or other Mahapujas) – See also Samudra Manthan Shaligram.

Descriptions

The Govardhana Shaligram is not specifically mentioned by name in the Puranic texts but is most often associated with Govardhana shila veneration as well as the veneration of a wide variety of other aniconic and natural murti, such as the Dwarka shila and the Shiva Linga.

In other Hindu traditions, the Govardhan Shaligram is considered to be a variation of the Samudra Manthan Shaligram.

Additional References

1. Rajasekhara Dasa 2001. Govardhana Hill: India's Most Sacred Mountain. Vedanta Vision Publications

2. Dev Prasad. 2015. Krishna: A Journey through the Lands & Legends of Krishna. Jaico Publishing House. pp. PT 147.

3. Haberman, David L. 2020. Loving Stones: Making the Impossible Possible in the Worship of Mount Govardhan. Oxford University Press.

HAMSA SHALIGRAM

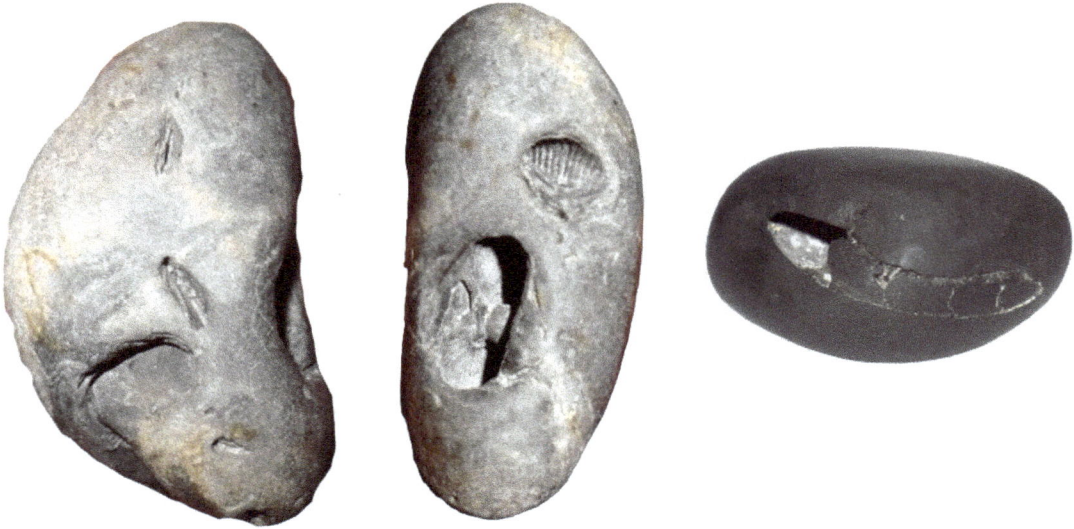

Saraswati-Hamsa Shaligram (Showing the swan's head and neck markings)

   The identification of the Hamsa Shaligram is contentious given the multiple meanings and translations of the word "hamsa/hansa." One of the most well-known depictions of the Hamsa is that of an open-hand or palm-shaped, five-fingered, amulet popular throughout the Middle East and North Africa, which is commonly used in jewelry and decorations.

   Depicting the open right hand often with an eye in the center, the Hamsa was an image used as a sign of protection throughout history. The Hamsa is also described by many religions, including Islam, Judaism, and Levantine Christianity, as providing defense against the evil eye.

   It has been theorized that its origins lie in Ancient Egypt or in Carthage (modern-day Tunisia) where it may have been associated with the Egyptian goddess Tanit. But for Buddhists and Hindus, the Hamsa as a hand symbolizes the interplay of the chakras, the five senses, the energy flow throughout the body, and the mudras (sacred hand gestures) that can affect that energy. The hamsa in Sanskrit, however, is the name of a migratory aquatic bird which is typically identified as a type of goose or a swan.

The icon of the hamsa-bird is also often used in Indian and Southeast Asian cultures as a spiritual symbol where it is identified with the Supreme Spirit, Ultimate Reality, or Brahman in Hindu theology. As such, the flight of the hamsa (as a swan) symbolizes moksha; final liberation from the cycle of samsara.

Additionally, the hamsa is also the vahana (a deity's mythical vehicle) of Saraswati; the goddess of knowledge and creative arts, and her husband Brahma; the god of creation. In practice, the most common interpretation of the Hamsa Shaligram among Hindus is that of Saraswati's swan. For Buddhists, the Hamsa-hand interpretation is more common.

Described as "bow-shaped" or occasionally as "shankha-shaped," with a slate grey or light bluish color, and whose chakras are joined together with a "lotus-like stem," the Hamsa Shaligram is primarily identified by shape and color. It usually contains a single opening with two chakras but it is also not unusual for this Shaligram to contain several smaller, less distinct, chakras elsewhere on the body of the shila.

Veneration of the Hamsa Shaligram is still primarily associated with goddess worship, specifically that of Saraswati or the Devi in general. Said to bestow blessings of enlightenment, divine favor, and to encourage proper ritual practice, these Shaligrams are often sought after by ascetics, sannyasis, and sadhus as well as by the wives of devout householders.

These Shaligrams are also popular more broadly in Shakta traditions of Hinduism and are associated with music, art, and other creative pursuits. In traditions that do not recognize the name-type of the Hamsa Shaligram, Shaligrams bearing the above-mentioned characteristics would be identified as Acyuta Shaligrams, especially if they contain three distinct chakras.

References

Pranatoshani Tantra pg. 351 – 356.

Descriptions

» Shaped like a bow with a mixed color of blue and white and having the marks of a discus and lotus on His body (P)

» Hamsa: D-Shaped body joined by 2 chakras; tinge of white. Or shaped like a shanka with mixed colors; chakra at the center; left side has a Kumuda flower and the right side has a bow markings. These Shaligrams have 1 vadana and 2 or 3 chakras.

» Hamsa: Shaped like a bow with a mixed color of blue and white and having the marks of a discus and lotus on His body. (P)

» Parahamsa: Shaped like the throat of a peacock, with a glaced (meaning polished) body and round opening. Inside the opening there are two circular marks with a sun-like print on the right side of them. There are also two linear marks forming the shape of a boar on His body. (P)

» The Vanamala Murti Shaligram, an occasional variation of the Hamsa Shaligram, is shila that appears sometimes in practice. It is described as being of a tawny (yellowish-brown) hue, and has an opening at the sides of which are fang-like structures and inside of which are two chakras; the opening is crooked and near its side is the vanamala line.

Additional References

1. Sonbol, Amira El Azhary. 2005. Beyond the exotic: women's histories in Islamic societies. Syracuse University Press

2. Bernasek, Lisa; Peabody Museum of Archaeology and Ethnology; Burger, Hillel S. 2008. Artistry of the everyday: beauty and craftsmanship in Berber art (Illustrated ed.). Peabody Museum Press, Harvard University.

3. Cush, Denise. 2007. Encyclopedia of Hinduism. Routledge. p. 697.

HANUMAN SHALIGRAM

Hanuman is a companion-in-arms to and a dedicated devotee of Sri Ram, the 7th incarnation of Vishnu. Hanuman is also one of the central figures of the Ramayana epic where he appears in various ways across multiple versions. His most famous and well-known appearance is that of the Vanara (monkey-man), wherein he participated in Rama's war against the demon-king Ravana. Hanuman is also one of the Chiranjivi, one of several immortal living beings in Hinduism who remain alive on Earth from ancient times and through Kali Yuga, the current and final age, until the end of the modern world.

He is mentioned in several other texts, including the Mahabharata, in various Puranas, and in some Jain texts. While some texts describe Hanuman as an incarnation of Shiva, he is more generally considered to be the son of Anjana and Kesari or as the son of the wind-god Pawan. By some accounts, he belonged to a tribe called "Vanar" residing in a deep forest. Because the Vanar were most often depicted as less civilized (including as humanoid apes) as compared to other communities of their time, there is some contention among scholars, theologians, and artists as to why Hanuman is portrayed as a monkey in a variety of sources.

The Hanuman Shaligram does not appear in all Shaligram interpretive traditions. But when it does, it either bears the overall shape of Hanuman, particularly in terms of his head, face, and arms or, conversely, the Hanuman Shaligram may only contain impressions of the distinctive face, with a slightly protruding lower jaw, wide nose, and broadly set eyes. This second formation is typically comprised of a single shale nodule that has a partial chakra embedded on the surface of one of its sides. The rest of the Shaligram then may demonstrate other features or markings. In either case, the Shaligram also often contains the marking of a gada (mace) located at the back of the main figure or near to his left hand or shoulder.

Despite being largely absent from mentions in Puranic texts, the Hanuman Shaligram is none-the-less comparatively popular in multiple Shaligram practices. The identification of this Shaligram largely focuses on two characteristics: the overall shape of the Shaligram, which should bear resemblance to the face and upper body of Hanuman's "monkey-man" incarnation, and markings of a gada (mace) on the back or top of the Shaligram. In other cases, impressions of the face of Hanuman are often seen on Sri Ram Shaligrams or on Sita-Ram Shaligrams.

Veneration of Hanuman Shaligrams is most often associated with those who are "submissive to God." As such, these Shaligrams are said to invoke deep senses of loyalty and to encourage a nature of service (both in terms of human relationships and with one's relationship to God). It is also said that worship of this Shaligram renders the devotee difficult to influence and shortly reveals lies and deception for what they are.

ADDITIONAL REFERENCE

1. Ludvik, Catherine. 1994. Hanumān in the Rāmāyaṇa of Vālmīki and the Rāmacaritamānasa of Tulasī Dāsa. Motilal Banarsidass.

2. Lutgendorf, Philip. 2007. Hanuman's Tale: The Messages of a Divine Monkey. Oxford University Press.

3. Richman, Paula. 2010. Review: Lutgendorf, Philip's Hanuman's Tale: The Messages of a Divine Monkey, The Journal of Asian Studies; Vol 69, Issue 4 (Nov 2010), pages 1287–1288.

4. Vanamali, Mataji Devi. 2010. Hanuman: The Devotion and Power of the Monkey God. Inner Traditions, USA.

Harihara (Shankara-Narayana)

Harihara Shaligram (top)

Harihara Shaligram (bottom)

Harihara is the fused representation of Vishnu (Hari) and Shiva (Hara) which often appears in iconography as a deity who is one-half Vishnu and one-half Shiva. Also known as Shankara-Narayana ("Shankara" is Shiva and "Narayana" is Vishnu), Harihara is venerated by Vaishnavas, Smartas, and Shaivas as a form of the Supreme God. Harihara is also sometimes used as a philosophical term to refer to the unity of Vishnu and Shiva as different aspects of Brahman (the Ultimate Reality). The Advaita Vedanta school of Hindu theology, for example, discusses this concept of the equivalence of various gods as variations of a single principle and the "oneness of all existence" as an understanding of Harihara.

Harihara Shaligrams are most often recognized through their combinations of a Shiva Linga and a Sudarshan Chakra in the same stone. In some variations of this Shaligram, the shila appears as a long, column-shaped, stone (lingam) with a chakra visible underneath the base and in other cases, the shila contains both a lingam marking and a chakra marking next to one another (a belemnite shell as well as an ammonite spiral, respectively).

As a result, Harihara Shaligrams are easily discerned by the simultaneous presence of a belemnite column and a whole (or intact but partially obscured) ammonite chakra-spiral. In other manifestations, Harihara Shaligrams have the overall shape of a Shiva Linga (with or without belemnite) but with a clearly visible ammonite chakra-spiral somewhere on the outer surface of the shila.

As a manifestation of both Vishnu and Shiva, Harihara Shaligrams are primarily associated with the healing of long-term illnesses and protection from accidental harm and other misfortunes. Worship of this Shaligram is also said to bestow improved decision-making abilities and the capability to discern multiple points of view regarding a single problem. Additionally, due to their dual-natured appearance, Harihara Shaligrams are often sought by practitioners whose families or personal religious practices incorporate rituals, ideas, and traditions from multiple religious traditions or lineages. As such, these Shaligrams are highly prized in families whose religious backgrounds are blended.

REFERENCES:

Pranatoshani Tantra pg. 348 and 361, Skanda Purana, Nagarekhanda, 244: 3-9

DESCRIPTION:

» Green in color, round in shape with one opening at the top. The lower portion of His body is marked with dot-prints. (P)
» (i) With two circular marks and a print like a Shiva linga on His front side
»(ii) With three circular marks on the sides, other things being the same as above.
»(iii) With four circular marks, other things being the same as above. (P)

»Shivanarayan: (i) a Harihara type with four different circular marks, and two openings. (ii) Without any opening, other things being the same as above. Both these varieties of Shivanarayan are forbidden to be worshipped; because they cause loss of wealth and land, and even they extinguish the family of their worshippers. (P)

»Shankaranarayana: Marked with the print resembling a Shiva linga either side on the right or the left side. (P)

»The Trimurti Shaligram is recognized in some traditions as a variation of the Harihara Shaligram. It is characterized by marks resembling a conch and discus (emblems of Vishnu), snake and battle axe (emblems of Siva) and lotus and water-pot (emblems of Brahma), along and markings that appear to be three garlands.

ADDITIONAL REFERENCES

1. Leeming, Leeming. 2001. A Dictionary of Asian Mythology, Oxford University Press. Pg. 67.

2. Rajarajan, R.K.K. 2021. "Rāmagiri Tēr Harihara and Harihara-Ekapāda Trimūrti". Journal of Indian History and Culture. 28: 187–213.

3. Rao, TA Gopinatha. 1993. Elements of Hindu iconography, Vol 2, Motilal Banarsidass. Pgs. 334-335.

HAYAGRIVA

Hayagriva, also transliterated as Hayagreeva, is a horse-headed avatar of Vishnu whose Sanskrit name typically breaks down to haya = Horse, grīva=Neck or Face. Conversely, he is also called Hayaśirṣa, which means haya=Horse and śirṣa=Head.

In a variety of traditions of East and South Asian Buddhism, Hayagrīva is also an important deity who originated as a yaksha (a type of nature spirit) attendant of Avalokiteśvara (the bodhisattva of compassion) or Guanyin Bodhisattva (a female equivalent who is the "goddess of compassion").

Appearing in the Vedas as two separate deities, Hayagriva was later assimilated into ritual worship and eventually became a Wisdom King in Vajrayana Buddhism. In Hindu theology, Hayagriva is worshipped as the god of knowledge and wisdom. His iconography is that of a man with a human body and a horse's head, white in color, with white garments and seated on a white lotus. Symbolically, the story of Hayagriva represents the triumph of pure knowledge, guided by the hand of God, over the demonic forces of passion and darkness.

The Hayagriva Shaligram is therefore most commonly identified as having two equally matched chakras (either internally or externally) and the general shape of a horse's head. Associated with the tale of Hayagriva rescuing the Vedas from beneath the ocean, these Shaligrams are said to encourage thinking and learning at a fast pace.

Worship of these Shaligrams is therefore meant to bestow knowledge, understanding, and confidence especially in cases where the practitioner seeks to learn something new or exceptionally challenging. For interpretation, the overall shape of a Hayagriva Shaligram should be reminiscent of a horse's head with the ridge of a chakra appearing out of the front or side of a shila (looking like a mane or a crest).

In some cases, it will also have a small vadana with two spiral imprints visible internally. In other appearances, Hayagriva Shaligrams are identified by two even "cheeks" with a central slate column obscuring the two internal chakras. In Himalayan regions, Hayagriva Shaligrams are highly sought after by horsemen and herdsmen who venerate these Shaligrams as representations of the horse's service, steadfastness, and friendship to mankind.

REFERENCES

Praanatoshani Tantra pg. 347-348, Brahmavaivartta (Prakritikhanda, Ch. 21), Garuda Purana (Panchanan Tarkaratna, Part 1, Ch. 45), Agni Purana; Bengavasi ed., Panchanan Tarkaratna, Saka 1812, Ch. 46

DESCRIPTIONS

» Two circular marks, shape of the face of a horse (BV).
» Big hole, big circular mark, five linear marks of a Kaustubha gem, an Anushka (spear head), several dots, and a dark spot (G).
i. Blue in color, shaped like a spearhead (Ankusha), and marked with a linear, a circular and several dot prints.
ii. With five linear marks, other characteristics being the same as above.
iii. Marked with a circle and a flag-print, other things being the same as above.
iv. Green in color, shaped like the head of a horse, and marked with a circle. (P)

In practice, there are also a number of regional and local descriptions of Hayagriva Shaligrams:
i. In South India, Hayagriva is described as having the form of a ripe jambu-fruit (rose apple, Eugenia Jambolana), with a face in the shape of an elephant goad. It has also longish spots on its body.
ii. Conversely, in central India, Hayagriva is described as having a C-shaped body with an elephant goad-like opening and well-defined dots or a berry shape.
iii. But the most common descriptions of Hayagriva are that the Shaligram has the shape of a horse's head and a central chakra opening. In these cases, the shila may be black or brown (tawny-colored) and have up to five dots and five lines on its body.

Additional References

1. D. Sridhara Babu. 1990. Hayagriva - The Horse-headed Deity in Indian Culture. Sri Venkateshwara University - Oriental Research Institute, Tirupati.

2. Dallapiccola, Anna L. 2004. Dictionary of Hindu Lore and Legend. Thames and Hudson.

3. Kapstein, Matthew T. 2002. The Tibetan Assimilation of Buddhism: Conversion, Contestation, and Memory. Oxford University Press. p. 170-174.

HIRANYAGARBHA

Hiranyagarbha, literally "Golden Womb" or "Golden Egg," (and often poetically described as the "universal gem") is the source of creation for the universal or manifested cosmos in Hindu theology. It is mentioned in one hymn of the Rig Veda (RV 10.121), where it is known as Hiranyagarbha Sukta, which suggests a single creator deity identified in the hymn as Prajapati.

This Shaligram expresses the creative urge of Narayana. The "Golden Egg" here is often interpreted as that from which all of the objective world emerges. The term thereby suggests that the entire creative power of the divine is but an expression of The Self; here meaning Narayana (Vishnu). This Shaligram is therefore linked with transcendental consciousness and Bhakti yoga practices.

In some Himalayan religious traditions, especially in Nepal, this Shaligram is identified as Chandra (The Moon) or as an expression of Shiva appearing as the full moon. It is therefore associated with asceticism, ancient knowledge, or the performance of esoteric rituals in much the same way as the Shiva Linga Shaligram. Depending on the specific markings present, there are also traditions that identify a golden colored Shaligram with this description as Hiranyagarbha, the same Shaligram without the golden coloration as Shiva-Chandra, and any other variations as a type of Kapila Shaligram.

Regardless, the Hiranyagarbha Shaligram is easy to identify and its characteristics are always relatively straight-forward. All variations of this shila are comprised of a single, rounded or cylindrical black shale, nodule which has typically fractured to reveal an equally round, central, nodule. In most cases, this central portion is also infiltrated by iron pyrites, giving it a "golden egg" appearance. In other cases, the central nodule may be the smoothed, internal surface of a large Belemnite chamber or the outer surface of an ammonite shell that has broken into a protruding cross-section and worn smooth.

In other Shaligram traditions, some variations of this Shaligram are referred to Jagdish Shaligrams, meaning one who was born (jah) at the beginning (aadi). Jagdish variations of this Shaligram, however, tend to be more completely rounded with less of the second, central, nodule visible from the outside; appearing more "womb-like" with similar characteristics to that of the Santan-Gopala Shaligram.

References

Praanatoshani Tantra pg. 348, Rig Veda 10.121, Vishvakarman Sūkta (RV 10.82), Manu Smrti 1.9, The Mahābhārata, Book 12: Santi Parva. Kisari Mohan Ganguli, tr. Section CCCIII.

Descriptions

The Upanishads call Hiranyagarbha "The Soul of the Universe" or Brahman, which floated in emptiness and the darkness of non-existence for a year before breaking into two halves which formed the Svarga and the Prthvi (the transitory plane for righteous souls and Earth, respectively) in Hindu cosmology.

In classical Puranic Hinduism, Hiranyagarbha is the term used in Vedanta for the "creator." It is also Brahma because he was born from a golden egg (Manu Smrti 1.9), whereas the Mahabharata calls it "The Manifest."

  i. With the color like that of honey and having a long shape. It has moon-like marks and several golden linear marks on His body.

  ii. Black in color and round in shape with a circular glaced opening. A sweet sound is always formed inside His body. It is marked with a charming Shrivatsa (a circle formed of hair) at its top. (P)

In practice, Hiranyagarbha has several descriptions but all of which agree on a similar set of characteristics. These are that the Shaligram should be round or moon-like in appearance, blue or black in color, with no vadana or openings, and with golden coloration around its center. In some Shaligram traditions, Hiranyagarbha shilas are considered to be the same as the Shiva-nabha Shaligram (See Shiva Linga Shaligram).

Additional References

1. Feuerstein, Georg. 2001. The Yoga Tradition: Its History, Literature, Philosophy and Practice. Arizona, USA: Hohm Press.

2. Schmiedchen, Annette. 2006. "The Ceremony of Tulāpuruṣa: The Purāṇic Concept and the Epigraphical Evidence". In Adalbert J. Gail; Gerd J. R. Mevissen; Richard Salomon (eds.). Script and Image: Papers on Art and Epigraphy. Motilal Banarsidass

3. Sircar, D. C. 1971. Studies in the Religious Life of Ancient and Medieval India. Motilal Banarsidass.

HRISHIKESH

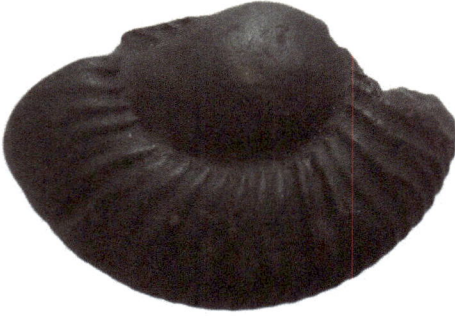

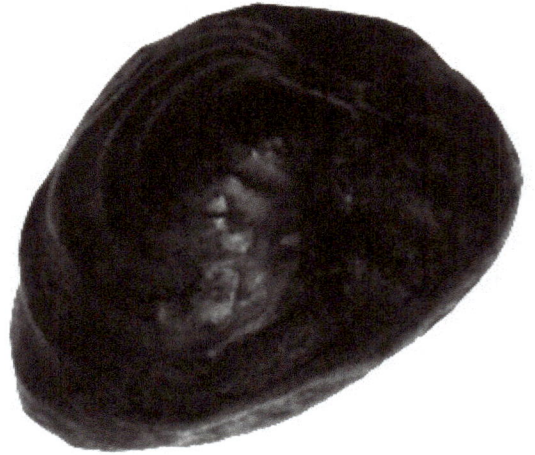

The Hrishikesh Shaligram, or conversely Hrishikesh Chandrama (Half-Moon Hrishikesh), is a manifestation of Hrisheeka+Eesa, "One who has coiled up his locks of hair." In Shaiva interpretations, this refers to Shiva as the ascetic, whose long, unkempt, locks are tied into a top-knot whereupon the phased half-moon and the river Ganga rest. In Vaishnava interpretations, Hrishikesh refers to Vishnu who manifests as the sun and the moon and is considered to be the Lord of All Senses/ Perceptions.

As the sun and the moon, Vishnu is also the deity who brings about the cosmic cycles of sleep and wakefulness and controls the rhythms of life. Lastly, as the 47th name in the Vishnu Sahastranama, according to Adi Shankara's commentary, the name has several meanings: 1) The lord of the senses. 2) He under whose control the senses subsist. And 3) He whose hair consists of the rays of the sun and the moon, which gives joy to the world.

The Hrishikesh Shaligram typically appears in one of two variations. The most common is the "half-moon" form; a prominent partial chakra crest with either a rounded central nodule or a second partial chakra spiral section above the first (almost like parallel layers). The second form, similar to the Aniruddha Shaligram, appears as one half of a fossil bivalve with large, well-spaced, concentric ridges that give the impression of uneven strands of wrapped hair.

Hrishikesh Shaligrams, like other Chandra (Moon) Shaligrams, are primarily associated with cycles of day and night, of moods, and of life in general. As such, these Shaligrams are especially sought after as wedding gifts to either the bride or groom. They are also commonly given to young men or women in search of marriage, family harmony, or who still hope to fall in love with a well-matched partner. In other cases, Hrishikesh Shaligrams are considered to be especially beneficial for individuals preparing to undergo rites of passage in their respective communities or for worship by ascetics who seek to moderate their earthly passions and attachments.

Lastly, Hrishikesh Shaligrams often substitute for Shiva Linga Shaligrams in many households who adhere to the "worship of the five forms" (pañcāyatana pūjā) system. Popularized by Adi Śaṅkarācārya, this puja system invokes the five deities Ganesha, Vishnu, Shiva, Devī, and Sūrya and is common throughout South Asia today, particularly in Nepal.

REFERENCES

Praanatoshani Tantra pg. 348, Skanda Purana, Nagarekhanda, 244: 3-9

DESCRIPTION:

i. Shaped like a half moon.
ii. With a single circular mark and also with marks resembling the hair of a boar. (P)

Some Shaligram traditions recognize two variations of the Hrishikesh Shaligram. The first is a dark blue (or black) shila that is described as being soft to touch and with 5 vadana and 10 chakras (similar to a Vishvarupa Shaligram). The second is a D-shaped shila that has "upward looking" chakras without striations and "downward looking" chakras that do have striations.

Additional References

1. The Garuda Purana part. 1. Motilal Banarsidass Publishers pvt. Delhi. Pp. 44–71.

2. "हृषीकेश / hṛṣīkeśa". Monier-Williams Sanskrit-English Dictionary. Last updated: May 19, 2014

JANARDHAN/JANARDANA

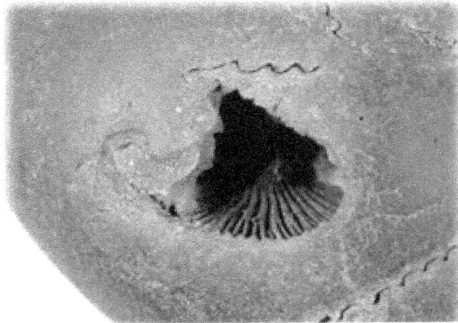

Janardhan, literally "one who helps people," is the 126th name of Vishnu in the Vishnu Sahasranama. According to Adi Śankara, Janardhana also means "One who inflicts suffering on evil men" or "He to whom all devotees pray for worldly success and liberation." As the liberator of the cycles of death and rebirth and as one who visits disaster on those who harbor malicious intentions, Janardhan Shaligrams are said to bestow protection to practitioners from anyone who wishes them harm.

As such, they are especially sought after by businessmen, politicians, or lawmakers and are common gifts, along with Ganesh Shaligrams, at weddings or following specific rites of passage. In other interpretive traditions, particularly in Nepal, Janardhan Shaligrams are revered as manifestations of Bhagwan Janardhan, or Vishnu as the Supreme God.

In Gaudiya Vaishnava traditions, it is also a common name of Krishna being addressed as such by Arjuna in the Bhagavad Gita and, as a result, these Shaligrams are sometimes considered to be a variation of the more common Krishna-type Shaligram. In practice, Janardhan Shaligrams are most often identified by the presence of four small chakra-markings or a large central chakra-marking ringed by three smaller chakras.

In some interpretive traditions, this Shaligram can be easily confused with a four-chakra Mahavishnu (see Multi-Chakra Mahavishnu Shaligram) but the difference between the two is most often ascertained by the type of chakras present: internal, dual-facing impressions in the Janardhan Shaligram and clearly visible, external, Sudarshan chakras in the Mahavishnu.

But because Janardhan Shaligrams are one of several types of aggregate fossil Shaligrams -- whole shale nodules which contain multiple open casts of eroded ammonite shells – these shilas also commonly contain a number of external seams or striated lines (rekha) and quartz infiltrates (vanamala markings or other features). The primary characteristic, however, is almost always that the body of the Shaligram is smooth and rounded with four distinct chakra-markings within two or more vadana (openings/mouths).

Due to this, it can sometimes be confused with the Sri Ram Shaligram.

There are also several variations of this Shaligram recognized by multiple Shaligram interpretive traditions:
1. Janardana Putralabha: Twi equal vadanas and four chakras.
2. Janardana Shira: Yellow and black coloration with two vadanas and four chakras.
3. Janardana Shriprada: One vadana on the right and one on the left with four chakras.
4. Janardana Utpalaprabha: Large in size, bluish and cold to the touch. This Shaligram is shiny and charming "like a water lily" with markings of a vanamala, a shanka, and a mace. Has two vadanas and four chakras.
5. Janardana Dvadasha Chakra: Six vadanas and twelve chakras with a vanamala.
6. Janardana Nilotpalajanardana: Blue in color and large sized with two vadanas and four chakras.

References

Praanatoshani Tantra pg. 348, Praanatoshani Tantra pg. 361, Skanda Purana, Nagarekhanda, 244: 3-9, Agni Purana; Bengavasi ed., Panchanan Tarkaratna, Saka 1812, Ch. 46

Description:

   i. With two openings marked with four circles.
   ii. With two circular marks on the sides and two others at the top.
   iii. With one opening at the front side, and another at the back side, each marked with two circles. (P)

Having 4 chakras (G)

Additional References

   1. Mahabharata, Section LXVIII and Bhagavad Gita, Verse 10.18
   2. The Skanda Purana: Chapters 28, 149, and 188. G. V. Tagare (Author), G.P. Bhatt (Editor), Ganesh Vasudeo Tagare (Translator). 1992. Motilal Banarsidass
   3. Mani, Vettam. 2021. Puranic Encyclopaedia: A Comprehensive work with Special Reference to the Epic and Puranic Literature. Motilal Banarsidass Publishing House.

KALKI

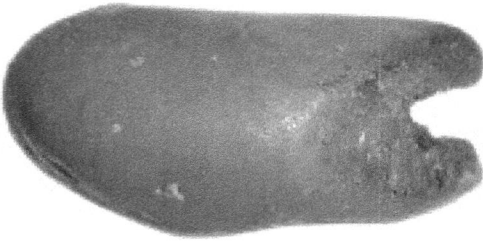

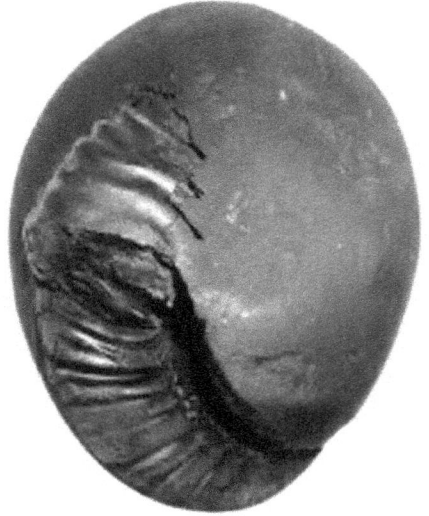

Kalki, the "Destroyer of Filth," the tenth and final avatar of Vishnu, is prophesied in the Kalki Purana to appear at the end of Kali Yuga, the current age. In the Puranic scriptures, Kalki will appear astride a white horse and carrying a blazing sword. As such, he is most often depicted as the harbinger of the end times in Hindu eschatology, after which he will usher in the next Satya Yuga (a.k.a. Krita Yuga, the first and best age) as the wheel of ages begins a new revolution.

In Tibetan Buddhism's Kalachakra tradition, 25 rulers of the Shambhala Kingdom also held the title of Kalki, Kulika or Kalki-king. During Vaishakha, the first fortnight of Shukla Paksha is dedicated to fifteen deities, with each day set aside for a different god. In this tradition, the twelfth day is Vaishakha Dwadashi and is dedicated to Madhava, another name for Kalki.

As a harbinger of the end of days, the Kalki Shaligram occupies an ambiguous place in Shaligram worship. Unlike the previous nine incarnations of Vishnu, Kalki has yet to actually manifest in the material world and therefore, the Kalki Shaligram is itself a direct manifestation of a yet as unmanifested incarnation of Vishnu. Because of this, these Shaligrams are said to bestow the ability to see into the future or predict the outcome of events as they unfold.

It is also said to bestow exceptional powers of observation and the ability to interact with others more effectively through understandings gleaned from these observations. This makes it especially useful to practitioners involved in speculative endeavors or who may often encounter dangerous situations (i.e., police, soldiers, etc.). Identifying the Kalki Shaligram is sometimes difficult as different interpretive traditions read these Shaligrams in slightly different ways. Regardless, it is generally accepted that Kalki Shaligrams have an oval or elongated appearance with a single chakra opening at the base of the śila that results in two extended points (much like legs astride a horse).

It should also contain white markings and at least two chakras. In other variations, this Shaligram may have no chakra marking at all and appear roughly in the shape of an upright, seated, man with discernable head, torso, and legs.

Practical identifications of the Kalki Shaligram involve several variations:
1. In some cases, Kalki is recognized by line-markings resembling a horse and a weapon called Kunta (lance), rather than by its shape. This shila is then white in color and has a long vadana.
2. Ankushakara Kalki: Blue color with an elongated body. This shila has a vanamala, a goad-shaped (hook-like) vadana, with several upward facing markings and a large chakra.
3. Kalyanamurti Kalki: This shila as a single large chakra with several upward facing markings and an overall sharp body.
4. Kuntayudha Kalki: A spear-shaped body (long and pointed end) that is white in color. This shila has have the appearance of a "long face" with two additional markings.

5. Mlecchanashi Kalki: This Shaligram is described as being very red in color with either minute vadana or a single large chakra. The entire shila should be stable when seated with a sword marking near the vadana or having a small vanamala.

6. Svarna Kalki: Described similarly to the standard Kalki but with golden and red colors mixed together.

REFERENCES

Praanatoshani Tantra pg. 348

DESCRIPTION:

i. With the color of a bee and printed with six circular marks, having a linear sword above the opening.

ii. Shaped like a horse and marked with three circular prints.

Some Vaishnava tradition consider Krishna-Vaasudev as the eighth incarnation of Vishnu, replacing of Sankarshan in other traditions. As such, they worship the Kalki Shaligram under different criteria including giving a Krishna name-type to it. With the passing of time this new type also was divided into different varieties and sub-categories.

ADDITIONAL REFERENCES

1. J. L. Brockington. 1998. The Sanskrit Epics. BRILL Academic. pp. 287–288 with footnotes 126–127

2. Dalal, Rosen. 2014. Hinduism: An Alphabetical Guide. Penguin.

3. Perry Schmidt-Leukel. 2017. Religious Pluralism and Interreligious Theology: The Gifford Lectures. Orbis. pp. 220–222

4. Johan Elverskog. 2011. Anna Akasoy; et al. (eds.). Islam and Tibet: Interactions Along the Musk Routes. Ashgate Publishing. pp. 293–310

5. Rinehart, Robin. 2011. Debating the Dasam Granth. Oxford University Press. pp. 29–30.

KALPVRIKSHA

Kalpavriksha, also known as Kalpataru, Kalpadruma, or Kalpapādapa, is the wish-fulfilling divine tree in Hinduism. It is also mentioned several times in Sanskrit literature from the earliest sources. Kalpvriksha as the divine "world tree" is furthermore a popular theme in Jain cosmology and in Buddhism. According to many accounts, both the sage Durvasa and the famous scholar Adi Shankara meditated under the Kalpavriksha. Additionally, the birth of Ashokasundari, the daughter of Shiva and Parvati, is attributed to the Kalpavriksha tree while another daughter, Aranyani, was later gifted to Kalpavriksha for safekeeping. By most accounts, the Kalpavriksha originated during the Samudra Manthan or "churning of the ocean of milk" along with Kamadhenu, the divine cow who provides for all needs (See Kamadhenu and Samudra Manthan Shaligrams). Finally, Indra, the king of the Gods, returned with this tree to his paradise where it is said to remain.

As such, Kalpavriksha is popular in numerous literatures and artistic renditions, where it is often identified with many living trees, such as Parijata (Erythrina variegata), Ficus benghalensis, the coconut tree (Cocos nucifera), Madhuca longifolia, Prosopis cineraria, Bassia butyracea, and the mulberry tree (Morus nigra tree). The Kalpvriksha Shaligram appears in numerous Shaligram traditions and is easily identifiable by it's smooth, chambered, appearance. The most common form of this Shaligram will not contain any easily discernable spiral but rather, the outer chakra-shell spiral will be completely without ridges in favor of evenly spaced striations (described as either rekha lines or "Tulsi" lines) all along the length of the outer circumference.

Other variations of this Shaligram will be almost completely smooth, with only the barest hint of lines or markings on the outer body of the shila. The distinctive appearance of the Kalpvriksha Shaligram is derived from the intricate patterns of sutures etched across the surface of the ammonite shell-spiral. These sutures were once junctures between the internal chamber walls and outer shell of the ammonite. The lines were then revealed when sand and mud filled the empty shell to form an internal mold and it is these primary shapes of "roots and branches" that now define the Kalpvriksha Shaligram in practice.

Veneration of Kalpvriksha Shaligrams is said to bestow the fulfillment of the devotee's deepest wishes. For this reason, these Shaligrams are often associated with the finding of a good marriage partner, with the birth of desired children, and with the resolution of long-term conflicts or arguments. These Shaligrams are also said to be able to unite long-lost relations and to spiritually join families together who are separated over great distances or who have suffered generational fractures.

ADDITIONAL REFERENCES

1. Agrawala, Vasudeva Sharana. 2003. Studies in Indian Art. Vishwavidyalaya Prakashan.

2. Beer, Robert. 2003. The Handbook of Tibetan Buddhist Symbols. Serindia Publications, Inc.

3. Dalal, Roshen. 2014. Hinduism: An Alphabetical Guide. Penguin Books Limited.

4. Randhawa, Mohinder Singh.1964. The cult of trees and tree-worship in Buddhist-Hindu sculpture. All India Fine Arts & Crafts Society.

5. Gupta, Shakti M. 1991. Plant Myths and Traditions in India. Munshiram Manoharlal Publishers.

KAMADHENU

Kamadhenu, also known as Surabhi, Shaval, Kamduh, or Aditi, is a cow-goddess who is called the Mother of All Cows. As a "cow of plenty," she provides her devotees with whatever they need and desire. In Hindu iconography, Kamadhenu is typically depicted as a white cow with a female head and breasts or as a white cow containing any number of other various deities within her body (or as markings on her hide). Additionally, as the earthly embodiments of the Kamadhenu, all types of cows are venerated in Hinduism as quintessential sacred animals. For this reason, Kamadhenu is generally not worshipped independently as a goddess (with few temples dedicated solely in her honor alone) but is rather honored more broadly by the sacred treatment of cows in general. For this reason, Kamadhenu Shaligrams are almost always paired with other sacred objects for ritual worship and are almost never kept alone.

A number of Hindu scriptures provide varying accounts of the origins of Kamadhenu. In popular Vaishnava mythography, she emerges from the churning of the milky ocean but in other stories and legends, she is described as the daughter of the creator god Daksha, as the wife of the sage Kashyapa, or as the pet of either Jamadagni or Vashista (two ancient sages).

In these versions of Kamadhenu's origin story, it is said that the kings who tried to steal her from the sage are later cursed to face dire consequences because Kamadhenu provides the milk that the sage uses in his ritual oblations to the gods. As such, Kamadhenu is also said to be capable of producing fierce warriors to protect either herself or the sages she serves. Lastly, in addition to dwelling in the sage's hermitage, Kamadhenu is also described as residing in Goloka (the celestial realm of the cows) and in Patala (the netherworld).

The Kamadhenu Shaligram is typically identified using the overall shape, which should be that of a seated cow resting with its legs drawn underneath the body. This Shaligram also typically has a small depression near the top of the shila; to mark the division between the cow's head and back hump, and markings or partial chakras which are reminiscent of folded legs.

Note, however, that the Kamadhenu Shaligram tends to be highly ritually and regionally specific and therefore may be easily interchangeable with other types of Shaligrams depending on the interpretive tradition involved. For example, this Shaligram is more commonly recognized in South India. A Shaligram with similar characteristics in North India and in Nepal is usually identified as a type of Hayagriva Shaligram. Shaivas, on the other hand, often interpret this shila as a Nandi Shaligram (Nandikeshwara or Nandideva), a manifestation of the bull mount of Shiva.

In these cases, Nandi Shaligrams are highly associated with travel, with the guardianship of thresholds, and with the movement of spirits after death. When associated specifically with the blessings of Kamadhenu, (such as in certain local Vaishnava traditions throughout South Asia), this Shaligram is said to bestow a variety of boons related to marriage (such as finding the perfectly matched spouse), the birth of healthy children (particularly daughters), and the protection of a householder's family from outside threats (such as infidelity, discontent, and disharmony).

ADDITIONAL REFERENCES

1. Mani, Vettam. 1975. Puranic Encyclopaedia: A Comprehensive Dictionary With Special Reference to the Epic and Puranic Literature. Delhi: Motilal Banarsidass.

2. Jacobi, H. 1908–1927. "Cow (Hindu)". In James Hastings (ed.). Encyclopaedia of Religion and Ethics. Vol. 4. pp. 225–6.

3. Biardeau, Madeleine. 1993. "Kamadhenu: The Religious Cow, Symbol of Prosperity." In Yves Bonnefoy (ed.). Asian mythologies. University of Chicago Press. p. 99.

4. Gopinatha Rao, T. A. 1997. Elements of Hindu Iconography, Volume 2. Motilal Banarsidass Publishers. p. 213.

KAMAL/KAMAL-NARAYAN

Kamala is a common Sanskrit name which usually refers to the Nelumbo nucifera, or the lotus. Variants include Kamal and Kamla (unrelated to the similar-sounding Arabic name). In Hinduism and Buddhism, Kamala is also a common praise name. For example, Kamalatmika, or Kamla, is a common epithet of the goddess Lakshmi. Additionally, a great number of Hindu deities are routinely praised in liturgical texts, prayers, and chants for being kamal or kamala: lotus, or having lotus-like attributes, such as beauty, purity, a transcendent demeanor, and a physically unsullied body.

These deities often include Shiva, Brahma, Shakti, Vishnu, Kali, and all of their avatars. Furthermore, 'lotus-feet' is a title often given to gurus (either male or female). The proper demonstration of respect to such a person is then to hold their feet in your hands and kiss their toes or the upper surfaces of the main part of the foot.

The Kamal or Kamal – Narayan Shaligram is generally considered to be a sub-type of the Lakshmi - Narayan Shaligram, or in other traditions is simply referred to as the Padma or Lotus Shaligram (though it differs in characteristics from the Padma Shaligram most often used along with Shankha, Gada, and Sudarshan Shaligrams – See Gadadhar, Madhusudana, and Shankha Shaligrams).

Rather, these Shaligrams are manifestations of Lakshmi (and Vishnu – Narayan) as the sacred lotus flower. As such, they are usually identified by their deep, central, opening, which typically contains "petal markings" (softer and more rounded than the "teeth" of Narasimha Shaligrams), white and gold coloration, and a rounded, smooth, main body to the shila.

Some variations of this Shaligram may also appear similar in characteristics to the Jagadyoni Shaligram, with a round body, a deep central depression, and a wide, stem-like, feature connection either side of the opening. In Kamal Shaligrams, however, this stem-like feature will have chakra – spiral markings on the outer edges rather than a smooth or ridged appearance.

Veneration of these Shaligrams is similar to that of other Lakshmi-type Shaligrams; said to bestow blessings of material wealth (including the ability to retain wealth) and life-long good fortune. In addition to this, however, Kamal Shaligrams are also said to connect the devotee with God more intimately (through the stem of the lotus) where it becomes easier for the devotee to discern his proper path in life and to undo or repay poor past karmas.

Lastly, worship of these Shaligrams is also described as more generally providing blessings of personal charisma, good physical health, and success in business ventures. It is important to note though that Kamal Shaligrams are generally limited to only certain Hindu or Buddhist traditions, specifically those that venerate the "Goddesses of Wealth or Fortune."

In most other cases, these Shaligrams would be interpreted as either Narasimha Shaligrams or as a combination of Narasimha and Padmanabha (Vishnu with the Lotus Growing out of his Navel). In general, however, a Kamal Shaligram should demonstrate some amount of white or golden markings on the interior of the main opening and be worn more smoothly than that of the sharper and more "aggressive" Narasimha types.

ADDITIONAL REFERENCES

1. Kinsley, David R. (1997). Tantric Visions of the Divine Feminine: The Ten Mahāvidyās. Berkeley: University of California Press.

2. Tattvālokah, Volume 18. 1995. Sri Abhinava Vidyatheertha Educational Trust.

KAPILA

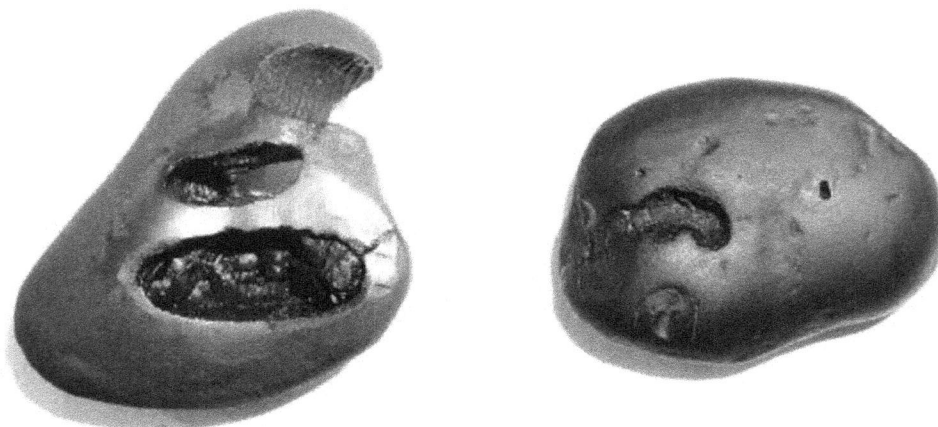

Kapila is the name of a wide variety of different individuals in ancient and medieval South Asian texts, of whom the most well-known is the founder of the Samkhya school of Hindu philosophy. Kapila of Samkhya fame is considered an extremely important Vedic rishi (sage), who is thought to have lived sometime in the late 6th century BCE or in the early 7th century BCE.

Rishi Kapila is credited with authoring the influential Samkhya-sutra: in which aphoristic sutras present the dualistic philosophy of Samkhya. But Kapila is also thought to have had strong influences on the Buddha and on the later development of Buddhist theology. In addition, many historic personalities in Hinduism and in Jainism, such as mythical figures, pilgrimage sites, and an ancient variety of cow all went by the name Kapila.

As such, the precise individual or individuals this Shaligram is said to represent is textually unclear, though many Hindu scholars take it to be a manifestation of the Vedic rishi more than anything else. The identification of the Kapila Shaligram adheres closely to the Puranic descriptions. Its most prominent characteristics are three rounded, open vadana or three open chakras in close proximity to one another. The overall shape of the Shaligram should also be reminiscent of a seated sage whose head is bowed in contemplation.

The Kapila Shaligram is similar in some respects to the Janardhan Shaligram as one of several types of aggregate fossil Shaligrams: whole shale nodules which contain multiple open casts of eroded ammonite shells. Because of this, the Kapila Shaligram may also demonstrate a number of external seams (rekha lines) and quartz infiltrates (vanamala markings or other features) but is almost always identified as having three distinct chakra-markings formed by three eroded ammonite casts.

In some interpretive traditions, this Shaligram can be easily confused with a three-chakra Trivikrama (see Trivikrama Shaligram) or a three-chakra Acyuta Shaligram but the difference between the two previous categories and the Kapila Shaligram is most often ascertained by the type of chakras present: internal, dual-facing impressions in the Kapila Shaligram and clearly visible, external, Sudarshan chakras in the Trivikrama and Acyuta Shaligrams (along with the absence of other defining features in the latter). In some traditions, the Kapila Shaligram is combined with the Yagnamurti Shaligram and is called Yagna-Kapila. Kapila Yagyamurti Shaligrams, however, tend to be multi-colored (red, green, or yellow mixed together). Furthermore, the left side of the shila will have two chakras at the opening while the right side will have the markings of the two sacrificial sticks (sruk and sruva) indicative of the Yagnamurti shila.

Kapila-Narasimha is also another possible variation. This Shaligram has a large chakra at the place where Narasimha's "tusk" would be located. Furthermore, the color of the stone is described as tawny (yellow or brown), with the potential marks of a vanamala. In the Sri Vaishnava tradition, these Shaligrams are restricted and can only be venerated by sannyasis (celibate ascetics) for the worldly prosperity of others or for salvation.

REFERENCES

Garuda Purana (Panchanan Tarkaratna, Part 1, Ch. 45), Agni Purana; Bengavasi ed., Panchanan Tarkaratna, Saka 1812, Ch. 46

DESCRIPTIONS

» Three dot-like marks on His body or at opening (G).

ADDITIONAL REFERENCES

1. Flood, Gavin D. 1996. An Introduction to Hinduism. Cambridge University Press

2. von Glasenapp, Helmuth. 1999. Jainism: An Indian Religion of Salvation [Der Jainismus: Eine Indische Erlosungsreligion], Shridhar B. Shrotri (trans.), Delhi: Motilal Banarsidass.

3. Jacobsen, Knut A. 2008. Kapila, Founder of Sāṃkhya and Avatāra of Viṣṇu: With a Translation of Kapilāsurisaṃvāda. New Delhi: Munshiram Manoharlal.

<u>K</u>ESHAV

According to Adi Śankara' s commentary on the Vishnu Sahasranama (of which Keshava is the 23rd and 648th name of Vishnu), Keshava has a variety of meanings:

1. One whose kesa or hair is long, uncut, and beautiful
2. The lord of creation, preservation, and dissolution (Vishnu).
3. Krishna who destroyed the demon Keśī
4. One who is endowed with the rays of light spreading within the orbit of the sun.
5. One who is himself the three: Kah Brahma; Ah Vishnu and Isa Shiva.

According to the Padma Purana, however, the name refers to Krishna's long, beautiful, unshorn hair. Additionally, in the Bhagavad Gita, Arjuna uses the name Keshava for Krishna a number of times, referring to him as the 'Killer of the Keśī demon' (Bhagavad Gita 1.30) after Keśī, in the form of a horse, was sent by the demon-king Kamsa to kill Krishna but was overpowered and slain (Vishnu Purana 5.15-16).

In other traditions, Keshav Shaligrams are associated primarily with the sun (kesa also meaning the sun's rays), where they are said to ward any and all uses of Nazar Dosha (the evil eye) and to protect devotees from all who might think badly of them. Worship of this Shaligram is also said to bestow wealth, social status and respect, and to facilitate worldly material comforts. Lastly, as one of several "sun" Shaligrams, the Keshava Shaligram is particularly useful for devotees seeking to "illuminate" their proper path in life by averting bad luck or dangerous omens.

Identification of Keshava Shaligrams is reasonably straight-forward. These shilas are typically "shankha" or conch-shaped overall with a single large chakra on their flattened upper side. The chakra should have clear, highly defined, ridges and striations (the kesa) that radiate outwards from the central spiral though, in all likelihood, the full chakra spiral will not necessarily be visible (see also Surya/ Suraj Shaligram). In some variations of this Shaligram, more than one chakra will be visible on the outer body of the shila but the entire Shaligram should generally sit flat with its main chakras facing upwards. In practice, Keshava Shaligrams have several descriptions depending on which story, deity, or deity mood (bhava) they are linked to.

In cases where they are more closely associated with Krishna, they are said to be blue-black in color with minute chakras; along with golden and silver spots or a mark resembling a vanamala. Keshava Shaligrams more closely associated with the sun are described as having a square or rectangular shape with two chakras, two red dots, and be black in color. These shilas are called Parshva in Jainism.

REFERENCES

Skanda Purana, Nagarekhanda, 244: 3-9. Garuda Purana (Panchanan Tarkaratna, part1 Chapter 45) & Praanatoshanitantra (page 348-351)

DESCRIPTION:

Marked with a circular print, and vanamala (G).
Shape as a conch and & mark with a circular print on lower middle portion (Sk)
  i. Marked with a small circular print, a garland and several golden dot prints.
  ii. Marked with a conch and a circle on the lower middle portion. (P)

ADDITIONAL REFERENCES

1. Dallapiccola, Anna L. 2004. Dictionary of Hindu Lore and Legend. Thames and Hudson.
2. Daniélou, Alain. 1991. The Myths and Gods of India: The Classic Work on Hindu Polytheism from the Princeton Bollingen Series. Inner Traditions / Bear & Co. p. 154.
3. Stutley, Margaret. 2020. The Illustrated Dictionary of Hindu Iconography. Routledge. p.71, 73.

KRISHNA-BALARAMA

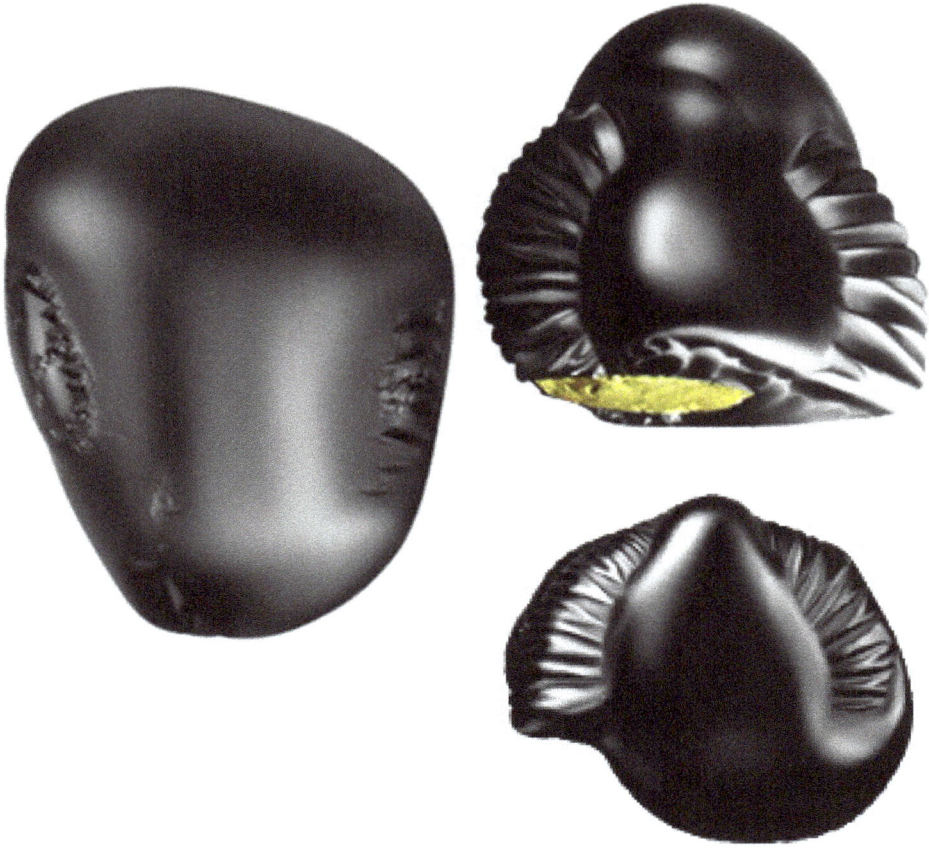

Balarama, who is also known as Baladeva (Jainism), Balabhadra, and Halayudha, is the elder brother of Krishna (the 8th avatar of Vishnu) and is often himself regarded as an avatar of Shesha. Balarama may have originated in Vedic times as a deity of agriculture and fertility. As such, he is often depicted with a drinking cup, a pitcher, a plow, or a shield and sword. In other Hindu traditions, Balaram is the Sankarshana form of Vishnu or is his 8th avatar on his own.

For this reason, the precise identification of Krishna-Balarama Shaligrams is highly dependent on the religious tradition in question. For example, these Shaligrams are often considered as variations of the Krishna-type Shaligram in Gaudiya Vaishnavism whereas in other traditions, such as among Madwas Brahmins or Sri Vaishnavas, they are variations of the Shankarshana and Ananta-Shesha Shaligrams respectively.

Krishna-Balaram Shaligrams are typically identified through one of two primary characteristics: a marking in the shape of a plow or as a single, smooth, rounded body (in the exact same fashion as a Krishna Shaligram) but with partially visible chakra ridges of roughly equal size and shape on either side. The central body of the shila, which should be largest portion of the Shaligram as a whole, is then typically slightly elongated or oval in shape.

In some Shaligram traditions, however, where Balaram Shaligrams are variations of the Shankarshana or Shesha Shaligrams, the defining characteristics are more in line with the respective Shaligram it relates to (See Shankarshana and Ananta-Shesha Shaligrams)..In general, Krishna – Balarama Shaligrams are said to act as advisors to their devotees, lending strength, conviction, and determination to challenging endeavors.

In other cases, Krishna-Balaram Shaligrams are associated with the retention of legal or political rights, with protection during political struggles, or in the resolution of issues revolving around personal and community identities (especially ethnic or religious identities). Lastly, these Shaligrams are also said to bestow good fortune and karma for the devotee's next seven births and to aid in uniting family members across successive lives.

Variations of this Shaligram in practice include the Balabhadra (Balaram) Shaligram, which is worshipped for obtaining celebrity and cattle wealth. This shila is blue-black in color and has the overall shape is that of a parasol or umbrella.

It is also smooth (even greasy) to the touch with a series of characteristics that are described as: an animate opening, a red spot or lines, with its fore-part being bulky and its body appearing to be soft and shining.

In other traditions, the Balarama Shaligram has marks of the plough-share and of a "pestle-like weapon" on it. It may be black or whitish in color, and has line-scratches of vanamala with dots like honey drops. This is then interpreted as the abode of Samkarshana. These variations may or may not have chakras on them as well but generally do not have vadana openings.

REFERENCES

Praanatoshanitantra pg. 348

DESCRIPTION:

Balabhadra: Marked with seven circular prints.
Balarama: With five linear marks on the top side and a bow and an arrow on the rear sides (P)

ADDITIONAL REFERENCES

1. Beck, Guy L. (Ed.) 2005. Alternative Krishnas: Regional and Vernacular Variations on a Hindu Deity. SUNY Press.
2. Doniger, Wendy. 1993. Purana Perennis: Reciprocity and Transformation in Hindu and Jaina Texts. SUNY Press.
3. Singh, Upinder. 2016. A History of Ancient and Early Medieval India: From the Stone Age to the 12th Century. Pearson Education.
4. Vemsani, Lavanya. 2006. Hindu and Mythology of Balarāma. Lewiston, New York: Edwin Mellen Press. pp. 30–31, 52–59, 68–69 with footnotes.

KRISHNA GOPALA/SANTAN GOPALA

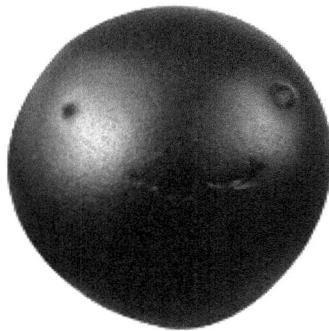

The Krishna Gopala (also called Santan Gopala, Bala Krishna, or Lakshmi-Gopala) Shaligram (Krishna as the Protector of Cows) is one of several formations of the Krishna-type Shaligram.

It always appears as an entirely black, smooth, and perfectly round, Shaligram with no other outward markings or characteristics save the possible emergence of two small points or holes on one side of the shila.

Additional markings on Shaligrams of this type are typically interpreted as the influence or presence of other deities or even other forms of Krishna but the ideal form is the "womb-like" appearance of the classic shila.

These Shaligrams are also occasionally referred to as Laddu Gopalas, referring to laddu or laddoo, the ball-shaped sweets popular in India that Krishna was said to relish.

As a manifestation of Krishna as an infant, this Shaligram is said to represent Krishna as both extremely small and as growing within the womb of his mother Devaki. Therefore, it is not uncommon to refer to Santan Gopala Shaligrams as "wombs."

This Shaligram is most often employed for blessings of fertility and the birth of obedient and virtuous children but it also bestows blessings of honorable austerity, the control of animal instincts, and the proper redirection of unseemly passions.

As a result, Santan Gopala Shaligrams are extremely popular in temple worship, where massive numbers of them can be collected into silver trays, and as companion Shaligrams on pilgrimage; where practitioners will carry one or more of them in pouches hung from their clothing.

In other instances, Santan Gopala Shaligrams are commonly gifted to women who have either lost children or who have had trouble conceiving. The presence of a Santan Gopala Shaligram within a household is therefore heavily associated with the care and rearing of young children or with the mischievous antics of childhood.

Ultimately, the formation of this Shaligram involves the weathering of a black shale nodule into a near-perfect ball-like shape. In many cases, these shale nodules contain ammonites within their interiors, some of which can be partially discerned by the flat end of the ammonite shell just beginning to protrude from one side.

Some traditions, conversely, describe this shila as Lakshmi-Gopala:

i. Lakshmi-Gopala is shaped like a hen's egg but has face markings and earrings. This stone is an extremely rare one and its worship assures progeny, prosperity and salvation.

ii. In other cases, Lakshmi-Gopala is shaped like a parasol, and is extremely unctuous: it has no openings but is spotted. It is also large, heavy, and brilliant.

Other variations include:

i. Madana-Gopala, which is partly black in color and partly reddish. It has a long opening on its left side and there are marks of a conch, a discus, a bow and a moon.

ii. Dadhi-Gopala-Vamana, which has a chakra on its top, with spots like honey-drops at the upper end.

iii. Kundala-Gopala has the shape of a jambu fruit (rose apple), is black in color, and has spots. At the rear of the shila, there is an opening and the marks of ear-rings (makara-kundalas). On the forehead of the stone, slanting to the left there may be the marks of an arrow and bow.

iv. Gopala-Murari has the marks of cudgel and a horn (which cowherds carry) on its sides, and at the head position can be seen the mark of a flute. The worship of this stone ensures progeny specifically. This shila is also blue in color and elongated in shape. It may have an opening that resembles an elephant-goad or a chakra.

REFERENCES

Praanatoshani Tantra pg. 347, Skanda Purana, Nagarekhanda, 244: 3-9, Garuda Purana (Panchanan Tarkaratna, Part 1, Ch. 45), Agni Purana; Bengavasi ed., Panchanan Tarkaratna, Saka 1812, Ch. 46

DESCRIPTIONS

Round in shape, flat upper side (G).

Gopala: Deep black in color, big in size with a good-looking opening. He has two circular marks, and the marks of vanamala and shrivatsa (either an inverted triangle or an "endless knot") on His upper side, and also teeth-like marks on a rear side (P).

ADDITIONAL REFERENCES

1. Hein, Norvin. 1986. "A Revolution in Kṛṣṇaism: The Cult of Gopāla." History of Religions, Vol. 25, No. 4 (May, 1986), pp. 296-317.

2. Klostermaier, Klaus K. 2005. A Survey of Hinduism. State University of New York Press; 3rd edition. pp. 206

KRISHNA GOVINDA

Krishna Govinda (Krishna as the Lord of Cows) is one of the most popular images of Krishna throughout the world and, as a result, has a variety of interpretations and forms. More broadly, Govinda and Gopala are names of Vishnu which mean "The finder of the Vedas" as well as "Protector of the Vedas" ('Go' is occasionally translated as "Veda," "Cow," and also "senses"). Therefore, Govinda and Gopala tend to refer to Vishnu/Krishna's youthful pastime as a cowherd or as the Protector of Cows or as he appears in stories and narratives describing his role as a spiritual herder.

The name Govinda also implies that this is the form in which God gives pleasure to the senses of devotees. Other traditions note that this name appears as the 187th and the 539th name of Vishnu in Vishnu Sahasranama. Regardless, Lord Vishnu or his complete incarnation as Krishna, in Krishnavite and Gaudiya Vaishnava traditions, is often regarded as the Supreme God or as a particularly prominent deity by a number of other traditions throughout modern day Hinduism.

The typical appearance of the Krishna Govinda Shaligram resembles that of the Krishna Gopala, involving a round, smooth, ball-like body and black coloration. The Govinda Shaligram however, always includes the distinctive white "cow-hoof" marking somewhere on the shila. The formation of this Shaligram therefore involves the weathering of a black shale nodule into a near-perfect spherical shape; though some Krishna Govindas may appear as oval or elongated as well (see photo 3, opposite).

The distinctive white "cow-hoof" marking though, contains a series of concentric quartz rings through the interior with a small indentation visible on one side which likely results from the cross-sectional breakage and wear of a fossilized belemnite or ammonite shell.

Veneration of this Shaligram is said to bring immense wisdom to the devotee, along with a harmonious family life, peace, and prosperity. In other traditions, this Shaligram is considered especially helpful in dealing with inter-family conflicts and in encouraging strong relationships among relatives.

The Krishna Govinda Shaligram is also associated with pastoralism and the concept of an idyllic life. As such, it is not uncommon for devotees to carry these Shaligrams somewhere on their person whenever they are travelling away from home or when they are undertaking pilgrimage.

Like many Krishna Shaligrams, Krishna Govinda has a wide variety of variations in practice. Some traditions describe this Shaligram as:

1. Dark blue like the blade of a fresh durva grass. It also has 10 apertures and 20 chakras; and there are scratches on its body which look like a vanamala.
2. A Shaligram that has 5 vadanas and 10 chakras
3. The same as a Santana Gopala but with a white cow-hoof marking.
4. A Shaligram that is black in color with a right-side gada marking, a left side mountain marking, and also has 5 vadanas and 10 chakras. May also have a small central depression.

References

Praanatoshani Tantra pg. 348, Skanda Purana, Nagarekhanda, 244: 3-9

Description:

i.   Black in color and very charming to look at. He holds the marks of a mace and a discus on His right side and that of a mountain on the left.
ii. Black in color and middle in size, having His central portion raised upwards. He has a big opening beautifully marked with circles, and His body is also decorated with five different circles. (P)

Additional References

1. Beck. Guy L. 2006. Alternative Krishnas: Regional and Vernacular Variations on a Hindu Deity. State University of New York Press.
2. Klostermaier, Klaus K. 2005. A Survey of Hinduism (3rd ed.). State University of New York Press. p. 206.
3. Sri Vishnu Sahasranama, commentary by Sri Sankaracharya, pgs. 69 and 115, translated by Swami Tapasyananda (Ramakrishna Math Publications, Chennai)
4. Klostermaier, Klaus K. 2005. A Survey of Hinduism. State University of New York Press; 3rd edition. pp. 206

KRISHNA

Mukunda Shaligram

Radha-Krishna Shaligram

Krishna is one of the most prominent and wide-spread of all Hindu deities who is worshiped in a variety of different traditions. In some cases, Krishna is recognized as the Svayam Bhagavan in his own right or as the complete incarnation of Vishnu in his eighth incarnation. Even today, Krishna is one of the most widely revered and popular of all Hindu deities worldwide. Krishna, like Vishnu, also goes by many names, including Govinda, Gopala, Mukunda, Madhusudhana, Keshava, and Vasudeva. Krishna is often described or portrayed as an infant eating butter, a young boy playing a flute as in the Bhagavata Purana, a young man along with his divine consort Radha, or as an elder giving direction and guidance in the Bhagavad Gita.

The stories of Krishna appear across a broad spectrum of South Asian philosophical and theological traditions which portray him in various perspectives: a god-child, a prankster, a model lover, a divine hero, and the Supreme Being. In Gaudiya Vaishnava Shaligram traditions, for example, there are several varieties of Krishna Shaligrams that represent Krishna's most recent incarnations of Chaitanya Mahaprabhu, Nityananda Prabhu, Advaita Acharya, Gadadhara Pandita, and Srivasa Thakura (identified by their various markings). Much like the deity whose manifestation they contain, Krishna Shaligrams appear in a wide-variety of shapes and sizes but in almost every case, Krishna Shaligrams are associated with ultimate expressions of love (both divine and physical), affection, and respect.

Because of this, they are said to provide the most direct path to moksha (salvation) and to cleanse the heart and mind of all sins, hateful thoughts, and to weed out foolishness and stupidity. As manifestations of Krishna the Cowherder, they are also strongly associated with agricultural pursuits and animal husbandry, bringing with them all the gentle affection and nurturing of the sacred cow. For this reason, Krishna Shaligrams are the most popular shilas given at weddings, at house-warmings, or at the birth of a child.Krishna Shaligrams are also as distinctive as they are deceptively simple. They are generally round to oval in shape, uniformly black in color, with no outwardly visible chakra markings.

They may, however, contain white quartz vanamala (garland) markings or occasionally small features reminiscent of a plow-share (indicating the presence of Krishna's brother Balarama). The variation of the Radha-Krishna Shaligram (called Neeladevi in the Sri Vaishnava tradition) has a series of striations or "Tulsi" lines. Lastly, many interpretive traditions have slight variations on the Krishna Shaligram wherein each shila's specific characteristics can be linked to any one of the many famous stories of Krishna's exploits and, as a result, this ostensibly basic black and unmarked Shaligram in practice can become very interpretively complex. See also: Krishna Govinda and Krishna Gopala Shaligrams

In some Shaligram traditions, there is another variation of the Krishna Shaligram called the Mukunda Shaligram ("One Who Gives Mukti"), which is characterized by having six vadanas (mouths) and twelve chakras. In rare cases, it may also reference king Muchkunda of the Mahabharata who gained a boon from Indra for battling the asuras (demons) as a representative of the devas (gods).

In practice, there are many Krishna Shaligram variations. Some of the rarer manifestations are:

Krishna Canuramardana, which has two red dots, a blue-black body, and an elephant trunk like shape with right side spots and striations or one vadana and two chakras.

Krishna Madhusudhana has markings of five weapons (the conch called Panchajanya, the discus called Sudarsana, the mace called Kaumodaki, the bow called Sarnga, and the sword called Nandaka). It may also have a vanamala and a lotus marking or several tiny chakras.

Krishna Madhava is honey-colored with a large chakra and one vadana. It may also have the mark of a mace.

Krishna Govardhana has a cow-ear shaped opening and may have golden or white spots with 2 chakras inside one vadana and a butter-pot marking.

In other appearances it may have four chakras like dots but they will not be four Sudarshan chakras.

REFERENCES

Praanatoshani Tantra pg. 347 (or pgs. 351-356), Skanda Purana, Nagarekhanda, 244: 3-9, Garuda Purana (Panchanan Tarkaratna, Part 1, Ch. 45), Agni Purana; Bengavasi ed., Panchanan Tarkaratna, Saka 1812, Ch. 46

DESCRIPTIONS

Round in shape, flat upper side (G).

Madhava: With a color like that of honey, and marked with a mace and a conch.

i.   Marked with a vanamala and a discus on His right side.
ii. Black in color with two equal circular marks at the opening.
iii. Small in size with a yellow spot and several dot-prints on His sides.
iv. With the upper side like that of a tortoise, and the entire lower middle portion resembling its mouth.
v.   Taarksya: (a) Black in color and long in shape resembling a pillar. (b) Shaped like a spear-head, and marked with two circles, one lotus, one ring, and one gem.
vi. Baalakrsna: With a long opening having dot-prints on His lower side.
vii. Gopala: Deep black in color, big in size with a good-looking opening. He has two circular marks, and the marks of vanamala and shrivatsa on His upper side, and also teeth like marks on a rear side.
viii. Madanagopal: A Gopala type holding a lotus mark on His upper or lower side.
ix. Santaanagopal: Long in shape, black in color with an opening of the half-moon shape.
x.   Govardhanagopala: With a comparatively less height and round upper portion. Marked with a stick, a garland, a whistle and long lines and also having silver dots all over His body.

xi. Lakshmigopal: Shaped like the egg of a hen and marked with a vanamala, a plough, a whistle, and a ring on different sides.

xii. Kaliyamardana: Marked with a golden line and three dot-prints.

xiii. Syamantahaarin: Big in size, with the color of a sword, and having the marks of a vanamala and shrivatsa on His upper side.

xiv. Chanooramardan: Green in color with two red spots and a linear mark on each of the right and left sides.

xv. Kamsamardana: Blue in color, having a different color either at the front or on a rear side (P)

ADDITIONAL REFERENCES

1. Beck, Guy L., ed. 2005. Alternative Krishnas: Regional and Vernacular Variations on a Hindu Deity. Albany, NY: SUNY Press.

2. Bryant, Edwin F. 2007. Krishna: A Sourcebook, Oxford University Press.

KUBERA

Kubera (Pali/later Sanskrit: Kuvera), also rendered as simply Kuber, is the Lord of Wealth and the god-king of the semi-divine Yakshas (a broad category of nature-spirits, usually benevolent, who are caretakers of the natural treasures hidden within the earth or in the roots of mystical trees. They appear in Hindu, Jain and Buddhist cosmologies). Kubera is also regarded as the "Regent of the North" (Dikpala) and as a protector of the world (Lokapala). Depending on the tradition in question, Kubera's many names indicate his continued rulership over a number of semi-divine species and his status as the owner of all the treasures of the world. Artistically, Kubera is most often depicted with a plump or rotund body, adorned with gold and jewels, and carrying a money-pot and a club.

Originally described as the chief of evil spirits in Vedic-era texts, Kubera acquired the status of a Deva (god) beginning in the Puranas and in the Hindu epics. Some scriptural references describe Kubera as having once ruled Lanka, but who was later overthrown by his demon stepbrother Ravana (Ramayana).

Subsequently, Kubera then went on to settle in the city of Alaka (or Alkapuri) in the Himalayas where he built a great city of riches and splendor. Kubera has also been assimilated into the Buddhist and Jain pantheons. In Buddhism, he is known as Vaisravana (a patronymic use of the Sanskrit Kubera) and is also equated with Pañcika. In Jainism, he is known as Sarvanubhuti.

The defining characteristic of the Kubera Shaligram is it's large, rounded, "belly." Also often referred to as Lakshmi-Kubera Shaligrams, the single chakra spiral present on the shila should be only half to one-third of a full spiral. These Shaligrams may then also have additional markings somewhere on the body of the Shaligram which are either reminiscent of a club or in the shape of a pot. Regardless of additional characteristics however, the primary and largest feature of the Shaligram should be the rounded, central, shale nodule forming Kubera's portly belly.

Kubera Shaligrams appear most often in the religious traditions of Nepal and in northern India, where their associations with the environment of the Himalayas makes them especially prized as household deities. In some ritual contexts, Kubera Shaligrams may also be buried at the base of sacred trees as offerings to the deities of the river or land.

Veneration of Kubera Shaligrams is primarily associated with blessings of wealth and material fortune, especially for business men, entrepreneurs, and those who work in finance or economics. To a slightly lesser-known degree, these Shaligrams are also associated with the workings of nature spirits and natural forces. For this reason, Kubera Shaligrams are often placed in strategic areas of the household or temple in order to ward off or pacify potentially harmful entities of the landscape, such as the Dakini, the fearsome wind spirits of the high Himalayas.

ADDITIONAL REFERENCES

1. Mani, Vettam. 1975. Puranic Encyclopaedia: A Comprehensive Dictionary With Special Reference to the Epic and Puranic Literature. Delhi: Motilal Banarsidass. pp. 434–7.

2. Prakash, Om. 2000. "Artha and Arthasastra in the Puranic Iconography and their symbolic implications". In Nagendra Kumar Singh (ed.). Encyclopaedia of Hinduism. Vol. 31–45. Anmol Publications PVT. LTD. pp. 41–4.

3. Sutherland, Gail Hinich. 1991. The disguises of the demon: the development of the Yakṣa in Hinduism and Buddhism. SUNY Press.

KUMARAMURTI

In practice, the Kumaramurti Shaligram is relatively uncommon, which is likely primarily due to its single late Puranic reference. In some South Indian interpretive traditions, the Kumaramurti Shaligram is considered to be a manifestation of Karthikeya; who is also called Murugan, Skanda, Subramaniyam, Cheyon, Senthil, Vēlaṇ, and Kumāran ("prince, child, young one"), the indigenous god of war. He is also the Commander-in-Chief of the army of the devas and is the primary deity of the Kaumaram sect of Hinduism.

In some Nepali Hindu traditions, however, the Kumaramurti Shaligram is described as a manifestation of the Kumari, the Living Goddess drawn from the practice of worshipping young pre-pubescent Buddhist girls as manifestations of the divine female energy or Devi; though this particular interpretation is highly regionally specific.

The Atharvaveda however, calls Kumāra Agnibhūta a form of Agni, who held him in his hands when Kumāra was born. The Shatapatha Brahmana however, refers to him as the son of Rudra (Shiva) and one of the six faces of Rudra. Conversely, the Chandogya Upanishad refers to Skanda as the "way that leads to wisdom" and the Baudhāyana's Dharmasūtra calls Skanda Mahāsena, meaning "Having a Great Army" and Subrahmaṇya as "beloved of Brahmins."

Additionally, the āraṇyaparvan (first section of the third book) of the Mahabharata relates the legend of Kartikeya Skanda in considerable detail. Whereas, the Skanda Purana is devoted to the narrative of Kartikeya. While textual references to Kumara are highly variable, the Kumaramurti Shaligram is most commonly associated with various endeavors related to politics, political struggle, and war.

On occasion, this Shaligram is given to political dissidents, artists, and protestors as a form of protection. In general though, worship of the Kumaramurti in households is taken as a protective action given how vigilant and guarding these Shaligrams are described as being. It is important to note that there is also a fair amount of disagreement as to the precise characteristics and details of the Kumaramurti Shaligram.

Broadly speaking, the general consensus is that this Shaligram is one of the "sky-colored" Shaligrams and should be grey, light blue, or dark blue in color and contain between two and six white (quartz) lines crossing the upper or central part of the shila. It does not typically contain chakras.

REFERENCES

Garuda Purana (Panchanan Tarkaratna, Part 1, Ch. 45) -- Not found in Agni Purana; Bengavasi ed., Panchanan Tarkaratna, Saka 1812, Ch. 46

DESCRIPTIONS

Big size, blue color, three linear marks or one or more dots (G).
As a result of this description, the Kumaramurti Shaligram is sometimes described as the only true "blue" Shaligram and that blue Shaligrams are always Kumaramurthi. In most cases, though, this is highly specific to certain traditions of Hinduism.

ADDITIONAL REFERENCES:

1. Dimmit, Cornelia and J. A. B. van Buitenen, eds. 1978. Classical Hindu Mythology: A Reader in the Sanskrit Purāṇas. Philadelphia: Temple University Press. pg 187.
2. Doniger, Wendy. 2004. Hindu Myths: A Sourcebook Translated from the Sanskrit. New York: Penguin Books.
3. Jash, Pranabananda. 1981. "Some Aspects of Karttikeya Worship With Special Reference to Bengal," Proceedings of the Indian History Congress 42 (1981): 163–70.

Kurma

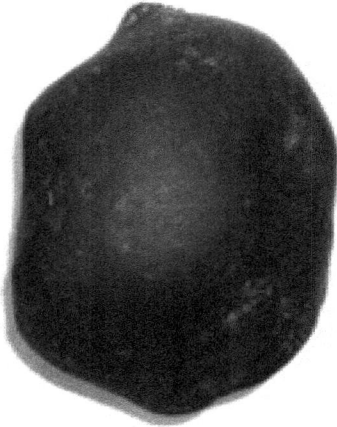

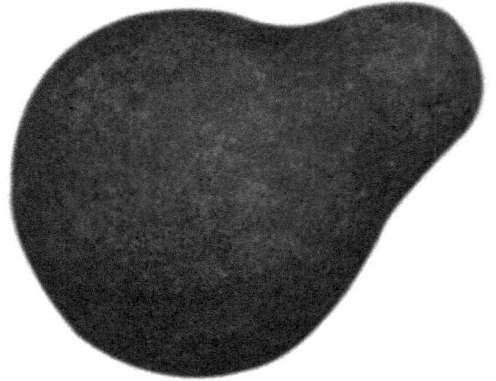

Succeeding Matsya and preceding Varaha, Kurma is the second incarnation of Vishnu. The story of Kurma begins in the Puranic scriptures where the sage Durvasa had given a garland to Indra, the king of Gods. But when Indra placed the garland around his elephant, the elephant immediately trampled it. Insulted, Durvasa cursed the gods (Devas) to lose their immortality and all of their divine powers. But the gods sought out Vishnu for help.

Vishnu advised the gods to drink the nectar of immortality to regain their glory. To obtain it, they would need to churn the ocean of milk, a body of water so large it required Mount Mandara as the churning staff and the serpent Vasuki (See Ananta-Vasuki Shaligram) for the churning rope.

Unfortunately, the Devas were not strong enough to churn the ocean alone and so declared peace with their historical foes, the Asuras, to enlist their aid (See also: Samudra Manthan Shaligram). Finally, Mount Mandara began to churn the ocean but the force was so great the mountain began to sink. Taking the form of a turtle, Kurma, Vishnu bore the mountain on his back as they churned the waters.

Fourteen precious things then arose from the turbulent ocean, but the most important was Dhanvantari, the physician of the gods, who brought with him the nectar of immortality. The Asuras immediately took the nectar and began to argue over it. In response, Vishnu manifested himself as a beautiful woman (Mohini) and tricked the Asuras to retrieve the potion, which he then gave to the Devas.

Though the Asuras realized the trick, it was too late and the Devas had regained their powers. The Asuras were subsequently defeated. Related directly to the Puranic stories, the Kurma Shaligram typically bears resemblance to the body of a turtle, with a small head emerging from beneath a rounded "shell."

This shell often contains one or more chakras or may be covered in a layer of gold or white markings. As such, the Kurma Shaligram bestows blessings of stability and a flow of wealth "like water." Kurma Shaligrams are also known to work as shields from misfortune or the ill intents of others and to act as foundational support from which new endeavors might be attempted.

Hence, Kurma Shaligrams are almost always described favorably for their stability, calm, and dedication. The formation of this Shaligram is that of a single ammonite weathering out of a shale nodule into the shape of a rounded stone, which is turtle-like, with a small additional nodule protruding from one side (or, occasionally, the markings of a small face).

Other versions of this Shaligram are completely round with the outer edge of the ammonite shell forming a visible ring around the central body of the shila. In some cases, these Shaligrams may be nearly completely obscured by golden (iron pyrite) infiltrates.

In practice, many traditions recognize a variety of sub-types of Kurma Shaligrams:

1. Kurma-Varaha has one chakra with two dots or the mark of conch (sometimes with another minute chakra nearby).
2. Putrapradayaka Kurma is round and shaped like tortoise shell with two large vadana and two chakras that serve as his navel.
3. Sarvakama Kurma is round, large, and golden-hued with two chakras and the mark of a Snuhi flower near the side of one of the chakras.
4. Manoratha Kurma has a tortoise-like face, a hump back, and is bright (usually meaning shiny) in appearance.
5. Kurma-Sudarshan has the same distinctive tortoise-like shape but with a full and complete chakra imprinted on its underside.

REFERENCES

Described as one of the 18 names of Shaligram. Praanatoshani Tantra pg. 348, Agni Purana; Bengavasi ed., Panchanan Tarkaratna, Saka 1812, Ch. 46, included in the Dasavatara

DESCRIPTION:

i. Shaped like a tortoise with the eastern side elevated.

ii. Green in color, round in shape resembling a tortoise, His upper side being higher and printed with circular markings.

iii. Shaped like a tortoise and printed with five different marks each resembling the sun.

iv. Marked with foot-prints of a cow on His sides.

v. Marked with a conch, a flag, and three golden dot-prints.

vi. Long in shape with openings on the left and right sides, and printed with five sun-marks.

vii. Shaped like a snuhi (emphorbia antiquorum) flower with circular marks on both the sides.

viii. Round and long in shape, having a circle and a tortoise printed on His sides. He has a mixed color of blue and red. (P)

ADDITIONAL REFERENCES

1. Gupta, Anand Swarup. 1972. The Kūrma Purāṇa (with English translation). All-India Kashi Raj Trust.

2. Krishna, Nanditha. 2009. Book Of Vishnu. Penguin Books India.

Lakshmi-Janardhan

In most cases, the Lakshmi-Janardhan Shaligram is relatively interchangeable with the Janardhan Shaligram (See Janardhan Shaligram). Janardhan, literally "one who helps people," is the 126th name of Vishnu in the Vishnu Sahasranama. According to Adi Śankara, Janardhana also means "One who inflicts suffering on evil men" or "He to whom all devotees pray for worldly success and liberation." As the liberator of the cycles of death and rebirth and as one who visits disaster on those who harbor malicious intentions, Janardhan Shaligrams are said to bestow protection to practitioners from anyone who wishes them harm. As such, they are especially sought after by businessmen, politicians, or lawmakers and are common gifts, along with Ganesh Shaligrams, at weddings or following specific rites of passage.

The Lakshmi-Janardhan, however, also demonstrates the presence of Lakshmi, Vishnu's celestial consort and the goddess of wealth, fortune, and prosperity. For this reason, this Shaligram is associated with success in business and the ability to discern deception. In other traditions, the Lakshmi-Janardhan Shaligram is a variation of the more common Lakshmi-Narayan Shaligram and is therefore associated with the acquisition of great wealth and material prosperity. Considered judgmental and aggressive in demeanor, these Shaligrams are said to create an atmosphere of obedience and a willingness to honor authority.

Similar to the Janardhan Shaligram in overall appearance, shape, and color, the presence of Lakshmi, however, is usually identified using one of two characteristics: either the presence of a wide, white, line near the top of the shila or a significantly larger opening (vadana) with two clear chakra-spirals on either side. What this means is that in traditions that recognize both types of Shaligrams, the Lakshmi-Janardhan Shaligram differs from the Janardhan Shaligram in that the former has clear chakras and the latter does not. In other cases, a Lakshmi-Janardhan Shaligram is identified as the same as a Janardhan Shaligram but with one additional chakra-spiral, for a total of five rather than four.

REFERENCES

Praanatoshani Tantra pg. 361, Brahmavaivartta (Prakritikhanda, Ch. 21)

DESCRIPTIONS

Single opening with four circular prints. Without mark resembling a vanamala (BV).
The same as Lakshmi-Narayan but without the mark of vanamala. (BV)
With one opening printed with four circles. (P)

ADDITIONAL REFERENCES

1. Lakshmi-Janardhan Temple: https://en.wikipedia.org/wiki/Janardanaswamy_Temple

LAKSHMI-NARASIMHA

Narasimha, or conversely Narsimha or Narsingh, is an avatar of Vishnu or Krishna who is considered to be the supreme God in certain traditions of Vaishnavism but is also a popular deity in Hinduism more generally. Narasimha commonly appears in early Hindu epics, iconography, and temple and festival worship and dates back to well over a millennium. Narasimha's appearance is particularly distinctive, usually depicted as having a human torso and lower body with the head and arms of a lion. Narasimha is also colloquially referred to as the god of "in-betweens" given his most famous appearance as the 'Great Protector' of the devotee Prahlada or as the protector of all devotees in their times of need.

For example, when Narasimha appeared to destroy the demon king Hiranyakashipu, he did so in such a way as to circumvent the demon's boon not to be killed by any living being created by Brahma, not to be killed at night or by day, on the ground or in the sky, nor by any weapon, human, or animal. Narasimha thus appears as the blending of a man and a lion, at twilight, at the threshold of the courtyard, places Hiranyakshipu on his thighs, and disembowels him with his claws.

As a variation of the Narasimha Shaligram, the Lakshmi-Narasimha Shaligram is easily recognized by the presence of a "fanged mouth" at the apex of the primary opening but which then also reveals two internal chakra-spirals typically characteristic of the Lakshmi-Narayan Shaligram.

This "mouth," then usually contains a row of "teeth" visible either along the outer edge of the upper part of the opening or encircling a second inner opening through the central column forming the end of the primary opening. This is because the "mouth" structures of these Shaligrams have been created by the partial wear of the ammonite out of the main shale nodule; leaving a spiral opening that still contains some of the original, interlocking, ammonite chambers inside it.

In short, this Shaligram has the same characteristics of Narasimha Shaligrams (with the distinctive "mouth-like" and "teeth" structures located at the top of the main opening) but contains visible chakra markings on the inside of the "mouth."

This is a particularly important distinction because, in many traditions, Lakshmi-Narasimha Shaligrams are permissible for home worship but Ugra-Narasimha Shaligrams (without the internal chakras), are not and can only be venerated in temple settings. (See also: Narasimha Shaligram).

As manifestations of Narasimha, worship of these Shaligrams is said to bestow protections from enemies and from attacks on one's faith. As such, Lakshmi-Narasimha Shaligrams are often sought after by those who live in regions where their particular religious tradition is in the political minority or by those who intend to immigrate to a country significantly outside of their usual cultural mores (such as America or the UK).

These Shaligrams are also said to bestow confidence, strength, and righteousness more generally and are considered highly desirable for inclusion in daily puja rituals.

In practice, there are a few recognized sub-types of the Lakshmi-Narasimha Shaligram:

In South India, Lakshmi-Narasimha Shaligrams are often described as having one or two chakras on the left side as well as being black in color with a few white or yellow spots. In other regions, Lakshmi-Narasimha is a tawny (yellow or brown) Shaligram with a large opening and single large chakra that has another, smaller, chakra inside of it.

Due to much of the ambiguity in some local descriptions however, it is not uncommon for people to identify any Shaligram with a very large vadana as a Narasimha Shaligram and to interpret the uneven ridges around the rim of the "mouth" (caused by the ammonite's imprinted striations) as the "teeth" required of this particular shila.

REFERENCES

Praanatoshani Tantra pg. 347, Brahmavaivartta (Prakritikhanda, Ch. 21)

DESCRIPTIONS

Large opening with two circular marks, glittering to look at, with vanamala mark (BV).

ADDITIONAL REFERENCES

1. See also: Lakshmi Narasimha Temple, Mangalagiri, Andhra Pradesh and Shri Laxmi Narsimha Temple, Maharashtra.
2. Blurton, T. Richard. 1993. Hindu art. Cambridge, Mass.: Harvard University Press. p. 123.
3. Flood, Gavin D. 1996. An Introduction to Hinduism. Cambridge University Press. p. 111.
4. Vasantha, Rangachar, 1991. The Nārāyaṇasvāmi Temple at Mēlkōṭe: An Archaeological and Historical Study. Directorate of Archaeology and Museums. p. 9.
5. Williams, George M. 2008. Handbook of Hindu Mythology. Oxford University Press. p. 223.

LAKSHMI-NARAYANA

Lakshmi Narayan or Lakshmi-Narayana (also Laxminarayana) is a manifestation of Vishnu along with his consort, Lakshmi the Goddess of Wealth and Prosperity. It is usually referring to a particular version of Vishnu, also known as Narayan, with his consort Lakshmi, in their celestial abode, Vaikuntha.

In most depictions, Lakshmi is shown standing next to a dark-skinned Vishnu, who is holding a conch, mace, lotus and the Sudarshana Chakra. Another depiction of Lakshminarayan portrays Lakshmi in the service of Narayan, who is reclining on the cosmic serpent Śesha, floating in Kshīrsagār, the Ocean of Milk.

According to the Vishnu Purana, this is one of the rarest Shaligrams but in practice, it is considered to be iconic of Shaligrams in general and is the type of Shaligram almost always rendered in art. The Lakshmi-Narayan Shaligram typically appears in one of two primary forms. The first is that of a large, round, whole Shaligram (see photo 1: opposite) which contains a central opening with large, clear, chakras imprinted on both sides of the internal space. These two chakras are then often joined in the center by a thin column.

The second form is the reverse of the first, comprising a single large chakra with visible spiral arch on both sides (see photo 2: opposite) and a smooth flat or rounded center (the central point of the spiral is obscured, which differentiates this sub-type from the Sudarshan Shaligram).

In ritual veneration, this Shaligram is most primarily associated with the acquisition of wealth and bestows blessings for starting or growing a business, to act against competitors, protections in one's professional life, successes in legal matters, and for household and workplace harmony.

In Nepal, these Shaligrams are more often referred to as Vaikuntha-Kamalaja; a combination form of Vishnu and Lakshmi depicted as half male and half female, split down the middle. The icon symbolizes the oneness or non-duality of male and female principles of the universe.

As an extremely popular Shaligram for home worship, there are several recognized variations of this shila in practice:

1. Lakshmi-Narayana-Garuda is a rare variation. It has one large vadana, two chakras, and the main opening has lines which resemble the feathers of the bird Garuda.

2. Lakshmi-Narayana-Sudarshan has a low or depressed look, is perfectly round, and is cold to touch. It also has a chakra on its head with two smaller openings that have four chakras either to the left or to the right.

3. Lakshmi-Narayana-Mahashakti is of a yellowish hue and its left side is rounded. There are four chakras somewhere on the body of the shila, along with markings of a pestle, a sword, a bow, a vanamala, a conch, a discus and a mace on the face and at the navel. This Shaligram is suitable for all prescribed rituals and will bring prosperity, and the accomplishment of one's desires.

REFERENCES

Praanatoshani Tantra pg. 347-348, Praanatoshani Tantra pg. 361, Brahmavaivartta (Prakritikhanda, Ch. 21), Garuda Purana (Panchanan Tarkaratna, Part 1, Ch. 45), Agni Purana; Bengavasi ed., Panchanan Tarkaratna, Saka 1812, Ch. 46

DESCRIPTIONS

In color, he resembles a new cloud and has a single opening marked with four circular prints. A linear mark resembling a vanamala (a particular kind of garland held by Lord Vishnu, or series of forests) is also printed on his body. (BV)

Round shape, single opening, four circular marks at opening and decorated with vanamala. One footprint of a cow, one golden linear mark (G). Having 2 chakras (G)

i.   It has a single opening with four circular marks (or with a vanamala)

ii. Round in shape big in size, having a glaced opening marked with a flag, a cross and a spear-head.

iii. Round in shape with a circular opening marked with four circles, and also printed with a flag, a cross, a spear head, and a yellow spot.

iv. Green in color, round in shape, and marked with one or four circular prints.

v.   Big in size with a comparatively high top, and marked with a flag, a cross, a spear-head, a garland and a few dot prints.

vi. With a small opening, having four circular prints and also marked with a garland.

vii. Marked with three circular prints.

viii. With the color of a new cloud and having a single opening marked with four circular prints, and also having the mark of a garland on His body. (P)

ADDITIONAL REFERENCES

1. Ellwood, Robert. 2007. Encyclopedia of World Religions. New York: Infobase Publishing. pp. 468.

2. Pal, Pratapaditya. 1967. "Vaiṣṇava Art from Nepal in the Museum". Boston Museum Bulletin. Museum of Fine Arts, Boston. 65 (340): 44–45.

3. Malla, Bansi Lal. 1996. "Vasudeva-Laksmi". Vaiṣṇava art and iconography of Kashmir. Abhinav Publications. pp. 45–9.

LAKSHMI MAHALAKSHMI

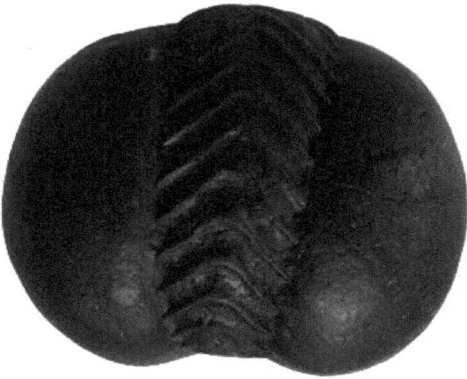

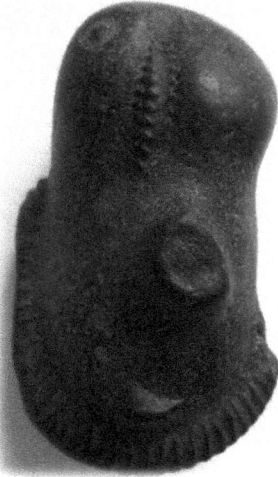

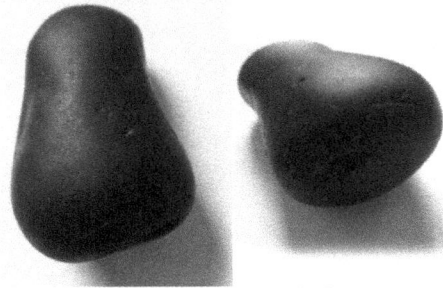

Lakshmi-Padam (Lakshmi's
Foot) Shaligram

Mahalakshmi Shaligram (top)

Lakshmi-Sudarshan Shaligram
(bottom)

Lakshmi is the Hindu goddess of wealth, fortune, marriage, and prosperity. She is also the wife and shakti (creative energy) of Vishnu. Additionally, Lakshmi is an important deity in Jainism and her iconography can be found in Jain temples throughout South Asia.

Lakshmi was also a goddess of abundance and fortune for Buddhists and can still be seen in deity representations on the oldest surviving stupas and cave temples of Buddhism. In Buddhist sects of Tibet and Nepal for example, the goddess Vasudhara displays a number of characteristics and attributes of the Hindu goddess Lakshmi with only minor iconographic differences.

Lakshmi is also called Sri or Thirumagal as a reference to her six divine qualities (gunas) but is more often worshipped as the divine strength and creative will of Vishnu. In some Hindu tales, she was born from the churning of the primordial ocean (See Samudra Manthan Shaligram) where she subsequently chose Vishnu as her eternal consort.

In other popular stories, when Vishnu descended to Earth as the avatars Rama and Krishna, Lakshmi descended as his respective consorts: Sita (Rama's wife) and Radha or Rukmini (Krishna's wife). More broadly, the marriage and relationship between Lakshmi and Vishnu as wife and husband is viewed as the paradigm for the relationship between bride and groom, husband and wife, and men and women generally.

For this reason, no manifestation of Vishnu is ever thought to exist without the corresponding presence of Lakshmi and this is also the case for Shaligrams. It is also important to note that Lakshmi is considered another aspect of the same supreme goddess principle in the Shakti tradition of Hinduism. As such, this Shaligram is also often called Mahalakshmi or occasionally Mahashakti and is the basis for many of the regional and traditional goddess manifestations and variations of Shaligrams (See Mahashakti Shaligram).

In fact, one of the primary distinctions of almost all Devi (goddess) Shaligrams is that they are formed from the Haplophylloceras ammonite species (notable for their deep chevron-shaped ridges), rather than the Blandfordiceras or Perisphinctes species more common is Shaligrams overall. Lakshmi Shaligrams thus tend to appear in one of two distinctive forms. The first (photos 1 and 2: opposite) is a wide, deeply chevron-ridged, spiral, the center of which may be obscured by rounded shale nodules on one or both sides.

These Shaligrams are then referred to as Mahalakshmi (photo 1) or Lakshmi-Sudarshan (photo 2) respectively. The second form is referred to as a Lakshmi-Padam or "foot of Lakshmi" and may contain one or two chakras, which can be either internal or external, adorning a roughly foot-shaped Shaligram (photos 3 and 4: opposite).

Lakshmi Shaligrams, in short, are easy to identify because they appear in one of two distinct forms, but are most often characterized by the presence of a large chakra-spiral associated with a smooth, black, shale nodule that is either rounded or "foot-shaped."

As manifestations of Lakshmi, these Shaligrams are typically said to bestow great wealth upon their devotees and to shield worshippers from monetary losses in business, especially those whose businesses deal in large transactions or in great financial risks.

REFERENCES

Praanatoshani Tantra pg. 361

DESCRIPTIONS

Lakshmipati: Either the front or any one of his rear sides is shaped like the throat of a peacock. He is dark in color with a big opening and a small circular mark. (P)

ADDITIONAL REFERENCES

1. Brooks, Douglas Renfrew. 1992. Auspicious Wisdom: The Texts and Traditions of Srividya Sakta Tantrism in South India. SUNY Press.
2. Gupta, Sanjukta. 2000. Laksmi Tantra, Motilal Banarsidass Publishers.
3. Isaeva, N. V. 1993. Shankara and Indian Philosophy, SUNY Press.
4. Om Lata Bahadur. 2006. John Stratton Hawley; Vasudha Narayanan (eds.). The Life of Hinduism. University of California Press

MADHUSUDANA

Madhusudana with Lotus
Markings

Madhusudana with Lotus
and Conch

Madhusudana with
Trishula Markings

Madhusudana with Lotus
and Vanamala

Anushka (Elephant Goad) Shaligram

Madhusudana is the 73rd name of Vishnu in the Vishnu Sahasranama. According to Adi Sankara' s commentary, Madusudana means the destroyer of the demon Madhu. Madhu and Kaitabha were Rakshasas (demons associated with Hindu cosmology) and both originated from one of Vishnu's ears while he was in the deep sleep of Yoganidra (additionally, a lotus sprouts from Vishnu's navel upon which Brahma, the creator, sits and contemplates the creation of the cosmos

In the Bhagavata Purana, Madhu and Kaitabha stole the Vedas from Brahma during the creation of the world and attempted to hide them beneath the waters of the primordial ocean. Vishnu, in his manifestation as Hayagriva (see Hayagriva Shaligram), subsequently killed them to retrieve the Vedas.

The bodies of Madhu and Kaitabha then disintegrated into twelve pieces (two heads, two torsos, four arms, and four legs) which are said to represent the twelve seismic plates of the Earth. In other legends, Madhu and Kaitabha are demons who set out to annihilate Brahma.

However, Brahma was aware of them and invoked the goddess Mahamaya in his own protection. This awakens the sleeping Vishnu and the two conspiring demons are killed. Hence the name Madhusudanah - the killer of Madhu. Descriptions of the Madhusudana Shaligram tend to vary in some details, but overall, the consensus is that these Shaligrams either appear as a single, smooth, shila with the markings of a conch shell and a lotus or in the shape of an astra; any one of several supernatural weapons owned by a specific deity. (In later Scriptures, astras can also mean any weapon which was used by releasing it from one's hand (e.g. an arrow or spear)).

For this reason, some traditions refer to Madhusudana Shaligrams by more specific titles, such as Padma Shaligrams (Lotus), Tulsi Shaligrams (tulsi leaf markings), Gadadhar Shaligram, Vajra Shaligram, Ankusha Shaligrams, or any other specific object or weapon name.

Madhusudana Shaligrams appear most often in Brahmanical worship and are comparatively rare outside of these contexts. Other Hindu traditions pair Madhusudan with Lakshmi, resulting in a Shaligram with similar characteristics to the Lakshmi-Narayan Shaligram but with the addition of conch-like or lotus-like markings.

For this reason, Madhusudana may commonly appear as an additional appellation of another name-type Shaligram and may not necessarily be identified on its own. Worship of this Shaligram is said to bestow liberation from temptations, particularly sensual temptations such as overindulgence in food or sex.

Madhusudana Shaligrams are also believed to aid in meditation and focus, to improve tolerance, to bestow great perseverance, and to improve on good karmas. For this reason, these Shaligrams tend to be highly sought after by householders looking to transition into ascetics or sannyasis or by those who wish to improve their religious practices overall.

Interpretation of the Madhusudana Shaligram is, therefore, a complicated endeavor. Since these Shaligrams can appear with the markings of a wide variety of weapons or other objects, their descriptions in practice are equally variable. In some cases, Madhusudana shilas are expected to have mixed colors (especially yellow or red) and a single chakra as their basis while other traditions interpret these Shaligrams as having a smooth, whole, body that is covered in all kinds of markings such as snakes, sacred threads, partial chakras, and, most importantly, weapons.

REFERENCES

Praanatoshani Tantra pg. 347, Skanda Purana, Nagarekhanda, 244: 3-9, Brahmavaivartta (Prakritikhanda, Ch. 21)

DESCRIPTIONS

Round in shape, middle in size, and charming to look at. He has two circular marks and a footprint of a cow on His body. (BV)

With a single circular mark at the opening and the marks of a conch and a lotus on His body. (P)

ADDITIONAL REFERENCES

1. "The Eternal Tatva". The Hindu. 3 November 2016. Retrieved 15 July 2020

2. "Essence Of Devi Bhagavatha Purana Vishnu destroys Madhu". www.kamakoti.org. Retrieved 15 July 2020.

Mahashakti/Devi

Mahashakti Durga

Seated Devi
with Mala

Eight-pointed
Mahashakti

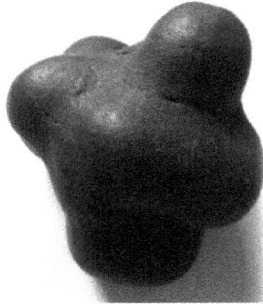

Classic Mahashakti

Shakti or Mahashakti, typically translated to "power" or "empowerment," is the primordial cosmic energy and creative forces of the universe. In Hinduism, Shakti is the concept or personification of the divine feminine in the broadest sense as well as the conceptualization upon which goddesses are said to manifest. Sometimes referred to as 'The Great Divine Mother,' Shakti is also known as Adi Parashakti or Adishakti. In familiar depictions of Hindu deities, Shakti most commonly appears as the female consort of male deities where she embodies creativity, fertility, or sometimes will or agency itself.

Shakti is not necessarily limited to the female form, however, and is said to also be present in males in a potential, unmanifest form. In Shakti tradition of Hinduism, Shakti is worshipped as the Supreme Being where she embodies the active feminine energy of Shiva and is identified as Tripura Sundari or her avatar Parvati. Mahashakti Shaligrams appear in a variety of forms. The most common shape is that of a woman seated in tapasya, or a meditative pose which conveys the performance of austerities.

This Shaligram may then contain any number of additional white lines or markings denoting which goddess is then said to be present, usually Lakshmi, Parvati, Saraswati, or Durga. The second most common form of Mahashakti Shaligrams is the Shakti Yoni, a uniform, rounded, shila with a central depression which may be smooth or may contain chakra ridges (this form is often either described as a "mother's womb" or as bearing resemblance to the "buttocks or udders of a cow").

Lastly, some rarer formations of these Shaligrams appear as "the face of the Devi" wherein the shila contains one or two "eyes" as well as a partial chakra in the form of a crown (see photo 1: opposite). Shaligrams of the last type are most often interpreted as manifestations of Durga and are generally sought after by Shakti or Shaiva devotees.

The blessings said to be bestowed by Mahashakti Shaligrams tends to vary with the specific goddess manifested: wealth and prosperity for Lakshmi, knowledge and speech for Saraswati, strength and courage for Durga and so on. Mahashakti Shaligrams are also highly varied in their interpretations and are the basis for many regional and colloquial goddesses manifest in some Shaligram traditions. For example, certain Hindu traditions identify the variety of Mahashakti Shaligrams as the various forms of Navdurga, Mahavidyas, Banmata, Kali, or Mariamman depending on the Shaligram's specific characteristics and features (see also: Navdurga Shaligrams).

As such, Mahashakti Shaligrams vary widely in appearance and structure. The most common of these forms however, is that of a somewhat triangular shape with a series of white quartz infiltrates as lines through the body of the stone. In other cases, the triangular shape may be interrupted by other nodule points or by markings interpreted as various weapons of the goddess in question. Lastly, the Shakti Yoni is easily identifiable by its round, smooth, appearance and a central depression which can be used to place ritual substances. In some traditions, the Shakti Yoni and Shiva Linga Shaligrams are paired to form the traditional Jaladhari Lingam-Yoni altar.

REFERENCES

Praanatoshani Tantra pg. 361

DESCRIPTIONS

Pitambara: Round in shape having some similarity with the buttock of a cow and printed with one circular mark.

ADDITIONAL REFERENCES

1. Boursier, Helen T. 2021. The Rowman & Littlefield Handbook of Women's Studies in Religion. Rowman & Littlefield.

2. Pattanaik, Devdutt. 2002. Lakshmi, the Goddess of Wealth and Fortune: An Introduction. Vakils, Feffer and Simons.

3. Pintchman, Tracy. 2001. Seeking Mahadevi: Constructing the Identities of the Hindu Great Goddess. SUNY Press. p. 9.

4. Vanamali. 2008. "3. Mahadevi." Shakti: Realm of the Divine Mother. Simon and Schuster.

MAHAVISHNU-DASAVATARA

Mahavishnu-
Dasavatara Shaligram

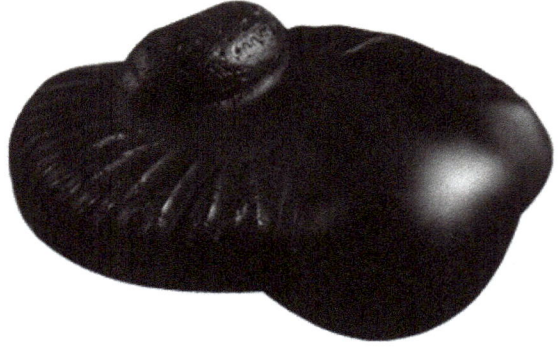

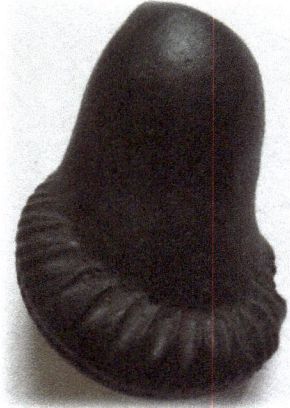

Vishnu Padam
Shaligram

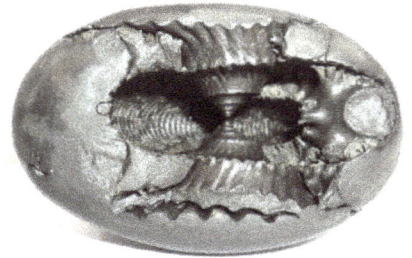

Mahavishnu Shaligram
– showing characteristics
of Narasimha, Narayan,
Kurma, and Lakshmi

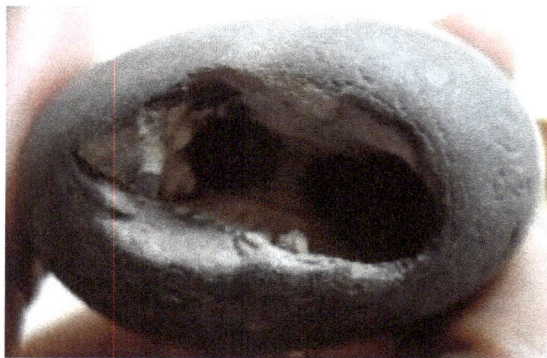

A Vatapatrashayi Shaligram from South
India

As noted in the Narayan Shaligram, Vishnu is one of the principal deities of Hinduism, and the Supreme Being in the Vaishnava tradition. Along with Brahma and Shiva, Vishnu is often venerated as part of the Hindu trinity (Trimurti). In Vaishnavism, Vishnu is identical to the formless metaphysical concept called Brahman, the Svayam Bhagavan, who appears as various avatars in order to preserve or protect the world whenever it is threatened with evil, chaos, and destruction. His most famous avatars include Krishna in the Mahabharata and Rama in the Ramayana but he is also known as Narayana, Jagannath, Vasudeva, Vithoba, and Hari.

Furthermore, he is one of the five equivalent deities worshipped in Panchayatana puja of the Smarta tradition of Hinduism. Lastly, while some Hindu traditions consider the Buddha to also be an incarnation of Vishnu (as part of the Dasavatara), it is not uncommon for Buddhists in Sri Lanka to venerate Vishnu as the custodian deity of the nation and as a protector of Buddhism. The Mahavishnu-Dasavatara Shaligram tends to be the most difficult category of Shaligrams for lay-people to identify without the help of a ritual specialist. This is primarily because Mahavishnu Shaligrams generally contain a wide number of characteristics joined together within a single shila, any of which may indicate the presence of one, several, or all of Vishnu's ten avatars (Matsya, Kurma, Varaha, Narasimha, Vamana, Parashurama, Krishna, Rama, and occasionally the Buddha, Balarama, and Kalki).

These Shaligrams may also contain characteristics of his consort Lakshmi or other attendant deities. Also included in this category is the Vishnu Padam or "Foot of Vishnu" Shaligram which is similar to that of the Lakshmi Padam Shaligram (See Lakshmi Shaligram) but with only a single visible chakra or with a marking that resembles a footprint on an otherwise unmarked shila. In practice, Mahavishnu Shaligrams are said to be especially potent in warding off ghosts, unclean spirits, evil magics, and snakes and to act as a powerful shield against misfortune, accident, or violent death. Mahavishnu Shaligrams are also often described as providing a generally calm and pleasant atmosphere and to act as stabilizing influences in the lives of their devotees.

REFERENCES

Praanatoshani Tantra pg. 361, Skanda Purana, Nagarekhanda, 244: 3-9

DESCRIPTIONS

1. Dasavatara: Having 10 chakras (G).
2. Vatapatrashaayin: Round in shape with a mixed color of white, red and blue. He has also one circular mark with a conch on His left and a lotus on His right side. There are also four circular marks and three dot-prints inside His opening. (P)
3. Saptavirashrava: Round in shape with a small circular mark and several golden dot-prints all over the body. (P)
4. Bahurupin: With many openings having the marks of a conch and discus in one of them. (P)
5. Swayambhu: Blue in color with a long and big opening, and having His body encircled by linear marks. (P)
6. Pitaamaha: He has four different openings with a circular mark in each of them. (P)
7. Chaturmukha: With four linear marks rising from the sides, and also printed with two circular marks on the middle portion of His body. (P) A name meaning "four faces."
8. Dattatreya: (i) With white, red and black spots all over His body and a mark of a rosary on the very topside (ii) Red and yellow in color, other things being the same as above. (P)
9. Chaturbhuja: He holds the color of a new cloud. It is round in shape with four circular marks on the body. (P) A name meaning "Four Arms."

ADDITIONAL REFERENCES

1. Jones, Constance and James D. Ryan. 2006. Encyclopedia of Hinduism. Infobase Publishing. pp. 491–492.

2. Flood, Gavin. 1996. An Introduction to Hinduism. Cambridge University Press. p. 17.

3. Tiwari, Kedar Nath. 1987. Comparative Religion. Motilal Banarsidass Publications. p. 38.

4. Wickremeratne, Swarna. 2012. Buddha in Sri Lanka: Remembered Yesterdays. State University of New York Press. p. 111.

MAHAVISHNU (MULTI-CHAKRA SHALIGRAM)

Four Chakra
Mahavishnu (Caturbhuj)

Five Chakra Mahavishnu
(Vaasudeva)

Multi-Chakra
Mahavishnu (Paramatma
13+)

A rare Multi-Chakra
Shaligram with white,
spiral, markings

The Mahavishnu Multi-Chakra Shaligram appears in a wide variety of forms. For many devotees, these Shaligrams are specific to Shaligram category-types listed in both the Pranatoshani Tantra and in the Skanda Purana, where the specific name of Vishnu associated with the Shaligram is determined by the number of visible chakras rather than by specific characteristics of shape or color. For this reason, many practitioners will identify multi-chakra Shaligrams using the name associated with their number of chakras followed by Mahavishnu (i.e., a four chakra Shaligram would be called Caturbhuja Mahavishnu, a ten chakra Shaligram would be called Dasavatara Mahavishnu, and so on).

This naming convention, however, can become confusing in cases where other Puranic texts use the same deity designations, such as Acyuta (three chakras) or Pradyumna (six chakras) to identify other types of Shaligrams in their own right. For example, Pradyumna Shaligrams are also mentioned in the Brahma Vaivarta Purana, but are identified by criteria other than their number of chakras.Also referred to as Chaturbhuj Shaligrams, Mahavishnu shilas are particularly sought after for their capacity to shield individuals and households from snakes, evil spirits, and restless ghosts.

In other cases, they are prized for their capacity to create atmospheres of holiness and devotion marked by creative energies, innovation, and good luck. In Shakti Hindu traditions, Mahavishnu Shaligrams are sometimes referred to as Sri Chakra or Sri Yantra Shaligrams. In this interpretation, the multiple interlocking chakras are seen as representations of a yantra of nine interlocking triangles that radiate outwards from a central point. As a junction point between the manifest (physical) and unmanifest (divine) world, these Shaligrams are therefore considered to be the form of the goddess Sri Lalitha or Tripura Sundari, "the beauty of three worlds" (an aspect, not of Lakshmi but of the goddess Parvati).

Multi-chakra Shaligrams are distinctive in that they are formed by concretions of ammonites (chakras) into a single mass. In other cases, these Shaligrams appear as a rounded stone with multiple spiral impressions covering their outer surface. Due to the high variability of their appearance, many Mahavishnu Shaligrams of this type are also often interpreted as multiple deities appearing in a single shila. As such, Mahavishnu Shaligrams may be named using multiple deity manifestations at a time, such as Lakshmi-Ganesha-Mahavishnu or Kurma-Mahavishnu.

References

Praanatoshani Tantra pg. 361, Skanda Purana, Nagarekhanda, 244: 3-9

Descriptions

There are multiple variations of textual descriptions of these Shaligrams depending on the specific number of chakras identified or the texts used in interpretation. See Chapter 1.

Chaturbhuja: He holds the color of a new cloud. It is round in shape with four circular marks on the body (P).

ADDITIONAL REFERENCES

1. Carman, John Braisted. 1994. Majesty and Meekness: A Comparative Study of Contrast and Harmony in the Concept of God, Wm. B. Eerdmans Publishing.

2. Dalal, Roshen. 2010. Hinduism: An Alphabetical Guide. Penguin Books India.

3. Krishna, Nanditha. 2010. The Book of Vishnu, Penguin Books India.

4. Vaswani, J.P. 2017. Dasavatara, Jaico Publishing House.

Matsya

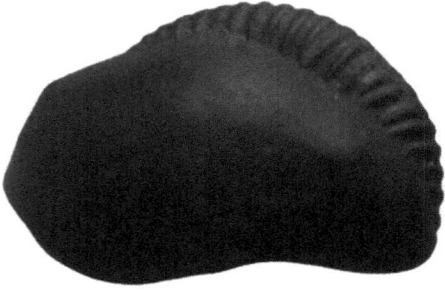

Matsya is the first avatar of Vishnu who appears in the form of a fish. Matsya is most often described Hindu stories as having rescued the first man, Manu, from a great deluge (a world-wide flood). In some cases, Matsya is depicted as a giant fish and in other cases he is anthropomorphized with a human torso and the bottom half of a fish. The earliest accounts of the legend of Matsya associate him with the creator god Prajapati (identified with Brahma). However, Puranic scriptures later incorporate Matsya as an avatar of Vishnu.

In these versions of the story, Matsya forewarns Manu about an impending catastrophic flood and orders him to collect all the grains of the world in a boat (or sometimes, all living creatures). When the flood destroys the world, Manu survives by boarding an ark, which Matsya pulls to safety. In later versions of the story, the Vedas are hidden by a demon, whom Matsya slays resulting in the rescue of Manu and the recovery of the scriptures. Matsya Shaligrams are reasonably distinctive in that they appear in the general shape of a fish with a top "fin" formed by the partial revealing of the chakra-shell spiral. In some cases, Matsya Shaligrams will also have a bottom "fin" where the lower half of the shell spiral is still visible.

Not to be confused with the similar looking Half-Moon Hrishikesh Shaligram, Matsya Shaligrams always have a substantial "body" to them with a clearly discernable head, body, and tail section. A Matsya Shaligram with a clearly definable tail is also sometimes called a Rohitah Matsya ("Red Matsya"). Matsya Shaligrams are almost always associated with the creation of a peaceful and meditative environment. These Shaligrams are also said to bestow sons to barren women, to remove misfortunes caused by an inauspicious birth, and to improve the lives and volume of living creatures within their vicinity.

For this reason, Matsya Shaligrams are often prized by fishermen, animal herders, and farmers. Conversely, in many Shaligram traditions, Matsya shilas are considered to be the best Shaligrams to initially acquire and to use in first learning ritual worship. For this reason, they are often gifted to children or to new devotees who are just starting to learn Shaligram practices or who have never done Shaligram puja on their own.

In practice, there are a few variations of this Shaligram:

1. Chitravarna Matsya is described as having a single chakra at the tail while the right side has fish-like markings. The left side then has lines, a long opening with 2 chakras in the middle, and a smooth body.

2. Kamsya Varna Matsya has a fish shape with a long body and three chakras. This shila may be yellow or copper in color.

3. In other traditions, Matsya has an overall form like the head of the fish with a chakra on the face. This shila also has marks of srivatsa as well as dots and scratches resembling a vanamala (garland of flowers).

4. In rarer variations, Matsya may also appear in combination with a Shiva Linga Shaligram. This shila will still have the shape of a fish and will be spotted but there will also be the mark of shakti-linga at the head which is unevenly situated or at the place where the mouth would be located.

REFERENCES

Praanatoshani Tantra pg. 348, Garuda Purana (Panchanan Tarkaratna, Part 1, Ch. 45), Agni Purana; Bengavasi ed., Panchanan Tarkaratna, Saka 1812, Ch. 46

DESCRIPTIONS

Long shape, lotus mark with two linear marks (G).

i.   Long in shape, golden in color, and marked with three dot-prints.

ii. Like bell metal in color, other characteristics being the same as above.

iii. With the color of sphatika (crystal) other things being the same as above.

iv. Green in color and marked with a fish, and two circles.

v.   Long in shape with three openings, having a circular mark inside the opening and another at the tail. He has the mark of a cart on His right side and a linear fish on His left side.

vi. With a long shape, having opening at the right side, and marked with three dot prints, one discus, one lotus and one conch.

vii. Shaped like a fish with a long mark on His head (P)

ADDITIONAL REFERENCES

1. Bandyopadhyaya, Jayantanuja. 2007. Class and Religion in Ancient India. Anthem Press. p. 136.

2. Dalal, Roshen. 2014. Hinduism: An Alphabetical Guide. Penguin UK.

3. Valborg, Helen (2007). Symbols of the Eternal Doctrine: From Shamballa to Paradise. Theosophy Trust Books. p. 313.

MURARI

According to Hindu legend, Saint Kashyap once had a son named Mura, who was rather annoyed by the fact that demons (asuras) were consistently beaten by the gods (devas). Thus, he decided to perform a tapasya (an ascetic feat) so that he might become stronger and to be able to request a divine boon. This tapasya was then to pray to Brahma constantly for several years. Shortly thereafter, Brahma agreed to grant him his boon. The boon he requested was that if a person touched him in any battlefield, that person would die immediately even if the person was immortal.

With this boon, Mura became invincible. He attacked Indra, who was then forced to leave his abode in heaven. Mura then attacked Yama, who immediately fled from the underworld to Vishnu to ask for help. As such, Vishnu asked Yama to send Mura to him. Mura agreed and went to visit Vishnu on the shores of the ocean. When Vishnu then asked Mura what it was that he truly wanted, Mura replied that he wanted to fight him. Vishnu responded that if Mura wanted to fight him, why was it that his heart trembled so badly. If Mura was frightened, Vishnu would not fight him. Confused, Mura tried to touch his heart to check if Vishnu was indeed right, and as soon as he did so, he fell down dead. Since that time, Vishnu has been called Murari (Mura = a demon, Ari = enemy of).

In another variation of this story, Krishna is called Murari after he frees the 16,000 princesses from Narkasur, whose chief minister is a demon called Mura. Though, in some colloquial accountings of the name "Murari," it is simply taken to mean "one who holds a flute" and it is therefore associated with the typical iconography of Krishna as a cowherd, playing a flute. The Murari Shaligram is typically identified as being small in size (smaller than a man's hand), with a single central vadana (mouth), two clearly visible chakras, and the markings of a lotus on the right side of the shila. In many cases, these Shaligrams are considered subtypes of either the Mahavishnu – Dasavatara Shaligram or of Krishna-type Shaligrams. As such, their veneration and blessings tends to follow similar practices depending on which specific deity manifestation they are attached to (See Mahavishnu – Dasavatara or Krishna Shaligrams)

For the most part, Murari Shaligrams are similar in appearance to many of the multiple variations of Mahavishnu or Krishna Shaligrams; that of a single, smooth, black shale nodule with one or more chakra-spiral markings and openings. In fact, one of the commonly defining characteristics of these shilas is an overall smooth appearance with very little irregularity around their vadanas as well as the presence of a straight or parallel line near the "mouth" of the Shaligram (representing a flute). Murari Shaligrams also tend to be more common among South Indian Vaishnava traditions than elsewhere. However, Murari as a manifestation of Krishna is widespread in northern India and in Nepal.

ADDITIONAL REFERENCES

1. "Murari," Cologne Digital Sanskrit Dictionaries: Cappeller Sanskrit-English Dictionary.

2. Bhumipati Dāsa. 2008. Chaitanya Bhagavata, Chapters 8, 10, and 20. Bhaktivedanta Book Trust.

Narasimha/Ugra-Narasimha

As described in the Lakshmi-Narasimha Shaligram, Narasimha, or conversely Narsimha or Narsingh, is an avatar of Vishnu or Krishna who is considered to be the supreme God in certain traditions of Vaishnavism but is also a popular deity in Hinduism more generally. Narasimha commonly appears in early Hindu epics, iconography, and temple and festival worship and dates back to well over a millennium. Narasiṃha's appearance is particularly distinctive, usually depicted as having a human torso and lower body with the head and arms of a lion.

Narasimha is also colloquially referred to as the god of "in-betweens" given his most famous appearance as the 'Great Protector' of the devotee Prahlada or as the protector of all devotees in their times of need. For example, when Narasimha appeared to destroy the demon king Hiranyakashipu, he did so in such a way as to circumvent the demon's boon not to be killed by any living being created by Brahma, not to be killed at night or by day, on the ground or in the sky, nor by any weapon, human, or animal. Narasimha thus appears as the blending of a man and a lion, at twilight, at the threshold of the courtyard, places Hiranyakshipu on his thighs, and disembowels him with his claws.

The general distinction between the Narasimha Shaligram and its more common counterpart, the Lakshmi-Narasimha Shaligram is not in the presence of a "mouth" and "teeth" but the inclusion of the visible internal chakra-spirals inside of the vadana. Therefore, true Narasimha Shaligrams should not have any visible chakras on the shila or on the inside of their "mouths." For the most part, Narasimha Shaligrams are sought after for their highly protective qualities. As manifestations of Narasimha, the god who defends his devotees in their times of greatest need, Narasimha Shaligrams are said to bestow protection from theft or the influences of evil or impure persons.

These Shaligrams are also said to aid in the healing of mental illnesses, especially anxiety and phobias, and to restore spiritual balance to persons caught in chaotic home situations. In some cases, Narasimha Shaligrams are also included in daily puja rituals for the sake of obtaining divine guidance before undertaking an especially challenging endeavor related to household or marital harmony. Depending on the tradition in question however, Narasimha Shaligrams may be restricted from home worship and therefore only appear in temples.

In some Shaiva traditions, this Shaligram is interpreted as the deity Bhairava, a fierce and terrifying manifestation of Shiva associated with annihilation. In a similar fashion, Vaishnava traditions sometimes call this manifestation Ugra Narasimha, a frightening and angry form of Narasimha whose famous statues reside at Hampi and Bangalore. Unsurprisingly, this Shaligram bears similar resemblance to the Lakshmi-Narasimha Shaligram, which is identified by the distinctive "mouth-like" structure located at the top of the main opening.

This structure is formed by the incomplete wearing of the ammonite shell out of the surrounding shale nodule, which leaves at least one cross-segment of the internal portion of the ammonite still in place as it breaks, piecemeal, out of the shell mold (resulting in the appearance of "teeth"). This variation on the Shaligram type, however, generally does not contain the two distinctive internally-facing chakra-shell spirals as is found in the Lakshmi-Narayan Shaligram and therefore, is considered the manifestation of only one primary deity.

REFERENCES

Praanatoshani Tantra pg. 347-348, Skanda Purana, Nagarekhanda, 244: 3-9, Brahmavaivartta (Prakritikhanda, Ch. 21), Garuda Purana (Panchanan Tarkaratna, Part 1, Ch. 45), Agni Purana; Bengavasi ed., Panchanan Tarkaratna, Saka 1812, Ch. 46

DESCRIPTIONS

Large opening with two circular marks, glittering to look at (BV).

Mark of a mace at center, circular mark in lower middle, upper middle portion comparatively bigger (G).

(i) With a big opening and two circular marks.

(ii) With a long opening and linear marks resembling the mane of a lion, and also with two circular marks.

(iii) Marked with three dot-prints other things being the same as above.

(iv) Uneven in shape with a mixed reddish color, having two big circular marks above it, and a crack at the front.

(v) Reddish in color and printed with several teeth like marks, three or five dot-marks and a big circular mark.

(vi) With a big opening, a vanamala and two circular marks. This type is popularly known as Lakshminrisimha.

(vii) Black in color with dot marks all over his body and two circular marks on His left side. This also is a variety of the Lakshminrisimha sub-type.

(viii) Printed with a lotus mark on His left side. This also is a sub-type of Lakshminrisimha.

(ix) When any of the above types of Narasimha is marked with five dot prints, He is popularly called Kapilanrisimha.

(x) Printed with seven circular marks and golden dots and also having openings on all sides. This type is called Sarvotmukhanrisimha.

(xi) Variegated in color, having many openings including a large one and marked with many circular prints. This type is popularly called Paataalanrisimha.

(xii) With two circular marks inside the main opening and eight others on His sides. This also is a variety of Paataalanrisimha.

(xiii) Aakaashanrisimha: With a comparatively high top and a big opening and also printed with circular marks.

(xiv) Jihvaanrisimha: Big in size, with two openings and two circular marks. He being the giver of poverty, His worship is forbidden.

(xv) Raakshasanrisimha: With a fierce opening and holes, and also marked with golden spots. His worship also is forbidden.

(xvi) Adhomukhanrisimha: With three circular marks one at the top and two on the sides, having His opening at the bottom.

(xvii) Jvaalaanrisimha: Marked with two circular prints and a vanamala, and having a small opening.

(xviii) Mahaanrisimha: Printed with two big circular marks and a few other linear marks one above the other. (P)

In practice, there is also:

1. Maha Jvala Narasimha, which is thick in shape, blue-black or tawny in color, and has a gaping mouth. This shila is fit for worship only by mendicants and ascetics.

2. Akasha Narasimha has unclear chakras at the center of the opening; a big belly; light weight with one vadana and two chakras.

3. Baddhachakra Narasimha is tawny colored with two joined chakras inside a single vadana.

4. Bala-Narasimha has a small opening with two chakras and a vanamala

ADDITIONAL REFERENCES

1. Chari, S. M. Srinivasa. 1994. Vaiṣṇavism: Its Philosophy, Theology, and Religious Discipline. Motilal Banarsidass. pp. 132–134.

2. Krishna, Nanditha. 2009. The Book of Vishnu. Penguin Books. pp. 50–53

3. Roshen Dalal. 2010. The Religions of India: A Concise Guide to Nine Major Faiths. Penguin Books. p. 148.

4. Soifer, Deborah A. 1991. The Myths of Narasimha and Vamana: Two Avatars in Cosmological Perspective. SUNY Press.

NARAYANA – VISHNU NARAYAN

Vishnu-Narayan Shaligram with
Anirudda appearing.

According to the Vedas, Itihasas, and multiple Puranic texts, Narayana is the Supreme God along with his many avatars. Most commonly venerated as Vishnu or Hari in Vaishnavism (or sometimes Krishna), Narayana is also called Purushottama or Purusha (the cosmic man or Self, Consciousness, or the Universal Principle) in the Bhagavad Gita, the Vedas, and the Puranas.

Narayana is an understanding of the divine as an infinite all-pervading form. While the Puranas present a seemingly divergent description of Narayana as an Enlightened Supreme Being, the fifth verse of the Narayana Sukta, a hymn in the Yajurveda, states that Narayana is an essence that pervades whatever is seen or heard within the material universe. Another important translation of Narayana is "The One who rests on Water." The waters are called narah and constitute his first residence (ayana). "Nara" can also refer to all human beings or living entities (Jivas). Therefore, another meaning of Narayana is "Resting Place for All Living Entities." As such, the close association of Narayana with water explains the frequent depiction of Narayana in Hindu art as standing, sitting, or sleeping on an ocean.

In practice, Narayan and Lakshmi-Narayan Shaligrams are virtually indistinguishable and both are used for similar ritual purposes. In fact, most ritual specialists explain that because Narayan (Vishnu) is never present without the corresponding presence of Lakshmi, any Narayan Shaligram could technically be interpreted using both categories. For the most part, many Shaligram traditions consider the divergent categories as more of an artifact of textual reference than any specific distinction in Shaligram identification. In Shaligram traditions that do make distinctions between the two categories, however, (such as some Brahmanical traditions), practitioners note that the Narayan Shaligram will contain a chakra-spiral on only one side of the shila, whereas the Lakshmi-Shaligram will have two chakras opposite one another. In other cases, the distinction between the Narayan and Lakshmi-Narayan Shaligrams is that Narayan shilas will have a single (partial) chakra spiral that encircles their outer edge (thus maintaining the one chakra characteristic) with a smooth, unmarked, center.

In South India, Narayan Shaligrams are sometimes described in one of two ways. Firstly, as a Shaligram with two chakras on each of its sides or secondly, as a very large Shaligram with equally large, clear, chakras that have fine striations and are black, blue-black, or brown.

In practice, there are also a few recognized variations of this Shaligram:
1. Acakra Narayana, which is blue-black in color with no chakras but three well-formed lines and a hole on the right side.
2. Vishnu Pushpa, which has a dark color along with the shape of a Vishnu-kranta flower (Clitoria Ternatea or Evolvulus Alsinoides). It may also have the marks of the five weapons of Vishnu, a vanamala, and a lotus.

REFERENCES

Praanatoshani Tantra pg. 348, Skanda Purana, Nagarekhanda, 244: 3-9, Garuda Purana (Panchanan Tarkaratna, Part 1, Ch. 45), Agni Purana; Bengavasi ed., Panchanan Tarkaratna, Saka 1812, Ch. 46

DESCRIPTIONS

Black in color, three linear marks at opening (G).

(i) He holds at His front side a good-looking opening marked with a necklace, a golden bracelet (keyura) and other ornaments.
(ii) It is marked with two circular prints on its either side with a clear circular mark at its opening. (P)
(i) Big in size and black in color with linear markings at the center of the opening.
(ii) With the mark of the mace at the center of the opening things being the same as Govinda. (P)

Green in color with a charming shape, having reddish circular marks at the opening and golden spots on His body. (P)

Rupinarayana: Marked with a pestle, a garland, a conch, a discuss and mace on his front side. It may also have the mark of a bow at His front. (P)

Chaturbhuja: He holds the colour of a new cloud. It is round in shape with four circular marks on the body. (P) The name Chaturbhuj is a derived from Sanskrit words चतु: = four and भुजा = arms, which literally means "One who has four arms," and refers to Vishnu.

ADDITIONAL REFERENCES

1. Clarke, Peter; Friedhelm Hardy; Leslie Houlden; and Stewart Sutherland. 2004. The World's Religions. Routledge. p. 748.
2. Ghosh, A. (2 March 2009). "Krishna: A Sourcebook. Edited by Edwin F. Bryant." The Journal of Hindu Studies. 2 (1): 124–126.
3. Holt, John Clifford. 2008. The Buddhist Viṣṇu: Religious Transformation, Politics, and Culture. Motilal Banarsidass Publishers. p. 268.

NAVAVYUHA

Though mentioned as a Shaligram name-type category in the Pranatoshani Tantra, in practice, Navavyuha more often tends to refer to Dvarka shilas and not to Shaligrams. The Dvararvati or Dvarka/Dwarka shila is a type of white or yellowish coral stone obtained from the Gomati (or Gomti) river near the city of Dvaraka. In the Hindu epics and in several of the Puranas, Dvārakā is called Dvaravati and is one of seven tirthas (pilgrimage sites) for spiritual liberation (the other six being Mathura, Ayodhya, Kashi, Kanchipuram, Avantika (Ujjain) and Puri). Dvaraka is currently located in the Jamnagar District of Gujarat at the mouth of the Gomati River as it flows out into the Gulf of Kutch.

Dvaraka shilas are coral with one or multiple chakra-markings as the most distinguishing feature, and hence they are called 'chakrankita-sila'. As aniconic representations of Hindu, Buddhist, and Jain deities, these stones share similar ritual contexts with Shaligrams, Shiva Lingas, Rudraksha seeds, Govardhana shilas (stones from the Govardhan hill), and other naturally occurring manifestations of the divine. They also often have solar or astrological significance, and their use in worship is very common among multiple Vaishnava, Shaiva, and Smarta traditions.

Dvarka shilas also have their own extensive list of name-types, ritual benefits, and categories for identification similar to that of Shaligrams but are generally associated with the cleansing of sins, the reversal of bad karma, and the fulfillment of spiritual desires. When the name appears in Shaligram interpretive practice, Navavyuha represents the collection of the nine forms of Vishnu: Vasudeva, Samkarshana, Pradyumna, Anirudda, Narayana, Hayagriva, Vishnu, Narasimha and Varaha. The first four forms are well known as "chatur-vyuha" (the four principal emanations of Narayana/Vishnu).

The twelve major forms of Vishnu are then derived from these nine forms, according to the Tantra Siddhanta, a division of the Pancharatra. In practice, however, the Navavyuha category of Shaligrams (those having 9 chakras) are typically subsumed under the Mahavishnu Multichakra name-type and share similar ritual qualities (See Mahavishnu – Multichakra Shaligram). In the same manner as the Mahavishnu Multichakra Shaligram, Navavyuha Shaligrams are formed by concretions of ammonite spiral shells/chakras into a single mass. In other cases, these Shaligrams appear as single rounded stones with multiple spiral impressions covering their outer surface; again, much in the same way as the Mahavishnu Shaligram.

However, a Shaligram identified as Navavyuha specifically has nine and only nine visible chakras. Due to the high variability of their appearance, many Shaligrams of this type are also commonly interpreted as multiple deities appearing in a single stone. As such, Navavyuha Shaligrams may be identified using multiple deity manifestations at a time in addition to their nine chakra markings.

REFERENCES

Pranatoshani Tantra pg. 361

DESCRIPTIONS

Having 9 chakras (G)

ADDITIONAL REFERENCES

1. Srinivasan, Doris. 1997. Many Heads, Arms, and Eyes: Origin, Meaning, and Form of Multiplicity in Indian Art. BRILL. pp. 209–210.

2. "Navavyuha" in Cologne Digital Sanskrit Dictionaries: Monier-Williams Sanskrit-English Dictionary.

3. Vihagendra-saṃhitā 4.17 of the Pāñcarātra corpus.

Navdurga

Skandamata
Navdurga
front and
back

Siddhidaatri
Navdurga
front and
back

Shailaputri
Navdurga
front and
side

Kaalratri
Navdurga

Kushmanda Navdurga

Chandraghanta
Navdurga

Brahmacharini
Navdurga

Mahagauri
Navdurga,
front and side

Kathyayini Navdurga

Navadurga, literally the "Nine forms of the Goddess Durga," in Hindu theology, is the manifestation of Durga, the Mother Goddess, in nine distinct forms:
- Siddhidātrī - the unmanifest Mother Goddess
- Kuśamāṇḍā – the Mother Goddess living within the Sun
- Brahmachāriṇī – Sati, the unmarried goddess. Betrothed to Shiva.
- Śailaputrī – The self-immolated goddess in the form of Sati
- Mahāgaurī – Sati at the age of 16, blessed with beauty and fair complexion
- Candraghaṇṭā - Married to Shiva, Mahagauri adorns her forehead with a half-moon (Chandra) shaped like a bell (Ghanta)
- Skandamātā – The mother of the God of War, Skanda. Son of Shiva.
- Kātyāyanī - To destroy the buffalo-demon Mahishasura, the Mother Goddess appears in her Warrior Goddess form.
- Kālarātrī - The fiercest and most ferocious form of the Mother Goddess, in which she manifests to destroy the demons, Sumbha and Nisumbha.

These nine forms are then worshipped together during the Navratri festivals (The Nine Divine Nights), that occur four times throughout the year. Durga is also known by a variety of other names, such as Devi, Shakti, Adi Parashakti and Parvati and as such, she is considered to be the primary form of the Devi in Shakta worship (see also: Mahashakti Shaligram, where the primary characteristic of Devi Shaligrams is the chevron-shaped lines along the chakras.).

The nine Shaligram manifestations of the Navdurga form a complex inter-relationship of forms, characteristics, and interpretations. More popular in Durga puja worship throughout India (esp. Gujarat and Maharashtra), in many of the goddess traditions of Tamil Nadu and Karnataka, in Bangladesh and West Bengal, and comparatively popular throughout Nepal, Navdurga Shaligrams are identified separately by characteristics iconic of the specific form of Durga they represent.

> » Siddhidātrī is described as a chakra – upon – chakra Shaligram (two layered chakra-spirals or one chakra spiral disappearing inside a second chakra spiral), demonstrating the formless motion of the goddess. In other Shaligram traditions, these Shaligrams are similar to Lakshmi-Narasimha Shaligrams in general appearance but tend to have a stark golden color apparent on the inside edges of the vadana (mouth).
>
> » Kuśamāṇḍā is described as having markings and features denoting the goddess's eight arms, holding a mala (garland/rosary) along with several other weapons, and having markings of her tiger mount (tiger tooth marks) or her solar aura (a golden color to the top portion of the Shaligram).
>
> » Brahmachāriṇī is a golden Shaligram, smooth in texture, with no blemishes or lines marking the surface. A single vadana (mouth) may be present on the lower portion of the Shaligram but the internal chakras should be almost completely smooth and flat.
>
> » Śailaputrī is described as having the shape of two hands, holding a trident and a lotus, and bearing the markings of her bull mount with an overall shape like that "of the mountains" to mark her status as the Daughter of the Himalayas (usually meaning a triangular shaped shila).

» Mahāgaurī is another golden Shaligram with a smooth outer body in the shape of the seated goddess, with a single "crown" or chakra-spiral ridge along the back or side of the Shaligram.

» Candraghaṇṭā is described as having the markings of ten hands and three eyes, a golden marking near the central opening (which has two internal chakras), with markings of the half-moon and of the ghanta (bell).

» Skandamātā is described as having the markings of three eyes and four hands, the markings of a lotus (or two), sitting aside her lion mount (a "mouth and teeth" feature similar to the Narasimha Shaligram) while holding her son, Skanda, in her lap.

» Kātyāyanī is described as similar to that of Kālarātrī but with the markings of multiple arms and weapons, including a chakra, conch, bow, sword, spear, club, trident, thunderbolt, and a lotus (or some combination of the nine). She should have the overall shape of the Warrior Goddess astride her divine tiger.

» Kālarātrī is described as a fierce Shaligram with a gaping mouth, bared teeth, and markings of claws or wounds somewhere on the body of the shila; representing her victory over demonic forces.

Veneration of Navdurga Shaligrams bestows a wide variety of benefits largely dependent on the combination of Shaligrams in question. In fact, across multiple Shaligram traditions, these Shaligrams have a wide variety of interpretations, characteristics, and additional mythologies attached to them including various cosmological meanings, links to local histories, and associations with other famous deities (such as Ram, Shiva, Parvati, and Lakshmi).

However, the worship of these Shaligrams is said to more generally provide blessings of harmony, specifically harmony between the private life of the devotee and the public life around him or her ("to make the internal universe the same as the external universe"). She is also associated with the phases of the moon, with the strength of womanhood, with protection from domestic or gender-based violence, and the destruction of evil occult, magical, or ghostly forces.

ADDITIONAL REFERENCES

1. "The Nine Forms of Goddess Mahadevi Durga". Times of India. Retrieved 3 May 2022.

2. Amazzone, Laura. 2010. Goddess Durga and Sacred Female Power. University Press of America.

3. Ramachandran, Nalini. 2020. Nava Durga: The Nine Forms of the Goddess. Penguin Books.

4. Srinivasan, Doris. 1997. Many Heads, Arms, and Eyes: Origin, Meaning, and Form of Multiplicity in Indian Art. BRILL. pp. 209–210.

5. "Navavyuha" in Cologne Digital Sanskrit Dictionaries: Monier-Williams Sanskrit-English Dictionary.

6. "The Nine Forms of Goddess Mahadevi Durga". Times of India. Retrieved 3 May 2022.

7. Amazzone, Laura. 2010. Goddess Durga and Sacred Female Power. University Press of America.

8. Ramachandran, Nalini. 2020. Nava Durga: The Nine Forms of the Goddess. Penguin Books.

9. Vihagendra-saṃhitā 4.17 of the Pāñcarātra corpus.

PADMANABHA

Padmahabha is one of the many names of Vishnu-Narayan and refers to the form of a reclining Vishnu from whose navel springs a lotus upon which Brahma the Creator is seated (this posture is referred to as Anantha Shayana; the eternal yogic sleep). The lotus also appears in a number of religions, including both Hinduism and Buddhism, as a symbolic representation of divine truth or any of its various manifestations. In the Yoga-sastras, for example, every idea is said to springs from the navel of the divine Self (Paraa) which then comes to be perceived (Pasyantee). Thereafter, ideas come to rest in the bosom as thoughts (Madhayamaa) before they are expressed (Vaikharee) in physical activities (idea becomes action).

Padmanabha, "One who has the lotus in his navel," is therefore most commonly used as a metaphor for all potential or unmanifest thoughts that come forth into consciousness, i.e., creativity. Conversely, some traditions translate Padmanabha as "He who is seated in the pericarp of the lotus," which refers to Vishnu as the original locus for the material manifestation of the world. Padmanabha Shaligrams typically only appear in Shaligram interpretive traditions that recognize the Tantras as sources of textual authority. In other traditions, this Shaligram might also be interpreted simply as the Padma or Lotus Shaligram, which is included in the representations of the four "weapons" of Vishnu (See Gada Dhar Shaligram).

Alternatively, this Shaligram is identified using the markings of Śesha (the world serpent) on the outer periphery or the markings of the Kalpvriksha (the world tree), which are then accompanied by the characteristic two-chakra markings of Lakshmi-Narayan visible inside the primary opening. Brahma may then appear as an additional chakra-spiral seated on Vishnu's navel (see photo 2, opposite). Padmanabha Shaligrams have a number of potential variations but the most common formation of this Shaligram mirrors the more common Lakshmi-Narayan Shaligram but with the inclusion of additional ammonite ridges across the top surface (Śesha), cracks or striations in the form of a tree (Kalpvriksha), or a wide, circular, section of flattened wear obscuring the cross-section of the ammonite on one side of the vadana (Lotus emerging from the navel; though this marking is also occasionally referred to as a "rose apple" marking).

The worship of Padmanabha Shaligrams is most often associated with a combination of potential blessings, including wealth (Lakshmi), protection from misfortunes (Vishnu), and knowledge and intelligence (Brahma). In this way, a single Padmanabha Shaligram can take the place of three or more other Shaligrams should the devotee be unable to properly acquire or venerate more than one Shaligram. For this reason, it is often popular with ascetics or frequent travelers.

In practice, there are a few variations of the Shaligram that are recognized by numerous traditions:

1. Padmanabha Shubhadayaka is a shila that is covered with a vanamala; Srivatsa (triangular) markings, and with a single vadana and two chakras.

2. Padmanabha Nabhicakra, conversely, has one chakra at the center with a "berry-shaped" and a "reversed plough" marking. This typically refers to the round "Lotus" shape on the side of the vadana as well as a crescent or pick-shaped line somewhere along the body of the shila. This Shaligram should also not have any more than one vadana and two internal chakras.

References

Pranatoshani Tantra pg. 361

Descriptions

(i) Reddish in color with a mark of a lotus on His body.

(ii) With a full and half circular mark, and also with the mark of a petal (of a lotus) but there is no hair mark on the body. (P)

Additional References

1. Bayi, Aswathi Thirunal Gouri Lakshmi. 1995. Sree Padmanabha Swamy Temple. Bharatiya Vidya Bhavan, Bombay, India.

2. Chinthu, I. 2019. A Contemporary Analysis on the Growth of Religious Tourism and the Role of Sree Padmanabha Swamy Temple. GIS Business, 14(3), 96-101.

3. Krishna, N. 2010. The Book of Vishnu. Penguin Books India.

4. Ponmelil, V.A. "Temples of Kerala – Sri Padmanabhaswamy Temple". Temples.newkerala.com.

PARAMESHTIN

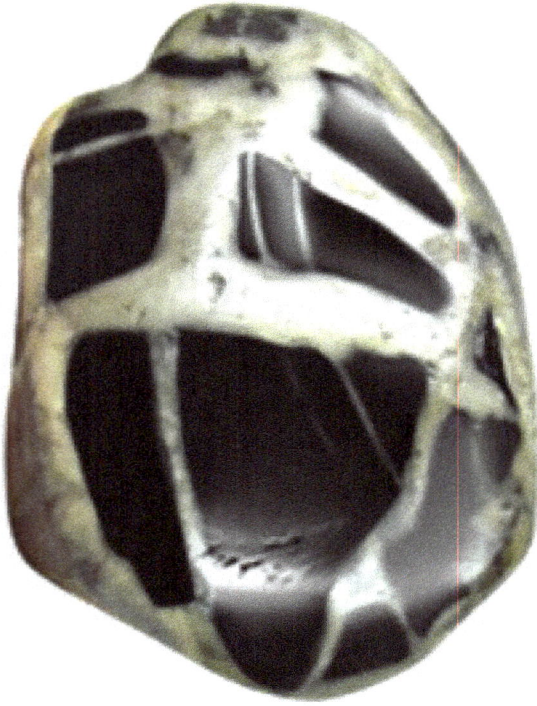

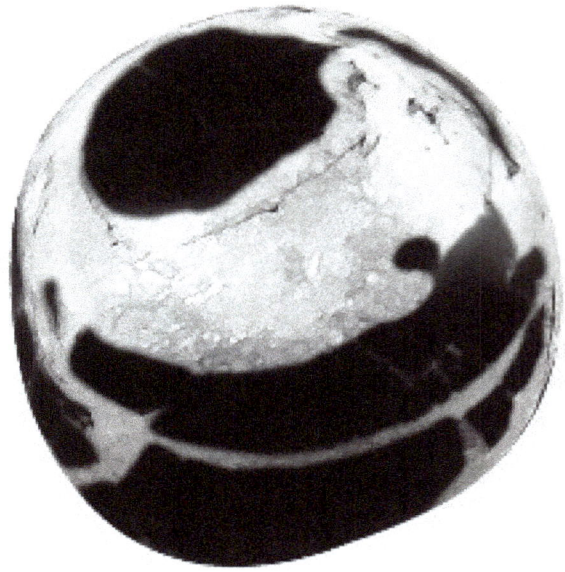

Parameshtin has a number of potential references related to various Shaligram traditions. In the Rig Veda, Prajapati Parameshtin refers to one of the patriarchs of the old Aryan society of the Vedic Age; one of several leaders who molded and shaped Indian Civilization in the early ages. Additionally, Panch Parmeshthi is the Sanskrit term for The Five Worships of Jainism and Purmeshthi is a king of Bharatkhanda or Viraj identified by the Atharvaveda – 4.11.7 with Indra, Agni, Prajapati and Parameshtin (A.V.iv.11.7).

Most Shaligram ritual specialists however note Parameshtin as another term referring to the Svayambhu, or the self-created Supreme Being who is without beginning, middle or end (Parameshtin meaning Supreme Ruler). In this interpretation, Parameshtin refers to the being who joins the Sun (the principle of fire) with the Moon (the source of Soma, the sacrificial potion). Together, they form the basis for the Cosmic Sacrifice, a standard Vedic ritual called the Yajnam. In related traditions, both the Sun and Moon are also considered to be two of the three eyes of Lakshmi (See Narasimha Taapaneeya Upanishad).

Like many Shaligram name-types referenced in only a single Puranic text, Parameshtin Shaligrams rarely appear in practice and are virtually unknown outside of specialist circles. When they do appear, most practitioners identify them as round or slightly elongated in shape with significant white markings and lines that cover almost the entire body of the shila, so as to make the Shaligram appear almost completely white in color. In other traditions, red, yellow, or white stones taken from the Kali Gandaki River along with more classical Shaligrams are occasionally interpreted as Parameshtin, though this is uncommon.

Parameshtin Shaligrams are formed by the wearing of a black shale nodule which contains significant quartz infiltrates. Some practitioners explain that these Shaligrams are only present in limited quantities that must be obtained by deep diving into the northern section of the Kali Gandaki River that immediately precedes the Damodar Kund, though others report that Shaligrams of this kind are occasionally found lower down in the river. Ideal types of this Shaligram should have even, concentric, white circles and be unchipped or otherwise unmarred.

The home worship of Parameshtin Shaligrams is uncommon. Devotees who do venerate these Shaligrams, however, describe them as bestowing exceptional atmospheres of meditative calm and patience, granting exceptionally long life spans, and encouraging the exploration of various paths to enlightenment. Others view these Shaligrams as the white Shaligrams referenced in the Skanda Purana, whose markings are representative of Krishna, Sridhara, Vanamala and Lakshmi or whose white color is a remnant of the droplets that fell during the churning of the milky ocean (See Samudra Manthan Shaligram).

For this reason, Parameshtin Shaligrams are also occasionally described as being copper-colored with a single lotus-shaped chakra and a hole in the base.

REFERENCES

Praanatoshani Tantra pg. 348. Agni Purana; Bengavasi ed., Panchanan Tarkaratna, Saka 1812, Ch. 46

DESCRIPTIONS

(i) With a hole at the top and having the marks of a lotus, a circle and several dots.

(ii) White in color, having a decent hole and a picture at the top and marked with a discus and a lotus.

(iii) Reddish in color with a circular and linear mark, and a hole at the top.

(iv) Round in shape, yellow in color with a hole at the top.

(v) Reddish or yellowish in color with the marks of a lotus and a circle on His body, its top portion being divided by a circular hole. (P)

ADDITIONAL REFERENCES

1. Jaini, Padmanabh S. 1998. The Jaina Path Of Purification. Motilal Banarsidass.

2. Pandit, M. P. 1988. Upanishads: Gateways of knowledge. Lotus Press.

Parashurama

Parashurama (lit. Rama with an axe) is the sixth avatar of Vishnu. The son of Renuka (a Hindu goddess primarily worshipped in South India, who is also considered to be an avatar of Parvati or Durga) and one of the saptarishis (seven great sages), Jamadagni. He lived during the last Treta and Dvapara Yugas (the third and fourth ages, respectively) and is one of the Chiranjivi (immortals) of Hindu lore. Parashurama, a Brahmin, received his famous axe after undertaking terrible penance to please Shiva, who in turn taught him Kalaripayattu (a type of martial arts originating in Kerala).

Parashurama is most well-known for repeatedly eliminating the world of malevolent kshatriyas (warrior rulers who had been living as tyrants) some twenty-one times over after the king Kartavirya Arjuna (not the Arjuna of the Mahabharata), killed his father, or in some cases, after he had stolen the holy cow Kamdhenu. According to the Mahabharata, Parashurama single-handedly conquered the entire world by killing thousands of kshatriyas before conducting hundreds of Ashvamedhas and giving everything away as alms to the sage Kashyapa. Parashurama also plays important roles in both the Mahabharata and Ramayana, serving as mentor to Bhishma, Drona, and Karna.

Unlike many of the other Dasavatara, Parashurama is not always included as a standard Shaligram name-type in the Puranic and Tantric texts. To some degree, this is likely to do Parashurama's late inclusion in the Dasavatara line-up but may also be in part due to his more regional South Indian popularity, where Shaligram traditions were also likely later in arrival. Parashurama Shaligrams, however, are relatively popular in ritual practice and appear in a number of oral Shaligram traditions. Said to bestow strength of will, courage, and vigilance (by virtue of his "prominent eyes"), veneration of these Shaligrams is said to tip unequal odds in favor of the devotee and to encourage the presence of good karma such that the merits acquired by the devotee in past lives will bear exceptional rewards in their present life as well as in the future.

Given their associations, Parashurama Shaligrams are typically identified through two characteristic features: the presence of "two eyes" on the body of the shila (either holes, indentations, or rounded markings) and the general shape of an axe head. This overall axe shape is then that of a rounded central nodule with a prominent, forward-facing ridge on one side and one or two smaller opposing ridges that make up the front blade and the back head and poll respectively. In some Shaligram traditions, this shila is considered to be the Shaligram described in the Pranatoshanitantra (pgs 351-356) as the Madhava Shaligram. In other variable descriptions, Parashurama is distinguished by lines or scratches resembling an axe (rather than a general axe shape). These shilas are further described as being dark blue-green "like the blade of the durva-grass" and high in stature because they are adorned with a small chakra near their navel.

Two additional variations of this Shaligram are:

1. Rajapujya Parashurama, which is black, white, or red in color with a large opening and two chakras. It might also have a spot on the chakra or a large chakra with the marks of an axe and fangs.

2. Parashurama Shanta is a plain shila but with a single mark of an axe on the bottom.

REFERENCES

Pranatoshani Tantra pg. 348, 351 – 356

DESCRIPTIONS

Madhava: With a color like that of honey and marked with a mace and a conch.

(i) Yellow in color and marked with a print resembling an axe.

(ii) With two prints resembling teeth, either at the top or on any two sides, other things being the same as above (P)

ADDITIONAL REFERENCES

1. Coulter, Charles Russell; Turner, Patricia. 2013. Encyclopedia of Ancient Deities. Routledge.

2. Jones, Constance and James D. Ryan. 2006. Encyclopedia of Hinduism. Infobase Publishing. p. 324.

3. Leslie, Julia. 2014. Myth and Mythmaking: Continuous Evolution in Indian Tradition. Taylor & Francis. pp. 63–66 with footnotes.

PARVATI/SHIVA-PARVATI

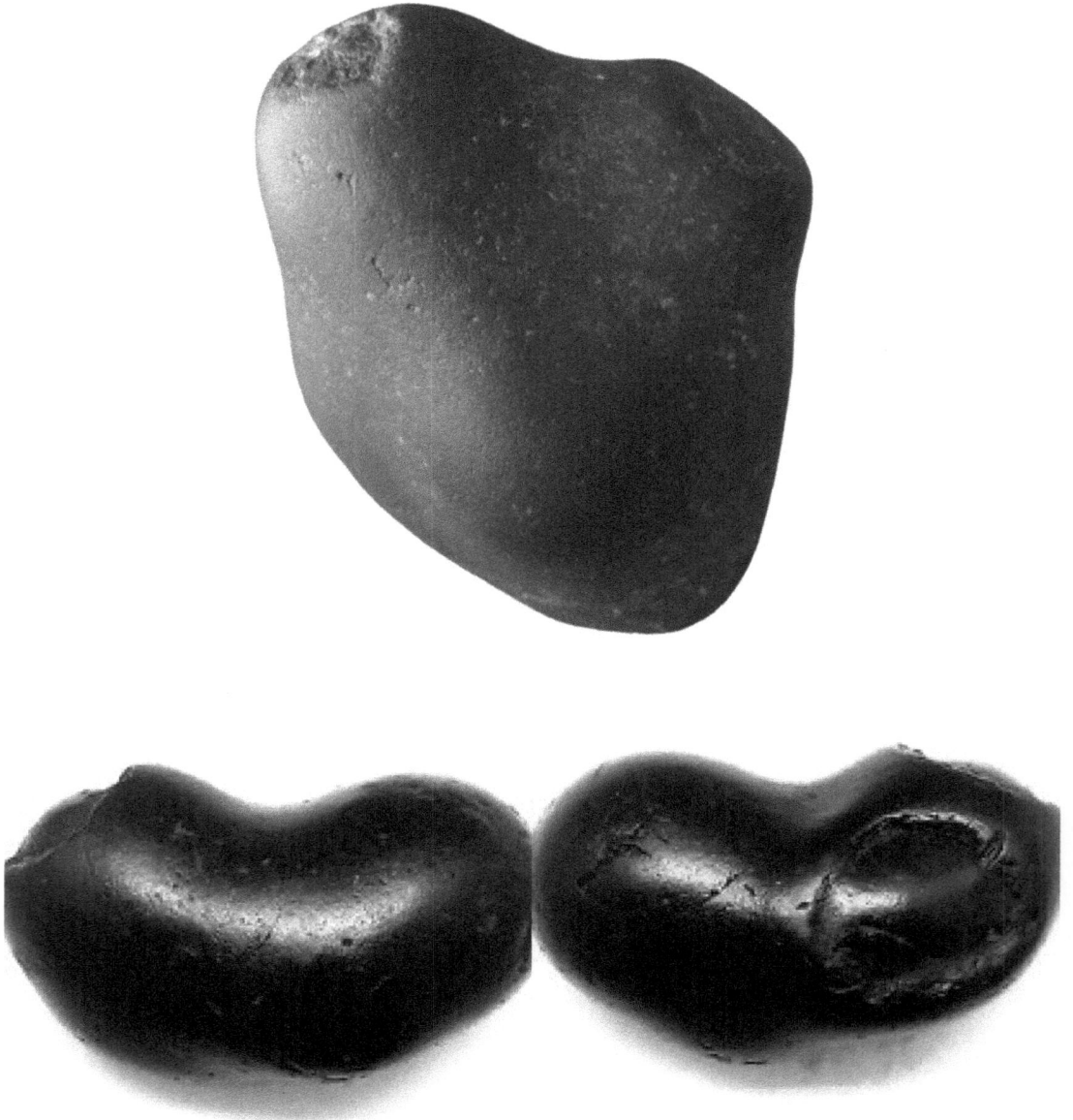

Parvati is the Hindu goddess of love and fertility as well as of divine strength and power. As a manifestation of Shakti, the Hindu conceptualization of the formless feminine divine, Parvati is most often depicted as a gentle and nurturing aspect of the Devi. As such, she is one of the central deities of the Goddess-oriented Shakta sect of Hinduism. Additionally, like many deities, Parvati appears in a number of different forms, each form or aspect identified with a different name. Along with Lakshmi (goddess of wealth and prosperity) and Saraswati (goddess of knowledge and learning), she forms the popular trinity of Hindu goddesses, the Tridevi, who are often depicted with their male consorts, the Trimurti of Vishnu, Shiva, and Brahma.

Parvati is also the wife of Shiva and the daughter of the mountain king Himavan and his consort Mena. Parvati herself is then the mother of the Hindu deities Ganesha and Kartikeya (Skanda). In some traditions, however, Parvati is the sister of Vishnu and is also identified as the river-goddess Ganga (Ganges). Along with Shiva, Parvati is a central deity in the Shaiva sect. In Shaiva tradition, she is the recreative energy and power of Shiva (his shakti), which means that she is therefore the cause of his actions in the world as well as the creator of the bond between all beings and their means of moksha, or liberation from the cycle of birth and death. In Hindu temples dedicated to her and to Shiva, she is symbolically represented as the argha or yoni, which then paired with the Lingam for worship.

In practice, the Parvati-Shiva Shaligram is either considered to be a variation of the Shiva Linga Shaligram (mainly in Shaivism) or a variation of the Mahashakti Shaligram (mainly in Shaktism). In either case, the Parvati-Shiva Shaligram is identified by its dual column formation; comprised of a Shiva Lingam on one side and a yoni or partial chakra-spiral on the other. In some versions of this Shaligram, the Shiva Lingam appears on one side while the other side is elongated and flattened (with a small depression in the center) as the manifestation of Parvati. Parvati-Shiva Shaligrams are formed by the joining of two shale nodules or by two ammonites at the base, giving the overall shila a smoothed heart-shape or, as is sometimes described, the shape of two hands pressed together but open at the palms.

Because these Shaligrams combine two particular sacred formations, a lingam and a yoni, they are also said to represent not only the union of male and female, but the manifestation of all universal knowledge in much the same way as the Satkona (the six-pointed star yantra) and the Yab Yum (a Buddhist representation of a male deity in sexual embrace with his female consort). Veneration of Parvati-Shiva Shaligrams are said to be especially powerful for married couples, and bestow blessings of a harmonious union, encourage marital equality or complementarity, and to bring about the birth of virtuous sons. Additionally, these Shaligrams are also said to reduce familial conflicts, to grant safety and security to women, and to prevent violence in the household (either by bringing about misfortune to the perpetrator or by causing them to leave the household).

ADDITIONAL REFERENCES

1. Dehejia, H.V. Parvati: Goddess of Love. Mapin.

2. Kinsley, David R. 1986. Hindu Goddesses: Vision of the Divine Feminine in the Hindu Religious Traditions. University of California Press.

3. Srivastava, A. L. 2004. Umā-Maheśvara: An iconographic study of the divine couple. Kasganj, U: Sukarkshetra Shodh Sansthana.

PITAMBARA SHALIGRAM

Pitambara with No Crown

Bagalamukhi or Bagala is one of the ten mahavidyas (great wisdom goddesses) in Hinduism. Bagalamukhi Devi specifically, is a goddess associated with the destruction of misconceptions and delusions (which may or may not be personified by the devotee's worldly enemies), where she is said to smash them with her cudgel. The word Bagala is derived from the word Valga; meaning the bit or bridle that is placed in a horse's mouth to control the movements of the tongue and the direction of the head. As with many deities in South Asia, this goddess has 108 different names (or in some traditions, 1108 names). However, Bagalamukhi is more commonly known as Pitambara Maa in North India, the goddess associated with the color yellow or with an overall golden hue and aura.

Pitambara also has a number of other meanings and connotations, from "one who wears a yellow robe," to Krishna's yellow dhoti in Vaishnavism, and in Buddhism as a reference to the yellow color of the cloth work by the Buddha at birth. In Shaligram traditions however, the Pitambara shila is almost always associated with Devi traditions where Bagalamukhi/Pitambara generally symbolizes the divine feminine, or the potent female primeval force of creation and agency in the universe (Mahashakti). Bagulamukhi is also sometimes taken to mean the back side of Shiva (usually the back of his head).

The principal temple of Pitambara is Srī Pītambra Pītha, a complex of Hindu temples (dedicated to the Shakta tradition – Mother Goddess worship), located in the city of Datia, in the Madhya Pradesh state of central India. It was, according to many legends, a 'Tapasthali' (a place of meditation) of many mythological as well as real life people. In practice, Pitambara Shaligrams are described as smooth, bright yellow, and round, with a single opening and two, clear, chakra-spirals. They are also one of the few Shaligram types not typically found in the upper Kali Gandaki region of Nepal. Rather, they appear more commonly further down in the river system, just south of the Himalayas.

The defining characteristic of Pitambara Shaligrams is their overall yellow or golden coloration. The Shaligram should also be generally round or oval in shape, with a single chakra-shell spiral opening near the side or base of the Shaligram. In some cases, the Shaligram may also contain a wide, ridged, crest formed by the back of the ammonite shell but this is not always necessary to the identification of this Shaligram. The presence of the ridge, however, is often referred to as the "Devi's crown" where it does appear.

The veneration of Pitambara Shaligrams is most commonly associated with goddess worship. More specifically, these Shaligrams are said to bestow blessings of wisdom, creativity, and the ability to discern reality "as it truly is." This means that the worship of these Shaligrams is designed to rid the devotee of false perceptions, misunderstandings, and mental conflicts. In some cases, these Shaligrams are also kept in the home as protection from personal enemies or from threats of deceit.

References

Praanatoshani Tantra pg. 351 – 356

Descriptions

Pitambara: Round in shape having some similarity with the buttock of a cow, and printed with one circular mark.

Additional References

1. "Pitambara," in the Cologne Digital Sanskrit Dictionaries: The Purana Index.
2. Sen, R., & Saktism, B. Category Archives: The Ten Mahavidyas.
3. Basumatary, P. 2020. Ambuvachi Festival:-A Socio-Cultural Study (Doctoral dissertation).

PRADYUMNA

Anirudda and Pradyumna Joined Together

In the Srimad Bhagavatam, Pradyumna is the son of Krishna and Rukmini. But along with Anirudda, Vasudeva, and Sankarsana, Pradyumna is also considered to be one of the four vyuha avatars of Vishnu (catur-vyuha) in Vaishnava theology (See Anirudda Shaligram). In other Hindu traditions, Pradyumna was an incarnation of Kama, the god of love and desire. Pradyumna is also a name of Vishnu, sometimes referred to as Vishnu Ankar Gupta. As such, he is listed as one of the 24 Keshava names of Vishnu referenced in the Mahabharata and in several Puranic texts. Finally, Pradyumna, as the son of Krishna, is identified as the twenty-first Kamadeva in the present half-time cycle (Avasarpini) in Jain cosmology.

In some Vaishnava traditions, Pradyumna is referred to as the "Transcendental Cupid" and is occasionally depicted in the regions of Dvaraka and Mathura in this fashion. As such, the Pradyumna Shaligram is often gifted to individuals whom others see as thinking more with their hearts than with their heads. Veneration of the Pradyumna Shaligram is also said to bestow greater reasoning and intellect as well as a stronger ability to resist emotional temptations of the heart. For this reason, these Shaligrams are commonly associated with qualities of dignity, confidence, concentration, and leadership and are thought to shift their specific blessings depending on the particular life-stage of the devotee: concentration and clear-headedness for youth, confidence and leadership for adulthood, and a renowned intellect and great austerities in old age.

Pradyumna Shaligrams are one of the few shilas actually identified by size. They are typically quite small with slightly elongated shapes and a single chakra-ridge along the top portion of the shila. The main body should be slim and somewhat flattened or, in some cases, paired with the distinctive Anirudda Shaligram as an additional ridge. Hence, in brief, Pradyumna Shaligrams should be small, oval-ish, shilas with a single top chakra ridge. They should not, however, be simply a broken piece of another Shaligram. Pradyumna Shaligrams are whole shilas in and of themselves and not fragmented sections of larger Shaligrams that have been damaged.

In practice, there are several variations of these Shaligrams:

1. Bahucchidrapradyuma has a small and elongated body, an elongated mouth, many holes, and one vadana with two chakras.

2. Krushnavarna Pradyumna is black in color with two dots somewhere on his body as well as one vadana and two chakras.

3. In South India, Pradyumna Shaligrams destined for temple worship are occasionally described as the color of a hibiscus flower (meaning red) with lines and scratches resembling a vanamala, a bow, an arrow or a lotus.

4. In rare cases, Pradyumna can also be bright yellow in color, as long as it maintains the same characteristics as noted above.

References

Praanatoshani Tantra pg. 348, Praanatoshani Tantra pg. 361, Skanda Purana, Nagarkhanda, 244: 3-9, Brahmavaivartta (Prakritikhanda, Ch. 21), Garuda Purana (Panchanan Tarkaratna, Part 1, Ch. 45), Agni Purana; Bengavasi ed., Panchanan Tarkaratna, Saka 1812, Ch. 46

DESCRIPTIONS

Color of a new cloud, small circular mark and several small holes over His body (BV).
Yellow color, long shape, and small opening (G). Having 6 chakras (G).
(i) Yellow in color with a small opening and having several linear marks both at the top as well as on the sides.
(ii) Blue in color with many holes at His small mouth, and having a comparatively long shape. (P)

ADDITIONAL REFERENCES

1. "Srimad Bhagavatam: Canto 10 - Chapter 55". bhagavata.org. Retrieved 11 July 2022.
2. Benton, Catherine. 2006. God of Desire: Tales of Kamadeva in Sanskrit Story Literature. SUNY Press.
3. Krishnamachariar, M. 1989 [1937], History of Classical Sanskrit Literature, Motilal Banarsidass.

PRTHU

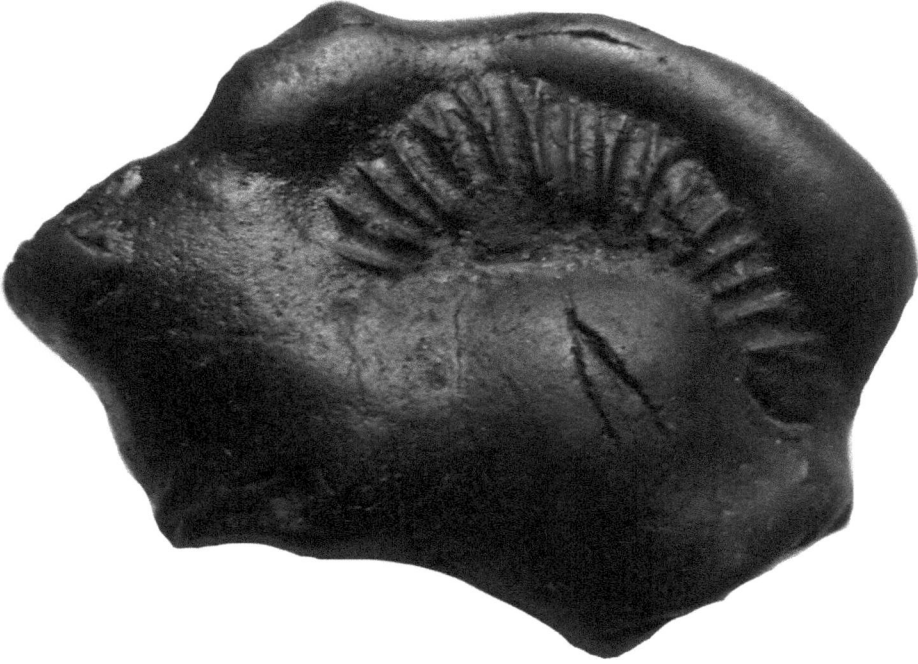

Prithu is the name of a sovereign (chakravartin), referenced in the Vedic scriptures. In some Hindu traditions, he is also an avatar of Vishnu, though not generally included in Dasavatara theology. Sometimes called Pruthu, Prithi and Prithu Vainya (Prithu the son of Vena) he is often celebrated as the first true king, from whom the earth received her name Prithvi. He is mainly associated with a legend that involves him chasing the Earth goddess, Prithvi, who attempts to escape him in the form of a cow but who eventually agrees to yield her milk as the world's grain and vegetation. The Mahabharata and the Vishnu Purana, however, list him among the avatars of Vishnu. The Prithu Shaligram is so rare in practice that only a few active versions of this Shaligram are generally considered to be in use. Additionally, because of its single, later, Puranic reference, many Shaligram traditions do not recognize this name-type at all and subsume its characteristics under any number of other avatar types, most notably the Padmanabha, Padma, or Mahavishnu – Dasavatara Shaligram categories.

When it does appear in practice, the Prithu Shaligram is typically associated with guardianship or stewardship of the environment (especially fields or orchards). Veneration of this Shaligram is said to bestow great healing to physical wounds in both human and animal bodies as well as to the world itself. It is also sometimes said to bestow liberation from the influences of evil spirits, especially in cases of possession. Due to its exceptional rarity in practice, there is no specific consensus on identifying this Shaligram. However, most ritual specialists agree that is should appear with a partial chakra-spiral, contain a rounded central nodule, a number of small holes or indentations, and a marking in the shape of a lotus flower somewhere on the main body of the shila. A number of Shaligram traditions, however, would not identify this Shaligram given the markings described above and would identify a Shaligram with said features as either Padmanabha, Padma, or Mahavishnu depending on the specific formation of characteristics present.

REFERENCES

Garuda Purana (Panchanan Tarkaratna, Part 1, Ch. 45) -- Not found in Agni Purana; Bengavasi ed., Panchanan Tarkaratna, Saka 1812, Ch. 46

DESCRIPTIONS

Long linear mark, circular mark, and a lotus. Has one or more holes (G).

ADDITIONAL REFERENCES

1. "Prthu," Monier Williams Sanskrit-English Dictionary (2008 revision). https://www.sanskrit-lexicon.uni-koeln.de/
2. Gonda, Jan. 1993. Aspects of Early Visnuism. Motilal Banarsidass Publ. p. 164.
3. Nagendra Kumar Singh. 1997. Encyclopaedia of Hinduism. Anmol Publications.

PUNDARIKAAKSHA

Pundarikaaksha
Pushkaraksha

Pundarikaaksha is the 111th name of Vishnu in the Vishnu Sahasranama and means "He who has lotus eyes" or conversely "He who is like eyes for those who dwell in the heaven called Pundarika." The name is similar to Pushkaraksha, which is 40th and also a variant of this form that appears as a Shaligram with the same general features described below but has smoothed, flattened, "eyes" that are more even and balanced. Like the majority of later-reference Puranic Shaligrams, Pundarikaaksha Shaligrams are relatively rare in practice. Madhwas Brahmins, however, recognize three distinct subtypes of this particular Shaligram: one with a single chakra and white coloration, one with two lotus-like markings, and one with a lotus marking near the primary opening along with two holes near the bottom or side of the Shaligram's "face."

Many Shaligram interpretive traditions, however, do not recognize this name-type category. As such, a Shaligram with the given characteristics might also be interpreted as a manifestation of Lakshmi-Narayan or Padmanabha, or, in cases where the outer body of the shila is rounded and smooth, Krishna. As a result, some Vaishnava traditions recognize these Shaligrams as a variant form (rupa) of the Madhusudana Shaligram. This is because the compound word is made up of pundarikam and aksham. Pundarikam means "a lotus flower, especially a white lotus." Aksham means "eye." Thus, the word Pundarikaaksha means "the lotus-eyed one" which is a common epithet for Krishna.

The veneration of Pundarikaaksha Shaligrams is said to bestow similar blessings to the worship of Narayana, Lakshmi-Narayana, and Mahavishnu Shaligrams and for those who actively seek these shilas, the benefits are described as compounded. Meaning, that the veneration of a Pundarikaaksha Shaligram can potentially bestow the benefits of all three types of Shaligrams if cared for properly. The formation of this Shaligram is somewhat complex in that it typically contains a single dual-chakra ammonite mold (vadana/opening) along with two holes reminiscent of eyes set high on a "face" or, alternatively, two rounded markings on either side of the vadana (sometimes referred to as lotus markings in other Shaligrams). Some practitioners also require that the "face" of the Shaligram be "smiling" in order to identify this particular name-type.

REFERENCES

Skanda Purana, Nagarekhanda, 244: 3-9, Praanatoshani Tantra pg. 351 – 356.

DESCRIPTION:

Pundarikaaksham: Printed with two eye-like marks either on a side or at the top (P)

ADDITIONAL REFERENCES

1. Bezbaroa, L. 2004. History of Vaishnavism in India. A Creative Vision–Essays on Sankardeva and Neo-Vaishnava Movement in Assam.

2. Jash, P., & Jash, P. 1979, January. "Vaisnavism In Ancient Southeast Asia." In Proceedings of the Indian History Congress (Vol. 40, pp. 932-942). Indian History Congress.

PURUSHOTTAMA

Purushottama can be interpreted to mean a number of things, including "Supreme Purusha (Being)," "Supreme God," "One who is the Supreme Purusha beyond the Kshara (The destroyable material world)," and "Akshara" (The undestroyable Atman)." Purushottama is also one of the names of Vishnu and is listed as the 24th name of Vishnu in the Vishnu Sahasranama. According to the Bhagavad Gita, Purushottam is described as above and beyond all other kshar and akshar purushas (material and celestial beings) or simply as the only truly omnipotent cosmic being. The Purushottama was also explained by the philosopher Haridas Chaudhuri (1913–1975) as representing that ineffable phenomenon which lies beyond the undifferentiated existence of God. Sri Ram, for example, the 7th avatar of Vishnu, is sometimes referred to as Maryada Purushottama and Krishna, his 8th avatar, is known as Leela or Purn Purushottama.

In the Garuda Purana, Purushottama Shaligrams are those Shaligrams which clearly demonstrate eight visible chakras. However, in practice, the identification of these Shaligrams tends to be done using a combination of characteristics, including a single large chakra with only the top section clearly visible, a wide, almost triangular base, and one or two white markings (vanamala) crossing the main body of the shila. Other traditions require Purushottama Shaligrams to have eight visible chakras (clear or unclear) which face upwards while the Shaligram is sits balanced on a flat surface. Because Purushottama is also often associated with both Ram and Krishna, however, some Shaligram traditions will identify the first formation type (single ammonite cast with white marking of the vanamala) as a Sri Ram Shaligram and not Purushottama alone. There are similar traditions involving the interpretation of Krishna Shaligrams as combinations of Krishna and Purushottama (both in characteristics and in name). For this reason, Purushottama Shaligrams often vary widely depending on the specific religious tradition in question and whether or not deities are combined in a single shila.

As a result, the formation of Purushottam Shaligrams depends on the particular tradition in question. Some versions of these Shaligrams are single ammonite casts embedded in a large, triangular, shale nodule which usually contains at least one line of white quartz crossing the main portion of the ammonite (pictures 1 and 2). The more common formation of these Shaligrams, however, is the single rounded shale nodule with multiple ammonite molds visible near the top and sides of the shila (picture 3 and 4, opposite). Veneration of Purushottama Shaligrams is said to create a general atmosphere of devotion and respect for society and communal decision-making. These Shaligrams are also said to bestow blessings of dignity (even in defeat), a strong will and sense of determination, and protections against gossip, a loss of social standing, or other social misfortunes.

In practice, there are several variations of this Shaligram:

1. Dvaracakrapuruhhottama has one vadana with two chakras at the entrance along with the markings of a noose and an elephant goad. Finally, there will be a circle mark somewhere inside.

2. Puranapurushottama is a grass-green shila with a minute opening. It may also be brown-black or reddish in color with many chakras.

3. Garuda-Purushottama has the markings of Garuda's wings or feathers, the markings of arrows and a chakra covering the vadana. The chakra should be on the top of the Shaligram and its shape determines which type of Purushottama it is (either Vishnu, Ram, or Krishna)

4. In other traditions, the Purushottama Shaligram is any shila with four vadanas and eight chakras.

REFERENCES

Skanda Purana, Nagarekhanda, 244: 3-9, Praanatoshani Tantra pg. 348, Praanatoshani Tantra pg. 361

DESCRIPTIONS

(i) golden in color with a circular mark at the middle portion of His body and a bigger circular mark at the top.

(ii) Yellow in color and marked with dot-prints on all sides.

(iii) With openings on all sides numbering about ten. (P)

Having 8 chakras (G).

ADDITIONAL REFERENCES

1. Rajaguru, S.N. 1992. Inscriptions of Jagannath Temple and Origin of Sri Purusottam Jagannath. Vol. 1–2. Puri: Shri Jagannath Sanskrit Vishvavidyalaya.

2. Sadhu, Paramtattvadas 2017. An introduction to Swaminarayan Hindu theology. Cambridge, United Kingdom: Cambridge University Press.

RADA RAM OR SRI RAM

Sri Ram Shaligrams showing white arrows.

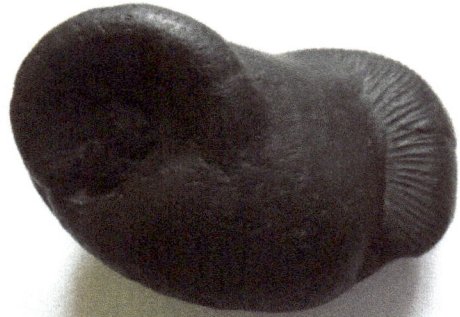

Ram-Sita Shaligram

Rama, Sri Ram, or Srī Rāmachandra is the 7th avatar of Vishnu and the central figure of the Hindu epic, Ramayana (Where Ram, the king of Ayodhya, defeats the demon-king Ravana in order to rescue his wife Sita). Ram is also an extremely popular deity whose representations in religious texts, scriptures, and historical narratives have been a formative component of numerous literary, artistic, and religious cultures throughout South and Southeast Asia. Along with Krishna, Rama is considered to be one of the most important avatars of Vishnu. In Rama-centric sects, he is sometimes considered to be the Supreme Being, rather than an avatar. Additionally, in some Hindu traditions, Rama and his brothers Lakshman, Bharat, and Shatrughna are recognized as another manifestation of the "chaturvyuha" expansions of Vishnu (Vasudev, Sankarshan, Pradyumna, Aniruddha).

Sri Ram Shaligrams are extremely popular and are identified in one of two ways; by the presence of an "arrow" or "bow" marking on the Shaligram or by the presence of a single chakra with a wide, white, marking (vanamala) crossing the body of the shila described as having the shape of a "hen's egg." There is occasionally some confusion regarding the first type because the "arrow" marking (a white belemnite fossil) is often interpreted as markings of the Shiva Linga in Shaiva traditions, though the "arrow" marking of Ram is generally accepted to be smaller, thinner, and slanted across the Shaligram rather than sitting upright in the form of a column.

Another popular variation of this Shaligram is the Sita-Ram Shaligram, which contains an additional smooth, rounded, chakra joined to the opposite side of the main chakra so that the two central spirals face away from one another. One final variation of this Shaligram is similar to a Krishna Shaligram: smooth, round, and unmarked but with a single central white vanamala marking crossing through the center of the shila (See also Raghnuath Shaligram).

The most common formation of Sri Ram Shaligrams contain at least one white "arrow" marking created by the fracture and wear of a belemnite fossil within the central portion of the shale nodule. Other formations of this Shaligram are either a single ammonite cast or, conversely, an unmarked black shale nodule both with a white quartz line bisecting the central part of the stone. Overall, however, the principal characteristics practitioners look for is a round, elongated, body (hen's egg), the markings of an arrow or bow, and blue-black or brownish color. Whether or not this shila has chakras also tends to be incidental. It can have no chakras, or several.

Veneration of Ram Shaligrams is said to bestow multiple blessings regarding strong ties with family members (particularly brothers and wives) and the ability to negotiate family tensions to a good outcome. These Shaligrams are also associated with leading a "kingly" life, with maintaining strong family honor, and with the formation of life-long friendships. As direct manifestations of Sri Ram though, they tend to act as a household's principal deity and are therefore, typically the largest Shaligrams allowed in home worship.

References

Praanatoshani Tantra pg. 347, Brahmavaivartta (Prakritikhanda, Ch. 21)

DESCRIPTIONS

» Round and middle in shape with prints of arrows all over His body. Must have two circular marks and prints of arrows or quiver (BV).

» Round and middle in shape with prints of arrows all over His body. He must have two circular marks and prints of a quiver with arrows on His body. (BV)

(i) Yellow in color and printed with the mark of the bow.

(ii) Green in color and glaced, having a stick like mark on the back side and two linear marks on the rear sides.

(iii) Ranaraama: Middle in size, round in shape and marked with two circles, and arrow, a quiver and several dot-prints.

(iv) Raajaraajeshvara: Round in shape, middle in size and printed with two circular marks at the opening. His body is marked with the prints of an umbrella, an arrow, a quiver, and several dots resembling the wounds caused by arrows.

(v) Sitaaraam: (a) Cloudy in color, with one opening, and printed with marks resembling teeth, bow, arrow, spear, umbrella, flag, chowry and garland. (b) With two openings each furnished with two circular marks and also with a circular print on His left side.

(vi) Dashakanthakulaantaka Raama: (a) Like an egg of a hen in size, green in color, and having two openings with two linear marks at each of them, and also with the mark of a bow. His top side is comparatively higher. (b) Printed with a linear mark resembling a bow on each side, other things being the same as above.

(vii) Viiraraama: Printed with an arrow, a quiver, a bow, an ear-ring, a garland, and a small circular mark decorated with petals.

(viii) Vijayaraama: Printed with an arrow, a bow, a quiver, and a big opening marked with red dots. A circular mark decorated with petals also is printed on His body or at the opening.

(ix) Raamamurtti: or Kavitavada Raama: Black in color and glaced, having one opening with a circular mark.

(x) Dushthararaama: Cloudy in color with the mark resembling one's knee, and also with a bow and arrow on the top side and footprints of a cow on the rear sides (P).

ADDITIONAL REFERENCES

1. Tulasīdāsa. 1999. Sri Ramacaritamanasa. Translated by Prasad, RC. Motilal Banarsidass. pp. 871–872

2. Valmiki. Ramayana. Gorakhpur, India: Gita Press.

3. Blank, Jonah. 2000. Arrow of the Blue-Skinned God: Retracing the Ramayana Through India. Grove Press; Reprint edition

RAGHUNATH

Raghunath - Sri Ram Shaligram (Sky-colored)

Raghunath Shaligram (front and top view)

Raghu is best known as one of the renowned kings of the Ikshvaku dynasty (whose father was called Dirghabahu). His son was Aja who begat a son named Dasaratha who was the father of the famous brothers Rama, Lakshmana, Bharata, and Shatrughna (See also Sri Ram Shaligram). Thus, Raghu was the great-grandfather of Sri Ram of the Ramayana. The name Raghu itself means "Fast One," said to be derived from his chariot riding abilities. He was a great heroic personality in his time who therefore passed his patronymic name onto his descendants.

As such, Raghunath translates as "Lord of the Raghus," or "Lord of the Dynasty of Raghu." Which also means, according to Hindu, Jain, and Sikh scriptures, when Mahavishnu or Shrihari was incarnated in the home of Dasaratha, in the family of Raghu, he appeared as the avatar Ram who is also called Raghunath (just as Krishna is also sometimes called Yadunath meaning Lord of Yadavas clan). Most Shaligram traditions recognize two versions of the Raghunath Shaligram. The first is nearly identical to the single chakra-white vanamala formation of the Sri Ram Purushottama Shaligram but with the exception of appearing as "sky-colored" (See photo 1, opposite).

In other words, a black, single chakra, Shaligram with a white vanamala marking crossing the central portion of the shila would be identified as a Sri Ram Shaligram/Purushottama Ram. The same Shaligram that is grey, slate-blue, or light blue in color is identified as Raghunath. The second variation is a round, black, Shaligram similar to the Krishna-type Shaligrams but with four prominent chakras arranged within two openings. Raghunath Shaligrams should ideally be formed from lighter grey or bluish slates rather than the characteristic black shales of most Shaligrams.

Additionally, most of these Shaligrams will contain either one or two prominent quartz-infiltrate lines (form 1) or contain a series of internal ammonite casts, with two casts taking up the majority of the shale nodule in a layered position (form 2). Veneration of Raghunath Shaligrams is said to bestow similar blessings to that of the Sri Ram Shaligram with the addition of being especially good for yogis, ascetics, or particularly religious devotees. This is because the worship of this Shaligram is said to provide exceptional meditative states from its position as a manifestation of the endless, joyous, consciousness of Paramatma, the Universal Soul.

REFERENCES

Pranatoshani Tantra pg. 347, Brahmavaivartta (Prakritikhanda, Ch. 21)

DESCRIPTIONS

Two openings, four circular marks, color of a new cloud (BV).
He has two openings with four circular marks. His body also is marked with the footprint of a cow, but not with any mark of vanamala. (BV)

ADDITIONAL REFERENCES

1. Vishnu Purana, 4:4

2. Mani, Vettam. 1975. Puranic Encyclopedia. A Comprehensive work with Special Reference to the Epic and Puranic Literature. Motilal Banarsidass Publishing House

Raj Rajeshwar

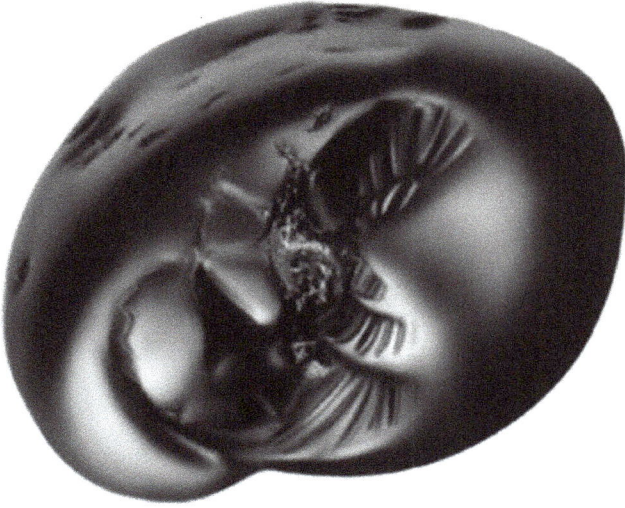

A Rare Sri Chakra/Sri Yantra Shaligram

Rajarajeshwari is the presiding goddess of Sri Chakra or Sri Yantra, a manifestation of the divine in the form of mystical diagram (yantra). The diagram is formed by nine interlocking triangles that surround and radiate out from the central (bindu) point. The two-dimensional Sri Chakra, when it is projected into three dimensions, is then called a Maha Meru or Mount Meru, a sacred mountain with five peaks in Hindu, Jain, and Buddhist cosmology; which is considered to be the center of all physical, metaphysical and spiritual universes. Sri Chakra also represents the goddess (Devi) in her form of Sri Lalita or Tripura Sundari: "The beauty of the three worlds" - Bhu, Bhuva and Swa. (Earth, Atmosphere, and Sky/ Heaven).

In most contexts, she is known as Tripurāsundarī (Beautiful Goddess of the Three Cities) but the Devi also has a variety of other names including Ṣhoḍaśhi ("Sixteen"), Lalitā ("She Who Plays"), Lilavati/Leelavati ("Playful, Charming"), and Rājarājeśvarī ("Queen of Queens, Supreme Ruler" or "Invincible One"). As such, Rajarajeshwari is one of a group of ten goddesses collectively called Mahavidyas or Dasha-Mahavidyas. She is the foremost and the most important in Dasha-Mahavidyas popular in the Shri Vidya school of Tantra and in the Shakti or Devi traditions of Hinduism. Her consort is Maha Kameswara Shiva and she is also considered to be the highest aspect of the Mother Goddess Adi Shakti. In some traditions, Parvati, the wife of Shiva, is the complete incarnation of Lalita Maha Tripura Sundari and Tripurasundari is the primary goddess associated with the Shakta Tantric tradition of Sri Vidya.

In practice, Raj Rajeshwar Shaligrams are described as being "umbrella-shaped" with a single or continuing chakra-spiral visible on the flattened bottom section or as having an elongated body with two chakra-spirals, one at each end. Additionally, the body of the Shaligram will have seven or more circular indentations or holes typically located on the top or sides (top and bottom being relative to how the Shaligram sits when placed on a flat surface; broader at the bottom, more angular or narrow at the top). Raj Rajeshwar Shaligrams are considered to be rare but are highly sought after by pilgrims and devotees of multiple religious traditions. Veneration of this Shaligram is said to reveal two-fold results.

The first, in relation to the goddess's aspect as one who bestows joy on all sentient beings, worship of this Shaligram brings tremendous good luck, worldly fame, respect of family members, and true insight into the Self. The second, in relation to her aspect as a righteous protector, worship of this Shaligram also brings destruction to foul thoughts or inclinations, metes punishment on those who cause harm to others, and reveals hidden evils present in devotees' lives. Finally, many ritual specialists explain that this Shaligram can only be properly worshipped through the yearly performance of a fire sacrifice (yajna) and anyone who is not prepared to adhere to a strict schedule of ritual veneration should not attempt to keep Shaligrams of this type.

REFERENCES

Pranatoshani Tantra pg. 347, Brahmavaivartta (Prakritikhanda, Ch. 21)

DESCRIPTIONS

Middle size, seven circular marks and marks of umbrella and grass or quiver (BV).

Middle in size, having seven circular marks and also the marks of an umbrella and grass (or quiver) on His body. (BV)

ADDITIONAL REFERENCES

1. Dikshitar, V.R. Ramachandra. 1991. The Lalita Cult. Delhi: Motilal Banarsidass.

2. Coburn, Thomas B. 1991. Encountering the Goddess: A Translation of the Devi-Mahatmya and a Study of Its Interpretation. SUNY Press.

3. Kinsley, David.1998. Hindu Goddesses: Vision of the Divine Feminine in the Hindu Religious Traditions. Berkeley: University of California Press.

4. Srivastava, M. C. 1979. Mother goddess in Indian art, archaeology & literature.

RATNAGHARBHA

With Light

With Light

Without Light

Without Light

The Ratnagharbha or Ratna Garva Shaligram is also sometimes referred to as the Red Jyoti Shaligram. This Shaligram usually appears as a small, black, pebble-like shila that, when light is shown through it (particularly sunlight), glows a translucent red or orange. Ratnagarbha Shaligrams typically do not contain any chakras or holes, and in fact, are not comprised of shale or slate. Rather, naturally occurring Ratnagharbha Shaligrams are almost entirely made of quartz. Additionally, Ratnagharbha roughly translates to "jewel-filled" or "jewel-like" and is commonly associated with Kubera, the Yaksha king of wealth and prosperity (See also Kubera Shaligram).

In practice, Ratnagharbha Shaligrams are believed to bestow knowledge regarding one's past lives and to be capable of freeing trapped spirits. In some traditions, it is also said that shining light through a Ratnagarbha Shaligram on certain auspicious Jayanti days will allow the devotee to see all ten Dasavatara forms (the ten incarnations of Vishnu: Matsya, Kurma, Varaha, Narsimha, Vaman, Parshuram, Ram, Krishna, Buddha and Kalki) on the day of their particular incarnations.

For the most part, this Shaligram typically forms as a single, round, pebble-like stone generally no bigger than a few centimeters in diameter. When held up to a light source, the otherwise dark stone will demonstrate a translucent quality and refract the light into red, orange, yellow, or most rarely blue, colors. As one of the rarest Shaligrams, the Ratnagharbha bestows spiritual protection and renders spaces free of angry spirits and bad karma. In other cases, this Shaligram is also said to grant devotees with a good internal intuition and improve the senses. Many practitioners therefore include the Ratnagarbha Shaligram on their altars when they desire protection from sudden losses and accidents, or wish to undertake significant philanthropic activities and begin a new practice of austerity.

REFERENCES

The Pṛithvī Sūkta or Bhūmī Sūkta is a celebrated hymn of the Atharvaveda (AVŚ 12.1) and is dedicated to Prithvi. Prithvi, meaning "the Vast One," is the Sanskrit name for the earth as well as the name of a devi (goddess) in both Hinduism and Buddhism. Ratnagharbha is one of the twenty-one epithets of Prithvi mentioned in the sūktas and means "repository of jewels."

There is some debate, however, as to whether or not the Ratnagarbha is actually a Shaligram. Some traditions include it, others do not.

ADDITIONAL REFERENCES

1. "Ratnagharbha" in the Cologne Digital Sanskrit Dictionaries: Edgerton Buddhist Hybrid Sanskrit Dictionary.

2. Leeming, David and Christopher Fee. 2016. The Goddess: Myths of the Great Mother. Reaktion Books.

3. Shaw, Miranda Eberle. 2006. Buddhist Goddesses of India. Princeton University Press.

SAMUDRA MANTHAN/SONA PARBAT

Also referred to as the Sona Parbat (Golden Mountain) Shaligram, Samudra Manthan Shaligrams are notably rare due to their combinations of relatively large size and gold (iron pyrite) color. Interpreted using a combination of markers such as the overall shape of the shila and the appearance of golden "droplets" or "golden flows" along the outer surface, Samudra Manthan Shaligrams are identified using the criteria in the Hari Bhakti Vilasa 5/257 from the Skanda Purana and sections 258-259 of the Srimad Bhagavatam 11. 27. 12-14.

In reference to these texts, Samudra Manthan Shaligrams are then said to appear in places where the nectar that flowed out of the sacred mountain while it rested on Kurma's back (see Kurma Shaligram) dripped down onto the physical world, hence the characteristic golden coloration.

In some cases, other gods and goddesses are also expected to manifest within these shilas, including any one of several "akrutis (forms)" of other gods or demons (asuras) or any one of the 14 Ratnas (gems or treasures) that emerged out of the milky ocean. These manifestations will then be represented by other markings and formations present on the Shaligram. As a result, Samudra Manthan Shaligrams are said to bestow exceptional spiritual enlightenment, strong concentration skills, and emotional and mental stability.

As a Shaligram strongly associated with amrita, the "nectar of immortality," Samudra Manthan Shaligrams are also associated, in practice, with protection from poisons or from spoiled food and are often presented in situations where pollution, disease, or pestilence has caused significant damage to crops, livestock, or water supplies.

Samudra Manthan Shaligrams appear in a variety of forms, but are most commonly identified using a significant presence of iron pyrites, which give the Shaligram its golden color. These Shaligrams also usually contain a large nodule of shale near the top of the stone or a smooth, wide, base that gives it an overall triangular or "mountain-like" appearance. Some formations of this Shaligram are therefore described as appearing like "a sun rising over a mountain," depending on what combination of features are present.

REFERENCES

Sanskrit: समुद्रमन्थन, lit. Churning of the Ocean. While the Samudra Manthan Shaligram is not mentioned by name in Puranic texts, the story of the churning of the milky ocean is one of the best-known episodes in the creation stories of Hindu cosmology. The story appears in the Bhagavata Purana, the Mahabharata, the Ramayana, and in the Vishnu Purana.

ADDITIONAL REFERENCES

1. Chaturvedi, B. K. 2006. Vishnu Purana. Diamond Pocket Books (P) Ltd.

2. Krishnan, K. S. 2019. Origin of Vedas. Notion Press.

3. Sinha, Purnendu Narayana. 1901. A Study of the Bhagavata Purana: Or, Esoteric Hinduism. Freeman & Company, Limited. p. 170.

SHANKARSHAN

Front & Side

According to the Bhagavata Purana, the cosmic serpent, Ananta-Śesha is also called Sankarshana, where he represents the tamasic energy (Tamas, meaning the quality of imbalance, chaos, and disorder) of Vishnu-Narayan. Dwelling deep within the inner layers of Patala (subterranean underworld), Sankarshana reigns as the nagaraja or the serpent-king of the nagas, the snake-race who bear gems on their heads (See also Ananta Shaligram). Sankarshana is also said to have existed since before the creation of the universe and when the universe is due to come to an end, he will create eleven rudras (meaning here "gods of the middle world," also envoys of Shiva) who will destroy the universe so that a new one might be created.

Additionally, in some Hindu traditions, Sankarshana is actually no different than Vishnu-Narayan himself (and is included in his four vyuha forms along with Anirudda, Vasudeva, and Pradyumna), having expanded to become Garbhodakshayi-Vishnu during the beginning of the universe and thus to create Brahma. Lastly, the identification of this Shaligram can become complicated given that Sankarshana is also a name given to Krishna's brother Balaram and occasionally to Rama's brother Lakshmana (who are avatars of Śesha as "brothers of Vishnu").

The defining characteristic of the Shankarshan Shaligram is in having two clearly defined chakra-spirals which join together on one side. Additionally, this Shaligram is identified by having reddish spots or a partial red coloration located somewhere on the body of the shila (or within the chakras, as is more often the case). One variation of this Shaligram has two joined chakras within a single primary opening, which differs from the Lakshmi-Narayan Shaligram only in that the two opposing chakra-spirals meet at the edge or at the bottom rather than completely facing one another. Lastly, in some Shaligram traditions, Shankarshan Shaligrams are Shaligrams with markings of the chakra (discus spiral), shankha (conch shell), gada (mace), and padma (lotus), in that order, but this interpretation is uncommon in practice.

The formation of Shankarshan Shaligrams comes from the wearing of a black shale nodule containing two partially attached ammonite casts, followed by the oxidization of the iron or iron pyrite deposits on the outer surface (giving it the reddish color). Conversely, it may contain a single complete ammonite cast where the two sides of the shell-spiral meet along the outer edge. In many cases, this Shaligram will also appear to have a full outline around the main vadana (created by the rest of the worn ammonite). This outline comprises the "gada marking" in the latter interpretive tradition.

Veneration of Shankarshan Shaligrams is similar to that of Ananta Shaligrams and is associated with wisdom, memory, and learning. This particular Shaligram, however, is also said to be best employed in rituals for the dead, to appease unquiet spirits, and to help prepare the terminally ill for death and possible rebirth. Shankarshan Shaligrams are also said to be particularly effective in circumstances of personal chaos and tribulation, where their presence helps to encourage the creation of new opportunities out of the loss of previous ones.

REFERENCES

Praanatoshani Tantra pg. 347, Praanatoshani Tantra pg. 361, Skanda Purana, Nagarekhanda, 244: 3-9, Brahmavaivartta (Prakritikhanda, Ch. 21), Garuda Purana (Panchanan Tarkaratna, Part 1, Ch. 45), Agni Purana; Bengavasi ed., Panchanan Tarkaratna, Saka 1812, Ch. 46

DESCRIPTIONS

Has two circular marks joined with each other on the top side of His body (BV).

Reddish in color, two circular marks joined with each other, and a mark of a lotus on east side of His body (G). Having 7 chakras (G).

(i) With two circular marks joined with each other on the top side.

(ii) Reddish in color with the glaced and spotless eastern side, and marked with two circles joined with each other.

(iii) Balabhadra: Marked with seven circular prints.

(iv) Balarama: With five linear marks on the top side and a bow and an arrow on the rear sides (P).

ADDITIONAL REFERENCES

1. Haq, Kaiser. 2015. The Triumph of the Snake Goddess. Harvard University Press.

2. Handa, Om Chanda. 2004. Naga Cults and Traditions in the Western Himalaya. Indus Publishing.

SHANKHA/LAKSHMI SHANKH

The Dakshinavarti Shankh or Sri Lakshmi Shankh, is a ritual object common in both Hindu and Buddhist ritual practices. Otherwise known in English as a conch shell, this is the shell of a large sea snail from the Indian Ocean (Turbinella pyrum sp.), but one that has the very rare reverse-turning spiral. In other words, when it is held with the spout (siphonal canal) pointed up, the Lakshmi conch's spiral twists rightwards (dakshinavarti) rather than very much more common form, which twists leftwards (vamavarti).

As such, the Shankha Shaligram appears similarly, with an ovoid tear-drop or conch-like shape and an opening or protruding ridge reminiscent of the rim of a shell. In some variations of this Shaligram, there is no visible opening but rather the ridge of chakra-spiral extending from the top of the rounded, central, body of the shila all the way down one side to form a conch-like lip at the base (some traditions interpret Shaligrams of this type as being combinations of the Lakshmi Shankh and the deity Kuber – See Kubera Shaligram). Lastly, some variations of the Shaligram are similar in appearance to the Surya Shaligram but contain a spiral which moves from thin to wide again in a similar manner to that of the conch shell.

The Shankha Shaligram is most typically used in conjunction with the Gada Dhar and Padma Shaligrams (See Gada Dhar Shaligram and Madhusudana Shaligram) during puja daily worship but can also be included in a home shrine alone, where it should be placed in the northern-most part of the altar. Veneration of this Shaligram is distinctly associated with blessing of wealth and good fortune. It is also associated with bringing about family harmony in cases of strife and with bestowing physical vigor and energy. Drinking water that has been used to bathe this Shaligram is often used in traditional healing rites and in some traditions of Ayurvedic medicine.

The most distinctive feature of Shankha Shaligrams is their characteristic shape, being that of a conch-shell. In Shaligram traditions that do not recognize this specific name-type, Shankh Shaligrams may alternately be identified as Lakshmi Shaligrams (when their chakra-spiral ammonite mold is clearly visible) or as another type of Surya or Mahashakti Shaligram (See Mahashakti Shaligram). Like most of the "object" Shaligrams, Shankh Shaligrams are not specifically referenced in Puranic texts but are none-the-less common in many Shaligram interpretive traditions.

Additional References

1. Ellingson, T. 1979. The Mandala of Sound: Concepts and Sound Structures in Tibetan Ritual Music. Ann Arbor, Michigan: UMI

2. Hornell, James. 1914. The sacred Chank of India: A monograph of the Indian Conch (Turbinella pyrum) – Online Book. The Superintendent, Government Press, Madras.

3. Jansen, Eva Rudy. 1993. The Book of Hindu Imagery: Gods, Manifestations and Their Meaning. Diever: Binkey Kok Publications. pp. 144.

4. Rao, T. A. Gopinatha (1985). Elements of Hindu iconography. Delhi: Motilal Banarsidass Publishers

SHASHIDHARA/CHANDRAMAULI

A variation of the Harihara Shaligram, Shashidhara or Chandramauli Shaligrams are a particular manifestation of Shiva as the "celestial ascetic." Most often identified by their combined characteristics of the white crescent-moon marking (a "Shashi" (moon)) and the general shape of a Shiva Lingam, these Shaligrams are considered to be comparatively rare in relation to the more typical Harihara Shaligram manifestation.

Shashidhara Shaligrams tend to be most highly sought after by Shaiva and Smarta Hindu traditions and are especially prized in Himalayan worship due to their associations with Shiva in his mountain hermitage. These Shaligrams are also said to prefer worship with water from the Ganges River more so than any other particular offering.

The most common appearance of the Shashidhara Shaligram is that of a smooth, black, shale nodule that contains a half-moon or crescent-moon marking which is created by the wearing of a white, quartz, infiltrate. In some cases, these Shaligrams also have gold spots or flecks resulting from the wearing of iron pyrites within the shale. Note particularly that Shashidhara Shaligrams do not contain chakra-spirals. Such a Shaligram would be identified as Harihara (See Harihara Shaligram)

Veneration of Shashidhara Shaligrams is said to bestow blessings of harmony between the body and the mind and to help in the healing of ailments related to the back, joints, and neck. These Shaligrams are also associated with proper respect towards familial obligation, such as the duty of children to care for their parents and the duty of parents to provide for their children.

As such, Shashidhara Shaligrams are said to spontaneously conjure boons of food, housing, and material wealth in times of need or where the livelihood of the family and community is directly in peril. Lastly, these Shaligrams are also particularly prized for their blessings of strong relationships due to the fact that their presence is said to improve the balance of energies between people and between people and their surroundings.

ADDITIONAL REFERENCES

1. Chakravarti, Mahadev. 1986. The Concept of Rudra-Śiva Through The Ages (Second Revised ed.). Delhi: Motilal Banarsidass

2. Flood, Gavin. 2003. "The Śaiva Traditions". In Flood, Gavin (ed.). The Blackwell Companion to Hinduism. Malden, MA: Blackwell Publishing.

3. Fuller, Christopher John. 2004. The Camphor Flame: Popular Hinduism and society in India. Princeton, New Jersey: Princeton University Press.

SHIMSHMARA

Shimshumara or Shimshumaramurti, which means scorpion (or sometimes, "dolphin"), is a somewhat obscure name of Vishnu. In his iconography, Shimshumara has characteristics similar to that of a scorpion but possesses a man's head and torso. In some traditions of Hindu cosmology, Shimshumara is the Cosmic Scorpion who stands upside down and holds all of the stars and planets within his legs with his tail arching overhead. Shimshumara is also the deity who decides the lifespan for Brahma. This is because Vishnu (Narayana) is the only truly eternal existence in creation. Even his consort Lakshmi only becomes immortal (as, nitya Sumangali, in the Vedas) when she is married to Vishnu-Narayan.

The Mundaakopanishhad 4.11 citation from the Brahamanda Purana in the Bhagavata - tatparyanirnaya 2.2.28 states that: "The Supreme hari, the support of an infinity of worlds and who is called Shimshumara, is saluted by all knowers of brahman on their way to the Supreme God." In Vedic astrology, the plane on which humans live is called Bhuloka. The plane above Bhuloka is called Antariksha Loka or Bhuvarloka. Bhuvarloka sits below another place called Swarga Loka which is where other planets, stars, and other celestial bodies exist. The entirety of Bhuvarloka is then said to be supported by Vishnu-Narayana in the form Shimshumara. His various limbs appear to us as various stars and planets. The tail of the scorpion is thus arched towards Swarga Loka and his head rests somewhere atop Mount Meru (See Raj Rajeshwari Shaligram). The edge of his tail also consists of Dhruva, the pole star.

Similar to some manifestations of Ananta-Sesha, the Shimshumara Shaligram is usually described as having an elongated or arched body (reminiscent of a scorpion with a raised tail), thick holes, and two chakra-spiral markings on the face side with one single chakra mark on the elevated tail side. Though, it is not uncommon in practice for these Shaligrams to only have one chakra entirely, which usually appears on their bottom portion. In traditions that do not recognize the Shimshumara manifestation of Vishnu, Shaligrams bearing the above-mentioned characteristics would most often be interpreted as a particular type of Ananta-Sesha Shaligrams. The primary difference between the two, however, is that the Shimshumara Shaligram does not contain the markings of the cobra's hood as the former type does.

Veneration of the Shimshumara Shaligram is most often associated with devotees seeking balance in their lives or who have a particular affinity to the Shimshumara manifestation of Vishnu. In practice, the inclusion of this Shaligram in home worship is comparatively rare but it does enjoy some regional popularity in central and south India. It is important to note however, that in Karnataka, this Shaligram actually may be read as the scorpion goddess Chelamma, where it is described as a shield against scorpion bites and infection by deadly viruses.

REFERENCES

Praanatoshani Tantra pg. 351 - 356

DESCRIPTION:

Shishmaarga: Long in shape, with a deep triangular opening and having one or two circular marks on the front side and another on the back side. (P)

ADDITIONAL REFERENCES

1. "Śiśumāra (शशिमार)," Cologne Digital Sanskrit Dictionaries: The Purana Index.
2. Frawley, David. 2000. Astrology of the Seers: A Guide to Vedic (Hindu) Astrology. Twin Lakes Wisconsin: Lotus Press.
3. Ohashi, Yukio. 1993. "Development of Astronomical Observations in Vedic and post-Vedic India". Indian Journal of History of Science. 28 (3).
4. Pingree, David. 1981. Jyotihśāstra: Astral and Mathematical Literature. Otto Harrassowitz.

SHIVA LINGA

Variations of this Shaligram may include an unbroken body with only the top and bottom of the shell-spiral visible on either end.

Shiva Linga Shaligram with the chambers of the belemnite fossil visible on both ends and on the sides.

Shiva (Śiva) is one of the three principal deities of Hindu theology. Shiva's most common depiction is that of "the transformer" or "the destroyer" within the Trimurti (including Brahma and Vishnu). In Shaivism, however, Shiva is the Supreme Being who creates, protects, and transforms the universe.

Even in the Shakti goddess tradition, where it is the goddess who is described as supreme, Shiva remains popular as a representation of her consort. Shiva is also one of the five equivalent deities in Panchayatana puja of the Smarta tradition.

In some Hindu traditions, Shiva is regarded as the formless, limitless, transcendent and unchanging absolute Brahman, and the primal Atman (soul, self) of the universe. Shiva also has a number of different depictions and manifestations, some benevolent and some fearsome.

In benevolent aspects, he is depicted as an omniscient Yogi who lives an ascetic life on Mount Kailash (or elsewhere in the Himalayas) as well as a householder with his wife Parvati and his two children, Ganesha and Kartikeya (Skanda). In his fierce aspects, he is often depicted slaying demons. Shiva is also known as Adiyogi and is regarded as the patron god of yoga, meditation, and the arts.

The Shiva Linga Shaligram (also called the Shivling or Shiv Nabha Shaligram) is one of the most distinctive Shaligrams and typically appears as a round, smooth, shila containing a central conical spiral, which can be black, gold, or with white markings. The variant of this Shaligram also appears as a columnar formation of black shale with a slightly segmented conical shape emerging wholly or partially from the top of the shila. In traditions that do not recognize the Shiva Linga Shaligram name type, these Shaligrams are interpreted as subtypes of the Harihara Shaligram.

The formation of this Shaligram is unique in that it usually contains a partially broken shale nodule with a prominently visible conical marine cephalopod of the Belemnoids group. In its "raw" formation, eroding out of high elevation fossil beds, these Shaligrams have clear markings of shell chambers and also typically contain iron pyrite or quartz infiltrates. This Shaligram is primarily associated with Shiva Linga worship and is therefore mainly sought after by Shaiva devotees. However, many Vaishnavas include the Shiva Linga Shaligram in their home practices in order to bestow blessings for meditation, protection, strength, and for normalizing a troubled family life.

REFERENCES

Praanatoshani Tantra pg. 361. Shivling Shaligrams are also a part of many local and regional Shaligram practices. While they are not mentioned by name in the Scriptures, many devotees consider Shivling Shaligrams to be a part of the Harihara category of Shaligrams.

DESCRIPTION

Praanatoshani Tantra pg. 361 - Because this Shaligram represents Lord Shiva (The One who is Eternally Pure) the life of the devotee is considered free from contaminations of Rajas and Tamas; where the non-apprehension of Reality is Tamas and the misapprehension of Reality is Rajas. However, in Reality Itself there can be neither of them. In the Upanishads, for example, Brahman and Shiva are declared as part of the Absolute Oneness, which is Vishnu.

Naramurtti: Yellow in color with the marks of a Shiva linga on one side and a sacred thread on the other. (P)

Shiva Linga

Shiva Linga - Belemnite from a shale nodule fractured by a fall into the Kali Gandaki River

Shiva Linga and Shiva-Parvati Shaligrams

In several Hindu traditions, Mahavishnu is described as a combination of Shiva and Parvati: as the non-relative and relative aspects of the divine respectively. If both are together, they are then called Mahavishnu. As a result, Shiva Linga worship is not uncommon in Vishnu devotion as a matter of course.

Even many Shaiva devotees incorporate icons and concepts of Mahavishnu practices into their own traditions and the complex interpretive traditions of these Shaligrams reflect that. In such Shaligram traditions, Mahavishnu and Shiva Lingam are not divided into two different deities and Shaligrams of both Linga and Mahavishnu types may be referred to as either Vishnu, Shiva, or Harihara.

Additionally, Shiva Linga Shaligrams are then considered to be concentrations of the Shiva-Mahavishnu in one shila. As such, Shiva Linga Shaligrams, as well as Shiva-Parvati Shaligrams, are treated as especially enlightened Shaligrams in these traditions where they bestow better awareness of an individual's soul as transcendental and formless.

They are also associated with a peaceful life (as Shiva is at peace and is partial to granting boons and favors to those who supplicate him). For this reason, these Shaligrams are commonly given as gifts in order to lessen suffering or to people who have experienced great hardship because they are said to bring about surprising or unexpected good fortune.

In South India, Shiva-Parvati Shaligrams are more commonly identified as Parvati or Maha Shakti/Maha Devi Shaligrams. They also appear as Gangamma (See Parvati-Shiva Shaligram).

ADDITIONAL REFERENCES

1. Issitt, Micah Lee; Main, Carlyn. 2014. Hidden Religion: The Greatest Mysteries and Symbols of the World's Religious Beliefs. ABC-CLIO.

2. Kramrisch, Stella. 1981. Manifestations of Shiva. Philadelphia Museum of Art.

3. Michaels, Axel. 2004. Hinduism: Past and Present. Princeton University Press.

4. Sharma, Arvind. 2000. Classical Hindu Thought: An Introduction. Oxford University Press.

Sridhar (Shreedhar)

Shridhar, Shreedhar, or Sridhara, meaning "possessor of Lakshmi" or "possessor of good fortune," is the name of Vishnu as he manifests along with his consort, the goddess Lakshmi. There is a great deal of variation in the identification of this particular Shaligram however, depending on the specific texts one takes into account while determining the Shaligram's characteristics.

In most cases, this Shaligram is identified as having a single clear, though small, chakra-spiral which appears near one edge of the main body of the shila and a somewhat elongated or oval shape. In other traditions, the Shridhar Shaligram has two visible chakras (usually one on either side) in addition to a white vanamala marking (a white quartz line).

In other words, the typical appearance of a Shridhar Shaligram is that of an elongated shale nodule with a single, small, but fully visible ammonite cast/chakra-spiral at one end which should be imprinted rather than raised. Some variations of this Shaligram contain two small chakra-spirals but it is more common to see the Shaligram with only one.

The presence of white quartz infiltrates (vanamala marking) is also not unusual but if a white line is present, it should appear near the middle of the Shaligram and should pass all the way around it completely. Veneration of Shridhar Shaligrams is heavily associated with both philanthropic or charitable pursuits as well as the accumulation of material wealth.

These Shaligrams are also said to bestow blessings of spiritual progress by encouraging the undertaking of sadhanas (daily spiritual practices), specifically those that involve dedicated practice in music, art, or religious philosophy.

For this reason, Shridhar Shaligrams makes popular gifts and are often exchanged or given to children following rites of passage or those who intend to undertake an extended period of study in either the arts or scripture.

In practice, there are several variations of this Shaligram that are recognized: In North India and Nepal, Sridhari Shaligrams are described as shining like fresh green grass but with uneven chakras and the mark of a vanamala. Elsewhere, Sridhara is recognized as having prominent markings of a vanamala and the shila's color being much like that of the Kadamba flower (Nauclea Cadamba, Orange). As a result, Sridhara Shaligrams in these traditions may be orange or reddish yellow with about two chakras, a vanamala, and other, smaller, lines.

REFERENCES

Pranatoshani Tantra pg. 347, Skanda Purana, Nagarekhanda, 244: 3-9, Brahmavaivartta (Prakritikhanda, Ch. 21), Garuda Purana (Panchanan Tarkaratna, Part 1, Ch. 45), Agni Purana; Bengavasi ed., Panchanan Tarkaratna, Saka 1812, Ch. 46

DESCRIPTIONS

Small in size with two circular marks and an additional mark resembling a vanamala (BV).

The same as Dadhivamana but with an additional mark of vanamala. (BV)

Five linear marks and a mace (G). Having 1 chakra. (G)

(i) Round in shape and decorated with five linear marks and a good-looking garland mark.

(ii) With linear marks standing upwards on His both sides, other things are the same as above.

(iii) Green in color, round in shape with a flat upper side and having a lotus mark at the opening.

(iv) Very small in size, and marked with two circles and a garland.

(v) Glittering like a gem, and having the marks of a flag and a circle.

(vi) He has a glaced body with the mark of vanamala on it, and there are also linear marks on the upper side on his body. (P)

ADDITIONAL REFERENCES

1. Śrīdhara (श्रीधर), Cologne Digital Sanskrit Dictionaries: The Purana Index.

2. See also: Sridhara Vishnu, 8th century AD, National Museum of Nepal. Kathmandu, Nepal.

3. Chandra, S. 2015. "Steps to Water: Stepwells in India." Chitrolekha International Magazine on Art and Design, 5(2), 40-46.

SHRIKARA

Krishna-Srikara
Shaligram

Radha-Krishna Srikara
Shaligram

"Srikara" is the name given to Krishna when he goes to fetch the Parijatha Pushpam from Swargaloka. There are, however, more than 150 different meanings and usages of the word 'Srikara' and different usages of the name imply different aspects of the deity or blessings he might bestow. For example, 'Sriyamkarothiiti Srikaraha' is He who creates wealth and prosperity. 'Srihikaranamyasmatsahaiti Srikaraha' means He who gives the right kind of wealth to those who intend to use it for dharmic purposes. 'Srihikareyasyasahaiti Srikaraha' is He who is the Lord of Lakshmi Devi (Sri), particularly one who seeks prosperity, health, proper devotion, and material wealth. In other usages, 'Srikaabhyam Ramayathiiti Srikaraha' is a name wherein Sri also refers to Saraswathi and Ka refers to Brahma the creator of the Universe. Srikara can then also a reference to the creation of the material universe. Finally, the usage 'Sripradaha Karahayasya Saha Srikaraha' means He whose hand (Kara) is capable of bestowing unimaginable wealth (Srihi).

Due to the high variation in the meaning of the name Srikara, few Shaligrams are ever identified using this name-type in practice. In most Shaligram traditions, Srikara Shaligrams are considered to be a particular variation of a Krishna Shaligram that bears the markings of a parijatha pushpa (night-blooming or coral jasmine) somewhere on the body of the shila.

Parijat (Nyctanthes arbor-tristis), appears in a number of Hindu religious stories and is often related to the Kalpvriksha tree (See Kalpvriksha Shaligram). In one story, for example, which appears in the Bhagavata Purana, the Mahabharata, and in the Vishnu Purana, parijat appeared as the result of the Samudra Manthan (Churning of the Milky Ocean) following which Krishna set about to battle against Indra to win possession of the parijat. Later on, Krishna's wife Satyabhama demanded that the flowering tree be planted in the backyard of her palace. However, it so happened that in spite of having the tree in her backyard, the flowers would only fall in the adjacent backyard of Krishna's favorite queen Rukmini because of her superior devotion and humility.

For the most part, Srikara Shaligrams are generally identified as Krishna Shaligrams (with smooth, black, rounded, bodies) which bear a marking in the shape of a flower's petals, leaves, or stem. In some traditions, Shaligrams with these characteristics might also be identified as "Tulsi Shaligrams" given the plant- or leaf-shaped markings, however, Srikara Shaligrams should demonstrate clear markings of petals. The "flower-like" or "petal" markings on a Srikara Shaligram should also be fairly clear somewhere on the main portion of the stone. These markings can either be the triangular appearance of a heavily worn set of ammonite ridges which form a ring of "petals" around the center or may be formed by deep striations within the shale nodule which create a series of winding grooves reminiscent of plant leaves.

Veneration of Srikara Shaligrams is said to bestow blessings of physical, emotional, and mental cleansing. Much like the use of the flower itself in Ayurvedic medicine, drinking water that this Shaligram has been bathed in is also said to relieve pain caused by sciatica, arthritis, and viral fevers. Conversely, these Shaligrams are said to bless households with great devotional fervor and to encourage humility, submission to God, and to be a comfort in times of sorrow.

REFERENCES

Pranatoshani Tantra pg. 348

ADDITIONAL REFERENCES

1. See also: Bhagavata Purana: "Krishna and Satyabhama steal Indra's Parijata tree." Pahari, early 19th century.
2. Hiremath, V., Hiremath, B. S., Mohapatra, S., & Das, A. K. 2016. Literary review of Parijata (Nyctanthus Arbor-Tristis Linn.) an herbal medicament with special reference to ayurveda and botanical literatures. Biomed Pharmacol J, 9(3), 1019-1025.
3. Smith, W.L. 2007. "Assam: Shankaradeva's Parijata Harana Nata." In Krishna: A Sourcebook. Edwin F. Bryant (ed.). Oxford University Press.

SUDARSHAN

The Sudarshana Chakra is the spinning, disk-like weapon, indicative of Vishnu. Literally meaning "vision of which is auspicious," and having 108 serrated edges, the Sudarshana Chakra is generally portrayed on the right rear hand of the four hands of Vishnu in his cosmic form (along with the shankha (conch shell), a gada (mace) and a padma (lotus)). The Sudarshana Chakra is also occasionally depicted as an ayudhapurusha, a divine weapon artistically shown in human form.

While the Sudarshana Chakra is usually shown to be subordinate to Vishnu himself, in many South Indian Vishnu temples, the Chakra as an ayudhapurusha is worshipped in its own shrine attached to the central temple. In the Puranas, the Sudarshana Chakra is primarily used for the ultimate destruction of an enemy, especially a particularly powerful or evil enemy. Lastly, the depiction of Vishnu with the Sudarshana Chakra in art is typically meant to represent Vishnu as the keeper and preserver of all celestial bodies and the heavens.

The Sudarshan Shaligram is probably one of the most common and most "iconic" of all Shaligrams. It is easily identified by its single, clear, fully revealed chakra-spiral and no other markings present on the body of the shila. Each section of the spiral, from beginning to end, should be markedly defined with no fractures, breaks, or interruptions. In most cases, Sudarshan Shaligrams will spiral in a right-hand, clockwise direction (denoting the direction of the rotation of the universe). Left-hand, counter-clockwise Sudarshan Shaligrams are especially prized in certain Buddhist and Bonpo practices.

Sudarshan Shaligrams most typically contain a single, entire, unbroken, ammonite which is clearly visible on at least one side (though two-sided Sudarshans are just as common). A lightly-worn cast of the ammonite-chakra shell, where the entire spiral is clearly defined, is also sometimes considered Sudarshan. However, in most Shaligram interpretive traditions, it is an imprinted spiral that is read as Surya, while a raised spiral is identified as Sudarshan. There is some variation in this reading however, in that some traditions consider any Shaligram with a single, complete, spiral to be Sudarshan, while Surya is identified as a partially complete spiral with the center obscured.

Veneration of Sudarshan Shaligrams is said to remove worldly worries and concerns and to aid the devotee in protecting the rights and lives of others. For this reason, it is often given to political leaders, businessmen, and physicians where it is said to act as a protector of society, as a shield against those who seek to do harm against the devotee and their family, and as a defense against physical misfortunes and illnesses. Given its iconic appearance however, Sudarshan is a particular popular Shaligram at all levels of worship and is kept in home shrines by practitioners of all kinds.

References

Praanatoshani Tantra pg. 347, Praanatoshani Tantra pg. 361, Brahmavaivartta (Prakritikhanda, Ch. 21)

DESCRIPTIONS

» Single circular mark (BV)

» (i) Green in color and glittering to look at. He holds the marks of a mace and a discus on His left side and two linear marks on His right side. A lotus printed with linear marks is also found on his body.

» (ii) A circular mark at the top and a big opening is deeply dark. (P)

» Chakrapani: Round and glaced in shape, with a small circular mark and many other prints. (P) – In some Shaligram traditions, this description is taken to mean that a Chakrapani Sudarshan Shaligram can have up to three vadana and eight chakras.

ADDITIONAL REFERENCES

1. Agarwala, Vasudeva Sharana (1965). Indian Art: A history of Indian art from the earliest times up to the third century A.D, Volume 1 of Indian Art. Prithivi Prakashan. p. 101.

2. Begley, W. E. 1973. Vishnu's Flaming Wheel: The Iconography of the Sudarsana-Cakra. New York.

3. Gopal, Madan. 1990. K.S. Gautam (ed.). India through the ages. Publication Division, Ministry of Information and Broadcasting, Government of India. p. 80

4. Monier-Williams, Leumann E, Cappeller C, eds. 2002. "Chakra". A Sanskrit-English Dictionary: Etymologically and Philologically Arranged with Special Reference to Cognate Indo-European Languages, p. 380. Motilal Banarsidass Publications.

SURYA/SURAJ

Surya means the Sun in Nepal and in India. Synonyms of Surya in ancient Indian literatures include Aditya, Arka, Bhanu, Savitr, Pushan, Ravi, Martanda, Mitra, and Vivasvan; names which are occasionally imparted onto the Surya Shaligram depending on the religious or regional tradition. Surya is also the name of the solar deity in Hinduism, particularly in the Saura tradition found in Rajasthan, Gujarat, Madhya Pradesh, Bihar, Uttar Pradesh, Jharkhand and Odisha.

Surya is furthermore one of the five deities considered to be an equivalent aspect and means to realizing the Brahman in the Smarta Tradition. His iconography is often that of a shining man depicted riding a chariot harnessed by seven horses, which represent the seven colors of the rainbow. In medieval Hinduism, Surya is an epithet for Shiva and Vishnu (what is now more commonly called Harihara). In some ancient texts and in the arts, Surya is presented syncretically with Indra, Ganesha or other local deities. Lastly, Surya is also highly revered in the arts and literature of both Buddhism and Jainism.

The Surya Shaligram typically comes in one of two variations. The first, and most common, is that of a complete round or half ammonite cast/imprint where the majority of the chakra-spiral is visible with the exception of the very center. The lines and ridges of the chakra-spiral then radiate outwards in a shape reminiscent of the rays of the sun or in a series of half-chakras in the appearance of the rising sun. The second variation is similar to a Sudarshan Shaligram, but contains such extensive iron pyrite infiltrates that the entire Shaligram is golden in color. In both cases, however, the central portion of the spiral is obscured by a rounded or flat nodule.

Lastly, one of the rarest variations of this Shaligram is the Red Surya, formed by the incomplete oxidization of the iron deposits in the shale, giving the shila a red or orange-red color overtop the black coloration beneath. Depending on the interpretive tradition, there can occasionally be some confusion between Surya Shaligrams and Sudarshan Shaligrams; the former however is generally identified by the more significant wear to the central spiral, resulting in clearer radiated lines which appear as deeply embedded in the surrounding stone.

Veneration of the Surya Shaligram is said to be particularly good for removing illnesses, especially those of the eyes, heart, or stomach. The "illumination" of this Shaligram is also said to allay worry, guilt, and fear and to be especially beneficial to those who suffer from mental illness. In fact, several Shaligram interpretive traditions, including Buddhist and Jain traditions, revere the Surya Shaligram for its ability to encourage "a clear mind" and many traditions practice meditation on its embedded spirals as a means of mental focus.

REFERENCES

Pranatoshani Tantra pg. 361

DESCRIPTIONS

Suryamurtti: With twelve different circular marks either on the body or inside His opening. (P)

ADDITIONAL REFERENCES

1. Blurton, T. Richard.1993. Hindu Art. Harvard University Press. p. 118.
2. Dalal, Roshen. 2010. Hinduism: An Alphabetical Guide. Penguin Books India.
3. Shimkhada, Deepak. 1984. "The Masquerading Sun: A Unique Syncretic Image in Nepal". Artibus Asiae. 45 (2/3): 223–229.
4. Vyas, R. T. and Umakant Premanand Shah. 1995. Studies in Jaina Art and Iconography and Allied Subjects. Abhinav Publications. pp. 23–24.

TARKSHYA

Tārkṣya is the name of a mythical being in the Rigveda. In some cases, Tarkshya is described as a horse using the epithet árișta-nemi; meaning "with intact wheel-rims" (RV 1.89.6, RV 10.178.1). Alternatively, Tarkshya is described as a great bird (RV 5.51) who is later identified with Garuda, Vishnu's celestial mount, in the Mahabharata and in the Harivamsha. Conversely, some traditions consider Tarkshya to be Garuda's father (Bhagavata Purana 6.6.2, 21) or one of the many offspring of Kashyapa who are counted in the Mahabharata (1.2548, 4830 and 12468). Lastly, Tarkshya is also the name of the hymn RV 10.178, which is ascribed to Tārkṣya Arișțanemi.

In practice, Tarkshya Shaligrams are comparatively rare and in many cases, are subsumed under the Garuda Shaligram name-type (See Garuda Shaligram). When they do appear, however, Tarkshya Shaligrams are described as shankha-shaped (shaped like a conch shell) with a single vadana (mouth) located on the underside of the shila. The two chakras within this opening are then described as smoothed-down, and with a clearer central spiral column rather than easily discernable chakra-shell markings. Tarkshya Shaligrams also tend to be larger in size than most standard home-altar Shaligrams (and it is their size that often differentiates them from Shankha Shaligrams), typically exceeding the size of an adult's palm by several centimeters.

Tarkshya Shaligrams are venerated in only a few Shaligram traditions, including by Madhwas Brahmins and in Sri Vaishnavism (among others). In other Shaligram traditions, a Shaligram containing the above-mentioned characteristics is likely to be interpreted as a Lakshmi-Shankha Shaligram or as a Garuda Shaligram. Veneration of Tarkshya Shaligrams is said to bestow blessings similar to that of Garuda Shaligrams: protection from snakes and other potentially dangerous animals (vermin) that can be found in the home, healing from poisons or toxic illnesses, and protection from political unrest. In addition to this, Tarkshya Shaligrams are also highly associated with travel and conveyance and are therefore popular among pilgrims, taxi and livery drivers, shipping drivers, traveling businessmen, and all those who must travel long distances for work or by other necessity.

ADDITIONAL REFERENCES

1. Tārkṣya (तार्क्ष्य), Cologne Digital Sanskrit Dictionaries: The Purana Index.
2. Bhagavata Purana 6.6.2, 21
3. Rig Veda: RV 1.89.6, RV 10.178.1

TRIVIKRAMA

Trivikrama is a name of Vamana, the fifth incarnation of Vishnu and the first incarnation to have appeared in Tretayuga the third age (See Vamana Shaligram). The name Trivikrama comes from the giant form Vamana took when he conquered the three worlds – sky, earth and underworld – by taking three giant steps.

As legend describes, Mahabali, a benevolent demon king, once created a utopian kingdom. Because of this, his fame spread worldwide, into the netherworld, and slowly into heaven. Indra, the king of the Devas and the ruler of heaven, felt threatened by this. In response, Aditi, his mother, observed a penance called payovrata so that she might help her son. Pleased with her devotion, Vishnu was born as the Brahmin dwarf, Vamana.

Vamana, carrying a wooden umbrella, then approached Mahabali who was conducting a yajna (a fire sacrifice). King Bali then asked Vamana to choose anything that he wanted from his kingdom. Vamana asked for just three steps of land and the king agreed, against the warning of his guru, Sukracharya. Suddenly, the dwarf grew into the skies and with one step covered the earth and with another step the heavens.

With no place to keep the third step, Mahabali, unable to fulfill the promise he made, then offered his head, which was pushed by Vamana down into the netherworld; granting the king immortality for his humility. In honoring Mahabali and his ancestor Prahlada (See Narasimha Shaligram), it is said that Vishnu thus conceded sovereignty of Patala, the netherworld. In other texts, however, Vamana does not step into the netherworld but instead gives its rule to Bali. In his giant form, Vamana is therefore known as Trivikrama.

In most cases, the Trivikrama Shaligram is comparatively larger in size than other Shaligrams (slightly larger than a man's palm) and contains at least one clear chakra-spiral which is partially ringed by additional chakra-spirals on either side (either right or left, or in some cases, top and bottom) – marking Trivikrama's three steps. This means that the main characteristic of these Shaligrams is the position of three chakras which should either appear in a "step" sequence or be layered over each other. While occasionally round in shape, Trivikrama Shaligrams are typically triangular or with one rounded edge and angular overall. It is also not uncommon for Trivikrama Shaligrams to have yellowish or orange-ish coloration on their chakra-spirals which may or may not extend to the body of the Shaligram itself.

Trivikrama Shaligrams sometimes have a series of smaller markings, such as a vanamala, the marks of a plough-share, a conch, a discus, or a mace. While none of these marks are required for the identification of this Shaligram, practitioners note that when they do appear, the shila in question may act as protection against untimely death. Veneration of Trivikrama Shaligrams is said to bestow blessings similar to that of the Vamana Shaligram: physical strength and the ability to face powerful enemies, confidence and wisdom. The Trivikrama Shaligram, however, is said to be especially beneficial to those involved in businesses or other endeavors related to land, reality, mining, or the working of precious metals and gems.

REFERENCES

Skanda Purana, Nagarekhanda, 244: 3-9, Garuda Purana (Panchanan Tarkaratna, Part 1, Ch. 45), Agni Purana; Bengavasi ed., Panchanan Tarkaratna, Saka 1812, Ch. 46.

Descriptions

Green color, circular mark on left side and linear mark on right side (G).

(i) Green in color, triangular in shape, and glittering to look at. He holds a single circular mark on His left side and a linear mark on His right side.

(ii) With two circular marks, other things apparently being the same as above. (Sk and P)

Additional References

1. "Sanskrit Dictionary for Spoken Sanskrit: 'Trivikrama.'" spokensanskrit. org. Retrieved 18 May 2022.

2. White YajurVeda (5.15)

3. Muir, John. 1873. Original Sanskrit Texts on the Origin and History of the People of India (Vol. 4) (in Sanskrit). Harvard University. Trübner. pp. 64, 67, 87, 122.

4. Rao. T. A. Gopinatha. 1993. Elements of Hindu iconography. Motilal Banarsidass. pp. 163–167.

UPENDRA

Upendra is typically translated to mean "younger brother of Indra." In some Puranic texts and in the Harivamsa, this refers to Vamana, the dwarf incarnation of Vishnu (See Vamana Shaligram). In other Puranic texts, however, such as in the Vishnu Purana Ch. XII, Upendra is a name given to Krishna who is called "Indra of the Cows" or Govinda (See Krishna Govinda Shaligram). For this reason, the Upendra Shaligram tends to vary considerably depending on the specific religious tradition involved in the interpretation of the shila.

In most cases, the Upendra Shaligram is considered to be a variation of the Vamana Shaligram with a similar short, crest-like, chakra along the top portion of the shila which is then seated on a wide, rounded, base. The Upendra Shaligram differs, however, in that one side of the rounded body of the stone is slightly more elevated than the opposite side, denoting that Upendra is superior to Indra, a representation of the superiority of the Self to the mind. In traditions that recognize Upendra as a name of Krishna, however, the Upendra Shaligram is subsequently described as similar to that of the Krishna Govinda Shaligram but with the addition of the crested portion of the chakra-spiral somewhere along the side of the Shaligram.

Upendra Shaligrams are rarer in practice than the Vamana or Krishna Govinda Shaligram types; categories under which they are often subsumed. When they do appear, however, they tend to be highly sought after for inclusion in family altars and are often given as gifts to children other than the first-born. Numerous devotees and pilgrims who did not inherit their parents' Shaligrams (because they were not first-born) often cite the Upendra Shaligram as their first Shaligram, around which they intend to build a new collection of Shaligrams to pass on to their own children.

Veneration of Upendra Shaligrams is said to bestow blessings of a large estate, especially in terms or land, prestige, or meaningful heirlooms. These Shaligrams are also said to be especially beneficial for resolving issues linked to inheritance, manners of title or ascension, the transfer of family goods, or for the elevation of younger sons and daughters to prosperity equal to that of their elder siblings.

In practice, there are two additional variations of this Shaligram:

1. Upendra Manivarnabha, which is blue-black in color with two small chakras inside a very small vadana.

2. Neela Upendra, which is blue in color but has the marks of a conch, a discus and a mace on its body.

REFERENCES

Praanatoshani Tantra pg. 361, Skanda Purana, Nagarekhanda, 244: 3-9

DESCRIPTIONS

Green in color and glittering like a gem. He has a glaced body with one or more circular marks on His sides. (P)

ADDITIONAL REFERENCES

1. Upendra (उपेन्द्र), (cf. Glossary page from Śrī Bṛhad-bhāgavatāmṛta).
2. Monier-Williams, Monier. 1899. A Sanskrit-English Dictionary: Etymologically and Philologically Arranged with Special Reference to Cognate Indo-European Languages. Oxford: Clarendon Press.

Vaikuntha

Vaikuntha (the Place of Non-Hindrance), Paramapadam, Vishnupada (Vishnu's feet), or Param Padam (the Supreme Abode) is the celestial home of Vishnu. In most of the Puranas, and in the majority of Vaishnava traditions, Vaikuntha is located in the direction of the Makara Rashi, a celestial formation which roughly coincides with the constellation of Capricorn.

Vishnu's eye is then said to be located at the South Celestial Pole. Vaikuntha Shaligrams are popular in practice but there is some debate as to the nature of their benefits. Oftentimes, the Vishnu Padam Shaligram (See Mahavishnu – Dasavatara Shaligram) takes its place or is identified itself as "Vaikuntha."

In other Shaligram traditions, however, the Vaikuntha Shaligram is identified by its distinctive "two-tiered" structure, where a small, central, spiral can be seen beneath the edge of a larger outer spiral or sunken down beneath the edge of the central shape nodule; representing the layering of worlds.

The formation of a Vaikuntha Shaligram typically comes about when the entire or nearly the entire ammonite mold has worn out of the shale nodule, leaving a clear chakra-spiral visible on the internal portion of the stone with an overhanging section still partially covering it.

It is also not uncommon for the central portions of these Shaligrams to contain significant iron pyrite deposits, lending the entire spiral a gold coloration. Furthermore, the somewhat odd shape of the central portions of these Shaligram's chakras is referred to as a "lotus stem," which is taken as further evidence of their otherworldly origins. Vaikuntha is also "the one who prevents men from straying down the wrong path" (Vikunthah) and the Shaligram itself is often described as a "seat of Vishnu."

For this reason, veneration of this Shaligram is said to bestow blessings of a strong 6th sense, to ensure moksha (liberation) for the devotee, and to protect the devotee from false information, poor teachings, or disreputable gurus. This Shaligram is often described as especially partial to requests for guidance or safety and, due to its association with the dwelling places of Vishnu, is taken on pilgrimages or other religious journeys undertaken by the devotee.

In more controversial practices, Vaikuntha Shaligrams are occasionally referred to as "Death Shaligrams" because of their use in funeral rites. For example, in some traditions, Vaikuntha Shaligrams are placed in the hands of the deceased during cremation so that they will be gathered up with the ashes and returned to the river afterwards. The Shaligram then accompanies the person to Vaikuntha before returning to the world in their place, thus freeing them from the karmic cycle of rebirth forever.

REFERENCES

Garuda Purana (Panchanan Tarkaratna, Part 1, Ch. 45), Agni Purana; Bengavasi ed., Panchanan Tarkaratna, Saka 1812, Ch. 46

DESCRIPTIONS

Blue color, lotus mark, a circular mark, glittering like a gem (G).

ADDITIONAL REFERENCES

1. Śrīmad Bhāgavatam 5.23.9.
2. Flood, Gavin. 1996. An Introduction to Hinduism. Cambridge University Press. p. 17.
3. Orlando O. Espín; James B. Nickoloff. 2007. An Introductory Dictionary of Theology and Religious Studies. Liturgical Press. p. 539.

Vamana

Vamana is the fifth incarnation of Vishnu and the first incarnation to have appeared in Tretayuga (the third age). Vamana is also the first avatar to appear in human form, that of a dwarf Brahmin bachelor (though some Puranic texts list his consort as Padma or Kamala (a manifestation of Lakshmi) and some texts describe him as a child rather than a dwarf). Vamana, sometimes transliterated as Vaamana, was born to Aditi (the mother of Indra) and Kasyapa and is the last deity listed among twelve Vedic Gods of the Adityas. Vamana is also the younger brother of Indra, who is known as Upendra.

The Srimad Bhagavata goes on to explain that Vishnu descended as the Vamana avatar in order to restore the authority of Indra over the heavens, mainly because it had been taken over autocratically by Mahabali, a benevolent demon King (See Trivikrama Shaligram). It is also important to note that Mahabali was the great grandson of Hiranyakashipu, the grand-son of Prahlada and son of Virochana (See Narasimha Shaligram). The Vamana Shaligram is generally recognizable by its small, segmented or partial chakra crests atop a wide smooth base. In some variations of this Shaligram, a white quartz vanamala line also appears on the main body of the shila but this is not always the case.

Veneration of Vamana Shaligrams is typically associated with blessings of physical strength and the ability to face powerful enemies,as well as confidence and wisdom. Vamana Shaligrams are also said to bestow success and material wealth but that such gains will not draw undue attention to the devotee, especially those who must maintain low social profiles or do not want accolades or recognition for their work (because Vamana acted to check Mahabali's pride). In some traditions, Vamana Shaligrams are also interchangeable with Trivikrama Shaligrams when it comes to blessings of land or precious metals.

Aside from their overall characteristic shape, Vamana Shaligrams often display a number of other, smaller, features related to the story of Vamana, Mahabali, and Trivikrama. This might include a white-quartz vanamala line marking his status as Brahmin, three successive indentations or impressions marking the form of Trivikrama, or other markings of small hands, feet, or eyes denoting his status as a dwarf or a child. In all, Vamana Shaligrams are often described by ritual specialists as being overall "short-statured" in appearance.

REFERENCES

Praanatoshani Tantra pg. 347-348, Skanda Purana, Nagarekhanda, 244: 3-9, Garuda Purana (Panchanan Tarkaratna, Part 1, Ch. 45), Agni Purana; Bengavasi ed., Panchanan Tarkaratna, Saka 1812, Ch. 46

DESCRIPTIONS

» Round shape, comparatively smaller, one or more beautiful circular marks (G).

(i) Round in shape, small in size and marked with five linear prints.

(ii) Small in size and glittering to look at. He has a circular mark on each of His above and below sides with the print of a Garuda bird near the circular marks.

(iii) Not very small in size. Marked with a circular print at the center and glaced to look at.

(iv) Yellow in color with a bit high top and having an indistinct circular mark.

(v) Cloudy in color, round in shape, marked with a vanamala and having a small opening.

(vi) Very small in size with the color of a cloud and marked with two circles. He is popularly called Dadhivaamana.

(vii) Yellowish in color, marked with several dot-prints with one or more at the opening. He also is a variety of the Dadhivaamana sub-type.

Regarding the shape of these Dadhivaamana varieties, the Matsyasukta (Matsyasukta quoted in Pranatoshanitantra, page 350) tells us that they may resemble either a vilva (woodapple) or vadara (berry) or even like the seed of any of these fruits. (P)

ADDITIONAL REFERENCES

1. "Satapatha Brahmana Part 1 (SBE12): First Kânda: I, 2. 5. Fifth Brâhmana". www.sacred-texts.com. Retrieved 18 May 2022.

2. Lochtefeld, James G. 2001. The Illustrated Encyclopedia of Hinduism, Volume 1. The Rosen Publishing Group, Inc. pp. 175.

3. Vaswani, J. P. 22 December 2017. Dasavatara. Jaico Publishing House. pp. 12–14.

Varaha

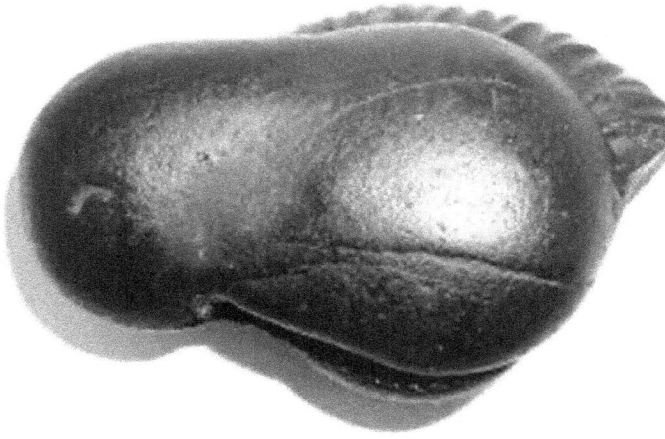

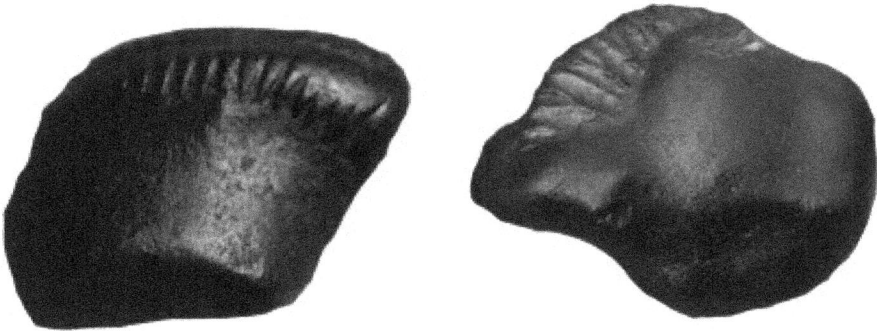

Varaha is the third avatar of Vishnu who appears in the form of a boar (or boar-man with the head of a boar and the body of a man). The story of Varaha begins when the demon Hiranyaksha stole the earth (typically personified as the goddess Bhudevi) and hid her in the primordial waters. Vishnu then appeared as Varaha to rescue her. Varaha killed the demon and retrieved the Earth from beneath the ocean, lifting it up on the tips of his tusks. From this vantage point, Varaha then succeeded in restoring Bhudevi to her proper cosmic place in the universe. In other versions of the story, it was the Vedas themselves that Hiranyaksha stole, thus requiring Varaha to return spiritual knowledge to mankind by rescuing it from the ocean.

Like the other Shaligram manifestations of the "animal" Dasavatara incarnations (i.e., Matsya and Kurma), the Varaha Shaligram is generally identified by its overall shape, which should resemble the head or head and body of a boar. Additionally, the Shaligram should have a clear, crest-like, chakra ridge and two lines, ridges, or markings to indicate the presence of Varaha's tusks. The presence of a rounded or nodule like front to the Shaligram (photo 1) indicates the presence of Bhudevi resting on the tusks. A rarer variation of this Shaligram will also contain a vadana (mouth) near the base of the shila which either indicates the additional presence of Narasimha (if the mouth contains visible "teeth") or Lakshmi-Narayan (if two chakra-spirals are present).

Veneration of the Varaha Shaligram is most often associated with blessings of intense sense experiences and with transcendental meditative awareness of the dissolution of the universe (oneness with the Atman). These Shaligrams are also said to be especially protective of forests, mountains, and rivers, particularly in cases where natural formations are also tirthas, or bridges to the divine. For this reason, Varaha Shaligrams are often associated with pilgrimage or pilgrimage activities.

Varaha Shaligrams can appear on their own or in combination with any number of other Shaligram types. For example, depending on the specific characteristics of the Shaligram in question, Varaha may simultaneously appear with Lakshmi, Lakshmi-Narayan, Surya, or as an addition to one of the Mahashakti Shaligrams. This is likely due to Varaha's close association with mother-goddess and earth-goddess worship, or with his Shakti-energy, the mother-goddess Matrika Varahi who is also depicted with the head of a boar.

In practice, there are several recognized variations of this Shaligram:

1. Bhu-Varaha, which has a raised body with a head shaped like an elephant goad. This shila also has a chakra at the bottom and near that chakra can be seen a structure like the single tusk.

2. Sveta-Varaha has a long snout and one tusk. It is also whitish in color and exceedingly clear with a single mark on its body which resembles a vanamala.

3. Golden Varaha is dark in color (black or blue-black) and has the rear part raised. This section is then adorned by a golden spot at the back. This variation also tends to have two chakras evenly located with a possible third minute chakra elsewhere on the shila.

REFERENCES

Praanatoshani Tantra pg. 348 and Garuda Purana (Panchanan Tarkaratna, Part 1, Ch. 45), Agni Purana; Bengavasi ed., Panchanan Tarkaratna, Saka 1812, Ch. 46

DESCRIPTIONS

Varahashaktilinga - Two circular marks of unequal size (G).

(i) Blue in colour, big in size, and printed with circular marks in odd number, as well as three linear marks.

(ii) Printed with even number of circular marks, of which at least one takes place on His right side, and also with a vanamala. This last variety is also called Lakshmi-varaha (P)

ADDITIONAL REFERENCES

1. Brockington, J. L. 1998. The Sanskrit Epics. BRILL Academic.

2. Lochtefeld, James G. 2002. The Illustrated Encyclopedia of Hinduism: A-M. The Rosen Publishing Group.

3. Nagar, Shanti Lal. 2005. Brahmavaivarta Purana. Parimal Publications.

4. Nanditha Krishna. 2010. Sacred Animals of India. Penguin Books India.

5. Rao, T.A. Gopinatha. 1914. "Dasavataras of Vishnu: The Varahavatara". Elements of Hindu iconography. Vol. 1: Part I. Madras: Law Printing House. pp. 128–145.

VENKATESHWARA/BALAJI

Balaji
Shaligram

Venkateshwara Shaligram (this
variation is similar in some respects to
Surya Shaligrams and may be interpreted
accordingly).

Venkateshwara
Shaligram

Venkateswara, also known as Śrīnivāsa, Bālājī, Veṅkaṭa, and Veṅkaṭācalapati, is a name of Vishnu which means "Lord of Venkata." The word is a literal combination of the words Venkata (the name of a hill in Andhra Pradesh) and isvara (Lord). In the Brahmanda and Bhavishvottara Puranas, the word "Venkata" means "destroyer of sins," deriving from the Sanskrit words vem (sins) and kata (power of immunity). Venkateswara's most prominent shrine is the Tirumala Venkateswara Temple located in Tirupathi, Andhra Pradesh in southern India where the central deity is said to wear a mala (garland) of these Shaligrams.

More common in South India than elsewhere, Venkateshwara Shaligrams, and their variation, the Balaji Shaligram, is identified as having very smooth, symmetrical, markings with clear, even, spacing. Sometimes mistaken for Hayagriva Shaligrams, the difference between the two is in the Venkateshwara Shaligram should have unusually smooth ridges which have straight, parallel, spacing. In some variations of this Shaligram, the parallel lines form a column which sits upright and extends from the top of the Shaligram nearly to the base.

The blessings of this Shaligram are said to be related to the loan Venkateshwara (Srinivas) took out from the deity Kubera in order to marry Padmavati (who is also called Alamelu Manga, a manifestation of Lakshmi who is the consort of Venkateshwara). The name Padmavati is Sanskrit for "she who emerged from lotus." In Jainism, she is also the protective goddess of Lord Parshvanatha. As such, veneration of this Shaligram is said to either bestow significant worldly wealth meant for the repayment of debts or to facilitate a good match in marriage. It is not uncommon, for this reason, for Shaligrams of this type to be given to young men or women who intend to marry into a caste or class hierarchically above their own.

Furthermore, Venkateshwara Shaligrams are often described as especially hospitable shilas and inclined to appear in whatever form a devotee has the greatest need of. Hence, these Shaligrams can also appear with the markings of Shiva, Vishnu, Brahma, Shakti, or even Skanda. In other traditions, these Shaligrams are also sometimes placed in the hands of the dead prior to cremation (similarly to the Vaikuntha Shaligram), where the Shaligram is said to ensure the passage of the soul to Vaikuntha and to keep the soul there in service to Venkateshwara for all eternity.

There is a somewhat significant degree of variation in the overall shape and appearance of Venkateshwara Shaligrams. The primary defining characteristic of any of them, however, is in the presence of clear, parallel or symmetrical, lines and markings. For this reason, these Shaligrams may have any variety of primary shapes, including rounded, elongated, or columnar, but should always display the requisite lines deeply eroded from the back or side of an ammonite cast.

Additional References

1. Krishna, Nanditha. 2000. Balaji-Venkateshwara, Lord of Tirumala-Tirupati. Vakils, Feffer, and Simons. p. 49.

2. Nair, Shantha. 2013. Sri Venkateshwara. Jaico Publishing House; 2013 edition.

3. Sitapati, Pidatala. 1968. "Sri Venkateswara, the Lord of the Seven Hills, Tirupati". Bharatiya Vidya Bhavan.

4. Tourist Guide to Andhra Pradesh. Sura Books. 1992. p. 21.

VISHVAKESHA

Though it is listed as one of the 18 names of Shaligrams in the Puranas, the precise meaning of Vishvakesha in relation to Shaligram practices is unclear. The meaning of Vishvakesh is also further obscured by its popularity in multiple languages, such as Hindi, Gujarati, Tamil, Telugu, Bengali, Marathi, Malayalam, Kannada, Oriya, Bihari and Rajasthani. It may refer to a regional deity name, an unused variant name to a well-known deity, or it may be a place name which has since fallen into obscurity.

Vishvakesha Shaligrams are functionally absent from most practices and are only rarely mentioned in oral tradition, and only then typically in reference to the Puranic list wherein the name appears. Though the name is also occasionally associated with Vrishabha (roughly correlated to Taurus) in Vedic astrology.

Unfortunately, no defining characteristics for these Shaligrams are given in the Scriptural texts and because they are virtually absent from oral tradition, there is no particular consensus as to what they look like.

Some Shaligram practitioners have suggested that Vishvakesh may possibly be a reference to a place where Shaligrams were once collected or conversely, may refer to Shaligrams with a wide variety of mixed colors, for example, a pearlescent ammonite fossil found elsewhere in the world. Others suggest that the modern usage of this name may be in an attempt to incorporate other types of ammonite fossils into the Shaligram taxonomy that would not normally be acceptable.

REFERENCES

Pranatoshani Tantra pg. 348

VISHVARUPA AND VISHVAMBHARA

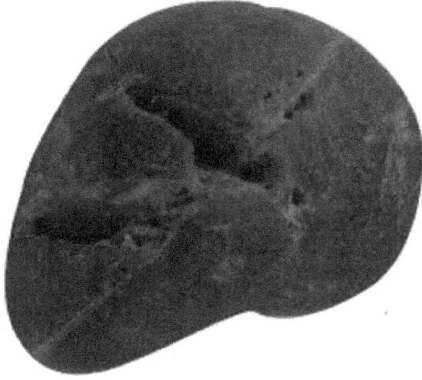

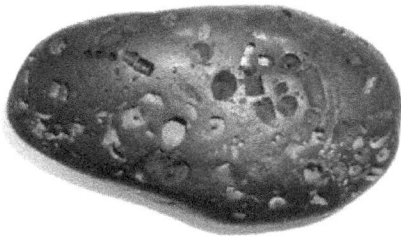

Vishvarupa, meaning "Universal form" or "Omni-form," conversely known as Darshan, Vishwaroopa, and Virata rupa, is an iconographical form of Vishnu or Krishna who is described as a particular kind of direct revelation of the supreme consciousness of the universe.

Though there are multiple Vishvarupa theophanies, the most well-known is in the Bhagavad Gita, where Krishna reveals his eternal, cosmic, form to the Pandava Prince Arjuna on the battlefield of Kurukshetra. In other instances, Vishvarupa is considered the supreme form of Vishnu, where the entirety of the universe is shown to be contained within him.

This iconography is then meant to demonstrate that the essence of divinity or God as He Actually Is, is present within all of the different gods of the Hindu pantheon and that God Himself is only one being. Vishwambharaa or Vishvambhara is generally translated as "The Goddess Who Supports the Universe" and most often refers to Bhumi Devi (the goddess of the Earth).

By an extension, Viswambhara also means the consort of Bhumi Devi, who fulfills roughly the same function, and is therefore often taken to be another name of Vishnu similar to Vishvarupa. In this way, Vishvambhara and Vishvarupa are occasionally used interchangeably.

The Vishvarupa and Vishvambhara Shaligrams are thus included together for two reasons. Firstly, because their names are relatively interchangeable. Vishvarupa being considered the "male" version of Vishvambhara, or vice versa. Secondly, because the descriptions of their Shaligram manifestations are identical save for the number of chakras appearing on the shila. In practice, Vishvambhara Shaligrams contain a total of 20 (or slightly less than 20) visible chakras while Vishvarupa Shaligrams contain more than 20 representing the deity's innumerable forms, eyes, faces, or mouths (See also Mahavishnu-Multichakra Shaligram).

As a result, Vishvarupa and Vishvambhara Shaligrams are easily discernible in practice as comprised of a single shale nodule with a large number (20 or 20+) of holes, indentations, striations, and other markings. Unlike Mahavishnu Shaligrams, these Shaligrams typically do not contain fully visible or easily discernible chakra spirals but are rather closer to descriptions of "circular marks."

Veneration of these Shaligrams is associated with a desire to obtain moksha (liberation) within a single lifetime. These Shaligrams are also said to bestow blessings of strong religious conviction, a steady mind capable of understanding great mysteries, and an ability to contemplate formlessness and selflessness. For this reason, they are commonly paired with other Shaligrams and aniconic divinities during worship so that their complex forms can help the devotee contemplate the icons and images they are using to represent the divine.

REFERENCES

Praanatoshani Tantra pg. 361 and 351 - 356, Skanda Purana, Nagarekhanda, 244: 3-9

DESCRIPTIONS

Vishvarupa: With one opening and many circular marks. (P).
Compare to, Vishvambhara: He has 23 circular marks on His body (P).
Visvarupa is known by its 12 apertures and 24 chakras. Conversely, Vishvarupa – more than 20 chakras and Vishvambara – 20 chakras

ADDITIONAL REFERENCES

1. Howard, Angela Falco. 1986. "Possible Brahmanic Influences in the cosmological Buddha". The Imagery of the Cosmological Buddha. Brill Archive. Retrieved 8 June 2022

2. Rajarajan, R. K. K. (January 2020). "Water, Source of 'Genesis' and the End Macro and Micro Viṣṇu in the Hymns of the Āḻvārs". The Medieval History Journal. 23 (2): 296.

3. Srinivasan, Doris. 1997. Many Heads, Arms, and Eyes: Origin, Meaning, and Form of Multiplicity in Indian Art. BRILL.

VISHVAYONI/JAGADYONI

Jagadyoni Shaligram

Red Jagadyoni

Vishvayoni, also known as Jagadyoni, means "Womb of the World" or "One Who Is the Creator Even of Lakshmi." According to H. P. Blavatsky, however, the terms Vishvayoni and Jagadyoni are not so much references to mother-goddesses or wombs but are meant to impart an idea which means something more akin to "Material Cause of the Universe." The meaning in practice, however, largely depends on the religious tradition. In Shaktism, for example, Vishvayoni Shaligrams are read as manifestations of the formless reality of the Devi, the goddess who creates the world. In other traditions, such as in Vedanta Hinduism or in Buddhism, the Vishvayoni is taken to mean "the ideal spirit of the cause of creation."

Vishvayoni/Jagadyoni Shaligrams are generally easy to identify, having a smooth, almost perfectly round, body (womb-shaped) and a single opening representing the yoni (vagina). Within the yoni, the Shaligram may contain chakra-spirals (an indication of the presence of the Shakti) or a spiral like ridge (the world emerging from the cause of creation or cosmic birth), or in many cases nothing at all. During ritual puja, it is not uncommon for milk, ghee, or scented oils to be poured into the Shaligram as offerings to the Devi.

Vishvayoni/Jagadyoni Shaligrams tend to be small, barely larger than the palm of an adult's hand, with a smooth, black, outer surface. The single vadana (mouth/opening) should be elongated or somewhat oval in shape with a deep space extending towards the back or bottom of the Shaligram. The inside of the opening is typically also smooth and unmarked, but can also contain one or two partial chakra-spirals or, in some cases, a spiral ridge

Veneration of Vishvayoni Shaligrams is more common in Shakti or Shaiva traditions (where it is often paired with the Shiva Linga during worship). In most cases, this Shaligram is said to be particularly potent for women, bestowing blessings of motherhood to the barren, strength and health to the mother, and good fortune and prosperity to the young woman. It is also highly prized by female ascetics and women seeking to leave family responsibilities, or those who do not wish to engage in family domesticity at all, to pursue a religious life. These Shaligrams are also closely associated with creativity, art, music, and having a fiery or fierce temperament.

In some Shaligram traditions, these shilas are considered to be a variation of the Hiranyagarbha Shaligram.

REFERENCES

Praanatoshani Tantra pg. 361, Skanda Purana, Nagarekhanda, 244: 3-9

DESCRIPTIONS

Jagadyoni: Red in color with a circular mark at the front of his opening. (P)

ADDITIONAL REFERENCES

1 Blavatsky, Helena Petrovna. 1993. The Secret Doctrine vol. I, Wheaton, IL: Theosophical Publishing House. Pg. 46.

2. Dyczkowski, Mark C. 2009. Manthanabhairavatantram, Kumarikakhandah 12 Vol. The Section Concerning the Virgin Goddess. Indira Gandhi National Center for the Arts and D. K. Printworld Pvt. Ltd.

3. Indradeva, Shrirama. 1966. "Correspondence between Woman and Nature in Indian Thought". Philosophy East and West. 16 (3/4): 161–168.

VITTALA/VITOBHA

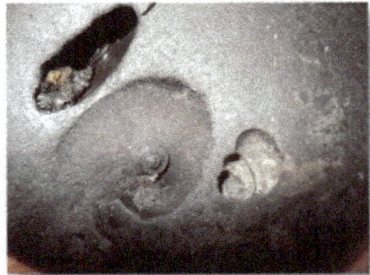

Close up of the chakra (top)

Vithoba, also popularly known as Vittala, Panduranga or Pandharinath, is a Hindu deity who is predominantly worshipped in the Indian states of Maharashtra, Karnataka, Goa, Telangana, and Andhra Pradesh. In most cases, he is generally considered to be either a manifestation of Vishnu or his avatar, Krishna. Vithoba, however, is most often depicted iconographically as a dark-skinned young boy, standing with his arms akimbo on a brick. He is also sometimes accompanied by his main consort, Rakhumai.

Vithoba is the primary focus of the monotheistic, non-Brahmanical, Varkari faith of Maharashtra and the Haridasa faith of Karnataka (Vitthal Temple in Pandharpur is his main temple). Additionally, Vithoba legends tend to revolve around his devotee Pundalik, who is credited with bringing the deity to Pandharpur and around Viṭhoba's role as a savior to the poet-saints of the Varkari faith. As such, the Varkari poet-saints are known for their unique genre of devotional lyric, the abhang, which is dedicated to Vithoba worship and is largely composed in Marathi. Other devotional literature dedicated to Vithoba includes the Kannada hymns of the Haridasa and Marathi versions of the generic aarti songs associated with rituals of offering light to the deity. The most important festivals of Vithoba are held on Shayani Ekadashi in the month of Ashadha, and Prabodhini Ekadashi in the month of Kartik.

The historiography of Vithoba and his veneration is an area of continuing debate among scholars and theologians, up to and including the meaning of his name. For example, various Indologists have proposed a prehistory for Vithoba worship where he was previously: a hero stone (which makes special note of possible early Shaligram traditions), a pastoral deity, a manifestation of Shiva, a Jain saint, or even all of these at various times for various reasons. Though the origins of both his worship and his main temple are likewise debated, there is clear evidence that Vitobha worship already existed by the 13th century.

Vitobha/Vittala Shaligrams are described as having a "dark complexion" (usually meaning blue-black in color), with protruding eyes (two holes or markings), and who is standing on a brick (a wide, heavy, somewhat flattened body to the Shaligram). This description tends to result in a large Shaligram, that is black or dark grey in color, with uniquely smooth chakras that have the general appearance of eyes. In many cases, like the deity manifestation it represents, it is often said that these Shaligrams are keen to "observe" the behavior of their devotees just as Vittala observed the service and devotion of Pundalik from his position on the brick Pundalik threw for him to stand on.

Veneration of these Shaligrams is also commonly associated with the performance of physical austerities where it is said that these Shaligrams can bestow blessings of improved physical senses, a strong sense of spiritual devotion and service to others, and proper admiration towards one's parents. Lastly, the blessings bestowed by this Shaligram are explicitly stated to come from its observation, unlike other deities who typically bestow blessings with their hands or words. For this reason, practitioners who keep Vitobha Shaligrams tend to house them in places where they can observe the family, such as high up on a shelf or in a wall niche.

Vittala Shaligrams are most commonly venerated in central and south India. Traditions that do not recognize the Vitobha/Vittala name-type tend to identify this Shaligram in accordance with the Mahavishnu type Shaligrams (See Mahavishnu – Dasavatara Shaligram).

ADDITIONAL REFERENCES

1. Deleury, G. A. 1960. The cult of Vithoba (Pune: Deccan College, Postgraduate and Research Institute -- Original from the University of Michigan) ed.). Magis Books.

2. Glushkova, I. P. 2018. Janabai: from a House Maid to Goddess: New Trends in Contemporary Hinduism. Vostok. Afro-aziatskie obshchestva: istoriia i sovremennost, (5), 113-124.

3. Iwao, S. 1988. The Vithoba Faith of Maharastra: The Vithoba Temple of Pandharpur and Its Mythological Structure. Japanese Journal of Religious Studies, 15(2), 183.

Yagnamurti

Yajna (or conversely, Yagna) literally translates as "sacrifice, worship, or offering," and refers, in modern Hinduism, to any ritual done in front of a sacred fire. The tradition has evolved considerably over time however, from the offering of objects and libations into a sacred fire to symbolic offerings in the presence of sacred fire (Agni). The word yajna appears throughout the earliest Vedic literatures (2nd millennium BCE) such as in the Brahmanas and in the Yajurveda. In the Rigveda, Yajurveda and others, it means "worship, devotion to anything, prayer and praise, an act of worship or devotion, a form of offering or oblation, and sacrifice." In post-Vedic literature, the term meant any form of rite, ceremony or devotion with an actual or symbolic offering or effort.

Yajna ritual-related texts are also called the Karma-kanda (ritual works) portion of the Vedic literatures, in contrast to Jnana-kanda (knowledge) portions contained in the Upanishads. The proper completion of Yajna-like rituals was the primary focus of Mimansa school of Hindu philosophy, though the performance of various types of yajna ceremonies have continued to play a central role in a Hindu's rites of passage, festivals, and community events. Modern major Hindu temple ceremonies, Hindu community celebrations, or monastic initiations may also include Yajna rites, or may alternatively be based on agamic rituals (meaning "received knowledge" or that which is required by a personal deity).

Yajnamurti Shaligrams are most often described as having markings of the two sacrificial sticks (sruk and sruva), which appear as straight, deeply embedded, grooves somewhere on the body of the shila. These Shaligrams then have a wide, flat, body and at least one (but occasionally two or three) large holes or depressions. These Shaligrams should also contain sections or portions of red to reddish-orange coloration. Generally considered to be a subtype of the Mahavishnu-type Shaligram, Yajnamurti Shaligrams are commonly sought after for inclusion in specific home or community yajna rites as a presiding deity. (Also, depending on the tradition, sometimes associated with or considered to be a subtype of Kapila Shaligrams).

Yajnamurti Shaligrams tend to be large in size (larger than an adult's hand) with a combination of black and red to reddish-orange coloration. The Shaligram should also rest stably when placed on a flat surface. This is because the holes or depressions within the Shaligram can be used to place offerings or pour libations during the yajna ritual as offerings made directly to the deity (the Shaligram is then usually bathed following the completion of the rite).

Veneration more generally also remains similar to other Mahavishnu Shaligrams, where they are said to ward off misfortune and to protect the family and community from evil spirits, unquiet ghosts, or from deceit through witchcraft or magic. As uninvoked, presiding deities at yajna rites, they are also said to ensure proper performance of the ritual and to ensure that the merits of the ritual are reciprocally rewarded. Not surprisingly then, many practitioners seek these Shaligrams as the literal foundation for the home worship and will place them in areas of high esteem within the house or temple.

REFERENCES

Pranatoshani Tantra pg. 351 - 356

DESCRIPTIONS

Yajnamurthi: Reddish yellow in color, with a small opening and two circular marks, one at the bottom and one the other side on the right side. (P)

ADDITIONAL REFERENCES

1. Gyanshruti; Srividyananda. 2006. Yajna A Comprehensive Survey. Yoga Publications Trust, Munger, Bihar, India; 1st edition.
2. Nigal, S. G.1986. Axiological Approach to the Vedas. Northern Books, pages 80–81.
3. Staal, Frits. 2009. Discovering the Vedas: Origins, Mantras, Rituals, Insights. Penguin. page 124.

Yogeshwara/Yogaraja

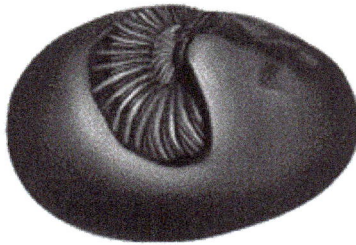

Vedavyasa Shaligram

Yogeshwara, typically, translated as "Master or Lord of Yoga" or "Master of the Mystic Arts," may refer to Shiva as the "Celestial Ascetic" or to Vishnu/Krishna (especially Krishna in the Bhagavad Gita) as the "Lord of Yogis." In Vaishnava theology, sense perception is the basis of knowledge but higher knowledge, that is an understanding of the divine, can only be gained when the mind is disciplined by concentration and meditation.

The praxis that then results from this conceptualization is called yoga; a set of bodily practices by which the experience of transcendental consciousness becomes possible. God, in this capacity, is the master of infinite yogic knowledge and it is out of this knowledge that he assumes suitable incarnations or avatars based on the needs of the particular time and place.

Yogeshwara is completely aware of the workings of the universe; everything from the movement of celestial worlds to the daily struggles of material beings. As such, many of the teachings and feats of deities throughout Hindu and Buddhist philosophy have been attributed to the perceptions of the deity in their capacity as Yogeshwara.

The Yogeshwara Shaligram is usually described as having a wide, flattened, shape with the presence of an open half or full-chakra located near the top of the shila. These particular characteristics are then described as forming a "stable seat" where the divine yogi has come to sit. In some Shaligram traditions, this name-type also forms the basis for reading Shaligrams as manifestations of specific gurus or historical figures related to the founding of certain religious traditions, schools of thought, or lineages (for example, Sri Chaitanya, Adi Shankara, or Guru Nanak; any of whom may manifest as Shaligram).

Yogeshwara Shaligrams are therefore described as "umbrella shaped," with a rounded base and a flattened top. When allowed to sit on a stable surface, however, they will not wobble or tip easily, regardless of which side (top or bottom) they are placed on. These Shaligrams should then contain one clear partial or full chakra which is "seat-shaped" or slightly half-moon in appearance. Veneration of this Shaligram is highly associated with ascetic practice and with the transition of householders to sannyasis (ascetics/hermits). For this reason, Yogeshwara Shaligrams are not often included in home shrines but are relatively popular during festivals or during community rituals. Yogeshwara Shaligrams are also said to bestow blessings of clear-sightedness, meditative calm, to encourage spiritual learning, and the ability to understand the complex meanings of religious texts. In some cases, Yogeshwara Shaligrams are also given to young or newly converted devotees who are actively seeking a teacher.

Some traditions recognize a variation of this Shaligram called Vedavyasa, or "Compiler of the Vedas;" a reference to the revered figure in Hindu traditions who is said to have authored the Mahabharata (as well as be a character in it), and the scribe of both the Vedas and Puranas. Vyasa is also considered to be one of the seven Chiranjivins (immortals), who are still in existence. According to the Vishnu Purana, "Veda Vyasa" is a title applied to the compilers of the Vedas who are avatars of Vishnu. Some 28 people have held this title so far. The only difference between a Vedavyasa Shaligram and a Yogeshwara Shaligram however, is that the former is described as having a "seat" that is raised up above the body of the shila, while the latter has a "seat" embedded into it.

REFERENCES

Praanatoshani Tantra pg. 361

DESCRIPTIONS

The type found at the top of the Shaligram mountain. (P)

ADDITIONAL REFERENCES

1. "Krishna the Yogeshwara". The Hindu. 12 September 2014.
2. Pattanaik, D. 2006. Shiva to Shankara: Decoding the phallic symbol. Indus Source.
3. Sethumadhavan, T.N. 2015. Srimad Bhagavad Gita: A User'S Manual for Every Day Living. Partridge Publishing. p. 339.
4. Swami Sivananda. 1964. Sri Krishna. Bharatiya Vidya Bhavan. p. 4.
5. Yogeshwar, G. 1994. "Swami Vivekânanda's concept of jnana yoga, raja yoga, karma yoga and bhakti yoga." Ancient Science of Life, 13(3-4), 261.

Biography

Holly Walters originally hails from a small, rural, town in Minnesota. A life-long storyteller, Holly is also a cultural anthropologist with a PhD from Brandeis University working in the high Himalayas of Nepal. While her ethnographic work focuses on fossil folklores and sacred ammonites in South Asia, her creative work pays homage to the dragons, unicorns, and fairy tales of her youth. When not writing, she can be found perfecting her Medieval archery skills, theorizing about movie plots, and forgetting where she left her tea cup. Today, she makes her home in Boston, Massachusetts, with a very unruly garden, a few equally cantankerous pets, a clever spouse, and a resident house ghost. And since her creepy sculpture hobby hasn't panned out thus far, she is looking forward to the publication of her first novel and the writing of many more.

The Three Little Sisters

The Three Little Sisters is an indie publisher that puts authors first. We specalize in the strange and unusual. From titles about pagan and heathen spirituality to traditional fiction we bring books to life.

https://the3littlesisters.com

www.ingramcontent.com/pod-product-compliance
Lightning Source LLC
Chambersburg PA
CBHW042335030426
42335CB00028B/3353